Spain and the American Civil War

Shades of Blue and Gray Series

Edited by Herman Hattaway, Jon L. Wakelyn, and Clayton E. Jewett

The Shades of Blue and Gray Series offers Civil War studies for the modern reader—Civil War buff and scholar alike. Military history today addresses the relationship between society and warfare. Thus biographies and thematic studies that deal with civilians, soldiers, and political leaders are increasingly important to a larger public. This series includes books that will appeal to Civil War Roundtable groups, individuals, libraries, and academics with a special interest in this era of American history.

Spain and the American Civil War

Wayne H. Bowen

University of Missouri Press
Columbia and London

University of Missouri Press, Columbia, Missouri 65201
Printed and bound in the United States of America

5 4 3 2 1 15 14 13 12 11

Cataloging-in-Publication data available from the Library of Congress.
ISBN 978-0-8262-1938-1

♾™ This paper meets the requirements of the
American National Standard for Permanence of Paper
for Printed Library Materials, Z39.48, 1984.

Designer: Kristie Lee
Typesetter: K. Lee Design & Graphics
Printer and binder: Thomson-Shore, Inc.
Typeface: Palatino

Research for and publication of this book have been supported by contributions from the Program for Cultural Cooperation between Spain's Ministry of Education and Culture and United States Universities.

To Percy C. Clark, Jr. (1925–2011)

Contents

Spain and the American Civil War

Introduction

> **Spain is the natural ally of the South. If the South has had a friend, from the beginning of her troubles, it has been Spain.**
>
> **—*Richmond Dispatch*, February 10, 1862**

The American Civil War was primarily a domestic conflict, pitting the southeastern slaveholding states against the more urban and industrial North and the antislavery West. Other nations, including major powers such as France and Britain and less globally significant ones such as Russia and Spain, did not intervene militarily or politically in any significant way. Even so, there was strong international interest and involvement in the conflict. The United States before its civil war was a rising economic and ideological power, especially in the Americas and the Atlantic world, so its division into two warring factions generated interest in overseas capitals. Some historians have noted the attention paid to the war internationally, but most publications have focused on diplomatic and economic relations between the two American republics—the United States of America and the Confederate States of America (CSA)—with the French empire and the United Kingdom. Negotiations between the Confederacy and these two European powers and the potential for their intervention on behalf of the Southern rebels have generated deserved attention. Only these two European states had the potential to broaden the conflict instantly—with British troops in Canada and the French in Mexico, as well as navies from both, able to lend immediate aid to the South should they choose to do so.[1]

However, one other nation was of comparable importance to the Confederacy and, in many ways, was more amenable to cooperation and even military collaboration: the kingdom of Spain. During the American Civil War, Spain was actively engaged in military expansion in the Caribbean. The nation worked to support slavery in its colonies and elsewhere, hoped for the defeat of the United States, provided tangible aid to Confederate warships, and even considered possibilities for an alliance with the rebels. After decades of foreign weakness and internal conflict, during the 1860s Spain was once again a nation of consequence. Its involvement, whether alone or in conjunction with its allies, could have transformed the American Civil War had it opted to align itself with the Confederacy, a viable option considered seriously in Madrid. Some at the time regarded Spain as likely to be "the last power to act," but even so there was a serious opportunity to engage it in the war on behalf of the Confederacy.[2] That it did not choose this path does not diminish the importance of understanding the history of Spain during this period, an understanding that will also enrich the overall picture of the global significance of the American Civil War.

Spain during the late 1850s and early 1860s stood at a moment of promise, in terms of its international position, economy, and military strength. This period, directly related to the temporary strength of the "Unión Liberal," between 1858 and 1863, "represented a culminating moment" in the foreign relations of the reign of Queen Isabel II, Spain's sole monarch. For a variety of reasons, Spain had relatively more freedom of diplomatic action during this period than at any other time in the nineteenth century. With British and French ambivalence and distractions elsewhere and the focus of the United States and the Confederacy on their own survival during the American Civil War, relative domestic peace within Spain made more action overseas possible. Temporary budget surpluses also meant Spain could afford to take actions such as building new warships, modernizing its army, and undertaking overseas expeditions and even wars in Asia, Africa, and the Americas. The nation's leaders were embarking on what one historian referred to as "a vivid, grandiose, and really Spanish foreign policy," for the first time perhaps since the seventeenth century.[3]

There was therefore, a brief moment when some Spaniards, and even foreign leaders such as Emperor Napoleon III of France, believed Spain could again become a great power as it had been in previous centuries. Certainly this was the ambition of Spain's most prominent prime minister during this period, General Leopoldo O'Donnell, whose experience as a senior officer in the Spanish empire had convinced him that his nation was destined to return to greatness. Britain was the superpower of the nineteenth century, and its toleration of Spanish ambitions was a contributing factor in making the Spanish dream possible. Although the rise of Spain seemed plausible, critics such as the Spanish writer Juan Bravo Murillo discarded the idea, saying caustically, "that pretension was as if a very short man proclaimed himself tall, against every evidence."[4]

This attempted revival of imperial power and prestige was built on Spain's preexisting interests, which included maintaining its colonies —especially Cuba—against US pressure and strength, preserving its cultural and political influence in Hispanic America, and asserting its economic and military strength in the Americas. While the Americas were much less important to Spain than Europe was in terms of its economic, political, and military significance, many Spanish leaders continued to mourn their loss of colonies during the Napoleonic era and immediate thereafter, hoping for a return to glory in this regard. New initiatives in North Africa and Asia were intended to contribute to this renaissance of Spain's global heritage, military power, and international prestige. Spanish politicians, chief among them Prime Minister O'Donnell, hoped that Spain would once again be counted as a Great Power, alongside its allies France and Great Britain. Efforts by the Spanish government in the 1850s and 1860s—including the temporary reannexation of Santo Domingo—should be seen in this context.[5]

In the United States, there was tremendous ambivalence about this European nation, the formerly powerful state with rediscovered ambitions. Spain occupied a special place in the imaginations of Southern politicians before and during the American Civil War. Prior to the conflict, Southerners such as Jefferson Davis plotted ways to seize Cuba from Spain and transform it into an additional slave state or states. Once the war began, these same statesmen attempted to convince Spain that it had no better friend than the Confederacy, and that their shared enmity for the Yankees could bridge their prior disagreements over the future of Cuba. That this putative alliance was seriously considered by both sides is a testament to the hostility and fear engendered by the United States in Spain and other European capitals; that it did not come to fruition is more evidence of the same. Even in the midst of a struggle for its own survival, the United States could instill concern in the minds of foreign leaders, faced with the possibility of war against it. It was in this context that Confederate diplomatic representatives, in Madrid and other foreign cities, attempted to make the case for international recognition and, perhaps, foreign intervention.

Despite considerable attempts to bring about a foreign alliance, or even recognition, from Spain and other European states, Confederate diplomacy during the American Civil War failed to attract significant support for the Southern Cause, but this was not because of a lack of strategy or effort. Southern plans depended on two factors: first, leveraging supplies of cotton to entice (or extort) support from European states and, then, winning enough major battles against the Union to gain international legitimacy and perceived viability as an independent state. Failures in both arenas doomed Confederate diplomacy, but leading US, Confederate, and European politicians in the early years of the Civil War did not necessarily see that future. Historians have discussed at length the reasons for the failure of the Confederacy's foreign policy, especially in regards to its two primary targets, France and the United Kingdom. Some have given primacy to the botched Southern campaign to wield the weapon of King Cotton, and others have looked at the failures of Confederate diplomats in London and Paris, missed opportunities for foreign mediation, the CSA's misguided expulsion of British consuls in October 1863, the lack of secure and expeditious communications between the Confederate State Department and its emissaries in Europe, or Jefferson Davis's and other Southern leaders' lack of interest in diplomacy. Given the Confederate States of America's stark inferiorities in industry, personnel, and military materiel, diplomacy and foreign intervention offered almost the only chance for a successful end to the war for the Southern rebels.[6]

At the same time, it was those very inferiorities that made it very unlikely that foreign states, particularly those with the power to have a decisive impact on the course of the war, would intervene on behalf of a weak partner. In a sense, the Confederacy would have been most likely to attract allies if it were able to prove it did not need them. One can imagine the Spanish, British, and French rushing to welcome the Confederacy into the family of nations with great dispatch had Robert E. Lee seized Washington, DC, captured Abraham Lincoln, and surrounded Manhattan Island with the Army of Virginia. While these events occurred only in the minds of Confederate partisans, they were within the realm of possibility in the early years of the American Civil War.

The early 1860s could have been propitious for the Confederacy, as the European powers each looked to the Americas—and more specifically, to the Caribbean—for possible imperial expansion. In 1861, Spain occupied Santo Domingo, the same year that France sent major forces to install an Austrian puppet in Mexico. Mexico itself suffered from ongoing civil war in this period, with possibilities for cooperation between the Confederacy and the various factions—including the French—attempting to control Mexico. France had broader aims as well, hoping to carve out territory from the southwest United States for an expanded empire joined to Mexico, and to consider reoccupying Haiti, which had been lost to a slave rebellion in 1804. With Spain controlling the eastern half of Hispaniola, some French and Confederate writers believed it was only a matter of time before the French section of the island invited their former colonial masters to return, or before the French invited themselves through some flimsy pretense, as they had done in Mexico.

Efforts by the Confederate States of America to attract support from Spain, however, have not attracted much scholarly attention, despite the advantages to both states that mutual assistance could have brought. In many ways, Spain was a far more likely ally than either the United Kingdom or the French empire under Napoleon III. The Spanish government had maintained slavery in its Caribbean territories and would do so until as late as the 1880s. It did not have close ties to Washington, DC, and was still unhappy over its loss of territory through the Latin American independence movements, efforts supported by the United States. So distant was the diplomatic relationship with the Union that at one point President Lincoln considered declaring war on Spain, because of the kingdom's provocative moves in the Caribbean, especially its 1861 reoccupation of Santo Domingo, Madrid's former colony in the eastern part of the island of Hispaniola. Elements of the Spanish governing classes, including Queen Isabel II and Prime Minister O'Donnell, were sympathetic to the Confederacy, and Spanish newspapers during the early phases of the war trumpeted Southern battlefield victories. With the close personal and economic ties of many of Spain's leading families to Cuban plantations and business interests, it was no surprise that many supported the Confederacy in its war against the Union. There were other international crises in Europe that drew the attention of Spanish diplomats and national leaders, such as the unification of Italy, the Polish insurrection in 1863, the war in Denmark in 1864, and the menacing signs of an impending Austro-Prussian conflict, but it was only in the Americas that Spain could reasonably expect to exert some influence over the resolution of events.[7]

Spain was also in the midst of a political, economic, and military revival. With its decades-long Carlist insurgency defeated, its economy improving, its military in the strongest condition since before the Napoleonic Wars, and under the leadership of the prime minister Leopoldo O'Donnell, a former general, Spain seemed poised to take back its previous status as a great power. Although this rise proved ephemeral in the end, it did not seem so in the late 1850s and 1860s. In quick succession, Spain intervened in Southeast Asia alongside France, dispatched forces to Naples, defeated Morocco in a highly popular war, reoccupied Santo Domingo, and joined Britain and France in a punitive military expedition against Mexico, forcing the Mexicans to agree to make good on their international debts. These seemed to be actions of a powerful state, with the prestige, political will, and military capabilities sufficient to exert global influence. This was a new kind of behavior, rather unlike the Spain that had been perceived as enduring perpetual imperial decline and defeat since the death of King Felipe II, the organizer of the Spanish Armada, in 1598.[8]

Despite the rediscovered strength among the Spaniards, however, and the desire in the Confederate capital of Richmond to forge ties with foreign powers, these and other factors favoring closer ties between the Confederacy and Spain were tenuous. During the American Civil War, there remained a well of mistrust and bad relations between the two. There remains the Spanish Question: why did these two "natural allies," as they were described by actors on both sides, not forge a closer relationship, which might have provided critical international diplomatic support for the Confederate States of America, and a means through which Spain could exact revenge on the United States of America? Historical evidence of this potential relationship in diplomatic, political, and military terms demonstrates that neither Spain, after two centuries of international retreat and weakness, nor the CSA, a new diplomatic entity, took sufficient advantage of the possibilities for cooperation between them, each preferring instead to wait for a weak moment in order to seize territory from the other. In the event, neither was able to take advantage of the other's weakness in this way—but the plans to do so reflected unrealistic ambitions on both sides, and their corresponding failure to appreciate the potential of a partnership and its possible advantages for both nations.

This project will address a major deficiency in the historical literature of the American Civil War. Despite thousands of books published since 1865 on all aspects of this conflict, there has yet to be a published book on Spain and the American Civil War, despite the critical role played by Spain in international diplomacy during this period and the fact that Spain could have changed the course of the war if it had aligned with the Confederacy. In the Library of Congress, for example, as of late 2010, there were over four thousand works under the keywords "Confederate States of America," but none that references this term—or any analogs—with "Spain" or "Spanish," much less in the context of foreign policy or military affairs.

This is remarkable when considered in the context of the time. Not only was Spain during the early 1860s the only remaining European slave-owning nation, it was hostile to the United States, controlled colonies (Cuba and Puerto Rico) in the direct sea routes to several major Confederate ports, demonstrated rising military and political strength, sheltered Southern blockade runners and smugglers in its harbors, acted on ambitious plans to restore its empire through force in the Americas and Asia, and engaged in negotiations with Confederate agents about potential future belligerency. Spain also boasted close ties to Portugal, itself a minor imperial power with long-standing ties to traffic in slaves and with its own African colonies that had long served as sources for the illegal slave trade to Brazil, Cuba, and even the Southern states. Britain certainly had greater imperial and industrial power (and so did France, to a lesser extent), but Spain was the nation most prepared by its geography, politics, and colonial means to lend direct aid to the Confederacy. Although it seems unlikely that

Spanish soldiers would have landed in Virginia to join in a combined assault on the Union Army, Spain could have provided use of its ports and facilities in Cuba to the Confederate navy, deployed its rapidly modernizing fleet against the US Navy, served as a conduit for arms and materiel from Europe to the South, and forced the Union to divert its resources to defend against the Spanish threat.

Foreign intervention was one of the few avenues for a possible Southern victory, given the Confederacy's inferiority in military capability, population, and economic strength when compared to the Union. Despite this, Confederate diplomacy has been a neglected area of research. Some of this reflects the relative lack of emphasis placed on foreign policy by the South itself. President Jefferson Davis and other Southern leaders did not devote significant resources to their agents abroad, other than what was necessary to purchase weapons and ships on the black market, especially in Europe. Lacking an experienced diplomatic corps, and without the venues afforded to sovereign states with international recognition, Southern agents in Europe and elsewhere were forced to skulk through palaces and government offices in the attempt to convince politicians, journalists, and other influential Europeans of the legitimacy and moral superiority of the Southern Cause. According to one historian of the Civil War, even Southern politicians groused that their government "never had a foreign policy, and never attempted any high diplomacy."[9] This argument is not quite correct, although Southern leaders did miss opportunities and remained wedded to ineffective foreign strategies, especially the self-defeating policy of relying on "King Cotton," long after their failures were evident.

This is not to say that the South did not have an argument that might have worked. The relatively new American Republic had not gained many friends in Europe, so there was an opportunity to make the case for its weakening, something that a permanent division of the United States would have accomplished. The rise of the United States as a commercial, manufacturing, fishing, and agricultural state, a rival in Western hemisphere markets, was not a welcome development for many Europeans. Support for slavery in Europe was clearly on the decline, especially after the British moved to abolish the practice in the 1830s, but there was still some identification by European aristocrats with the Confederate ruling classes. Even more important, the hope that the secession of the South might slow the dramatic growth of the United States made it seem that support for the Confederacy would be in the interests of many European governments and private interests. To paraphrase a more modern opinion often expressed ironically about a divided Germany during the Cold War, the Europeans loved the United States so much that, early in the American Civil War, they hoped there would be two of them.

Some historians have noted the political efforts of Southern agents overseas. The main thrust of Confederate diplomacy was to force France and Great Britain to intervene in the war through refusing to sell cotton to the Europeans, a policy described in Frank Owsley's *King Cotton Diplomacy*. This classic work, revised in 1959, argued that this attempt to use cotton as leverage ultimately failed because the Europeans were able to develop other sources for their textile imports. Owsley also examines the impact of relatively inexperienced and underfunded Southern agents in sophisticated European capitals and, especially, the more adept machinations of US secretary of state William Seward with Britain and France. Even the most able of diplomats would not have been much more successful, however, given the ongoing failures of the Confederacy on the battlefield and the constraints imposed by Jefferson Davis and other Southern leaders on their agents. King Cotton was not a winning strategy, no matter who was charged with articulating it in Madrid, London, or Paris. Other classic works, including James Morton Callahan's *Diplomatic History of the Southern Confederacy* and Edwin DeLeon's *Secret History of Confederate Diplomacy Abroad*, argue that the failure of cotton diplomacy—and of Confederate foreign affairs in general—owed more to defeat on the battlefield than to any inability to move foreign opinion, which had initially been sympathetic to the rebels. Callahan's work, in particular, retains significant validity, even as the diplomatic and archival record becomes more complete.

As these and other works have demonstrated, however, no amount of diplomatic skill, personal connections, financial resources, or charisma on the part of Southern advocates arguing for their cause in Europe could deny the inexorable march of Union armies into Confederate territory, or the increasingly effective blockade of Southern ports by the Union navy. For the CSA, it was not enough merely to survive—they needed to bring tremendous battlefield pressure against the Union in order to encourage the European powers to become actively engaged in mediating an end to the war. The South did achieve notable tactical and operational victories, but the Confederacy was never able to rout the Union, capture a major Northern city, or cause sufficient panic in Washington, DC, to pressure Lincoln to negotiate a settled ending to the war.

More recent works include Charles Hubbard's *The Burden of Confederate Diplomacy* and Dean Mahin's edited *One War at a Time*, which argue that diplomacy could have offered the South real opportunities to gain foreign intervention had it been coordinated more closely with battlefield operations and attempts to defeat the Union naval blockade of Confederate ports. With more experienced diplomatic hands at work, along with better intelligence in the European capitals and more rapid communications with the Confederate government, there very well could have been conditions for outside intervention in the American Civil War. Just as there was a general balance of power in Europe in the nineteenth century, so too there was a general balance of opinion. Some lesser powers—such as Belgium and Portugal—were strong supporters of the Confederacy. Some states, such as Russia, were more pro-Union, while others, such as Denmark and Prussia, were fully engaged in continental wars and effectively indifferent to events across the Atlantic. France and especially Britain were the states with some room for autonomy and with the means to intervene decisively should they have chosen to do so. Spain was in an intermediate position, with limited global means but significant strength in the Caribbean, which could have been of great assistance to the Confederacy. Just as important, Spain had key leaders with genuine enthusiasm for the victory of the Southern rebels. Ultimately weaker than the United States and unable to confront it directly by itself, Spain still could have lent enough leverage to make a difference in determining the outcome of the American Civil War had Britain and France looked favorably upon such actions on behalf of the Confederacy.

Other specialized works on diplomacy have focused on the British role during the conflict. As the nineteenth century's global superpower, British intervention on behalf of the South could have been decisive. The British also wielded an effective veto over French or Spanish intervention on behalf of the Southern rebellion, making their role in Confederate diplomatic failures even more important. Monographs that examine Confederate stumbles in these efforts include Eugene Berwanger's *The British Foreign Service and the American Civil*

War, Howard Jones's *Union in Peril: The Crisis over British Intervention in the Civil War*, and Frank Merli's *The Alabama, British Neutrality, and the American Civil War*. While the story in these books is one of Southern failures, they also illustrate the opportunities that were before the Confederacy, making it possible to imagine an alternative course of developments that might have led to European recognition of and intervention on behalf of the rebellion.

The British are also the focus of *Lincoln's Man in Liverpool: Consul Dudley and the Legal Battle to Stop Confederate Warships* by Coy Cross II, where he examines the discipline, consistency, and broad approach followed by Union diplomats in Europe, contrasting this with the poorly prepared and inadequately funded Confederate agents, who hoped to procure weapons and allies for the Southern cause. Confederate agents, lacking the training, funds, and legitimacy of US diplomats, were at pains even to have consistent communications with their administration in Richmond, and consequently had to rely on their own, often misguided, initiative. The venue for most of this diplomacy was the United Kingdom, the chief maritime power in the mid-nineteenth century. Britain has received the attention of most historians, as is appropriate given its dominance of the seas and global trade, but there has been some work on France and the Civil War, most of this contained within more general studies of diplomacy.

A recent exception is John Bigelow's *France and the Confederate Navy, 1862–1868: An International Episode*, but the relatively narrow focus of this text does not take into account the broader outlines of French foreign policy, and its close collaboration with the British. France's significance was not just as a potential base to arm the South surreptitiously but as a potential level to nudge Britain toward intervention, as well as to be itself nudged by Spain. In *The Union, the Confederacy, and the Atlantic Rim*, editor Robert May and authors such as Howard Jones and James Macpherson argue for a greater place in historiography for the international context of the American Civil War, a position supported by this book as well. Attempting to expand the picture of Confederate diplomacy beyond the capitals of London and Paris, the essays in May's work also include interviews with the authors, a conversational device that makes the work more accessible.

An earlier book, Philip van Doren Stern's *When the Guns Roared: World Aspects of the American Civil War*, ranges widely in its coverage of the international context of the conflict. It briefly describes reactions to the Civil War in such far-flung nations as Japan and Russia, but the focus is (as with most works) on the efforts of both Confederate and Union representatives in Paris and London to create momentum for their respective causes, and on the reactions of French and British diplomats to events in the American Civil War. Given the comprehensiveness of this 1965 book, it is remarkable that references to Spain and Cuba are made only in passing, while letters President Lincoln sent to the Republic of San Marino and the King of Siam are quoted at length. Although these documents are illustrative of the character of Abraham Lincoln, they shed little light on the real issues and foreign states with the most direct bearing on the American Civil War.[10]

The hemispheric context of the Confederacy has fortunately received increasing attention by historians in recent years. The rebellion by the slaveholding region of the United States did not occur in isolation but occurred in the context of a global struggle over slavery. While Britain worked to end the slave trade and slavery worldwide, nations such as Brazil, Spain, Portugal, and the Ottoman empire benefited from the industry and hoped to maintain slavery, if not the trade itself. Gerald Horne, in *The Deepest South*, examined the critical importance of Brazil, in the minds of Southern politicians, as a potential ally and eventual refuge after the end of the American Civil War. Horne argues for a larger role in the historiography for slaveholding Brazil as well as other parts of the Lusophone world in our understanding of the context for the Confederacy. Along with Cuba, Brazil was a slave state, but with its immense size and political independence it held an outsized role in the mentality of Southern politicians before and during the American Civil War.

Brazil continued to hold a special place in the minds of slave-owning Southerners as a refuge for some intransigents after the war's end. The ongoing, albeit illegal, slave trade coming from Portuguese colonies in Africa and the Ottoman empire was an additional complicating factor in the history of slavery in the Western hemisphere. Global British efforts to put a complete end to the slave trade, as well as to slavery itself, consumed a surprising amount of British resources, from Royal Navy contingents patrolling the west coast of Africa to diplomats pressuring foreign governments to adopt significant legislation against the entire industry. In addition to Horne's important work, promising future publications by young historians such as Matthew Karp and Michael Schoeppner, on the international and hemispheric context of slavery and race relations, should also enrich the field.

There have been a handful of works on Spain during the period of the American Civil War, but few of them have been recent publications. For example, the primary work on public opinion in Madrid concerning the sectional conflict was published over seventy-five years ago. This is Edwin Pratt's article, "Spanish Opinion of the North American Civil War," in the *Hispanic American Historical Review*, published in February 1930. More recent scholarly efforts in Spain have produced two articles—Joaquín Navarro Méndez, "Anexión y abandono de Santo Domingo, 1861–1865," in the *Revista de Historia Militar*, and Juan Batista Vilar, "Las relaciones internacionales de España, 1840–1874," in *España siglo XIX*—and one monograph, Jamie de Jesús Domínguez's *La anexión de la República Dominicana a España*. In these three examples, the focus of the historiography is on the broader developments in Spain's attempted imperial revival, in which the flirtation with the Confederate States of America receives little to no attention.

One author, James W. Cortada, has written twice on the subject of Spain during the 1850s and 1860s, in two respected works published over twenty-five years ago. The pamphlet *Spain and the American Civil War: Relations at Mid-Century, 1855–1868*, and the monograph *Two Nations over Time: Spain and the United States, 1776–1977*, examine the difficult relations between Spain and the United States during the American Civil War and the decades prior to and following this conflict. Cortada's two works provide a good general introduction to the diplomatic history of these two nations during key crises, including the American Revolution, the Latin American Wars of Independence, and tensions over US ambitions to annex Cuba and other Spanish territories. The two publications cover much of the same ground but do not take advantage of current research or documents from Spanish diplomatic and political archives that have been released more recently.

The recent digitization of millions of pages of Spanish periodicals from the nineteenth century has greatly improved access to Spanish publications from the time of the American Civil War. These online documents, the Hemeroteca Digital (Digital Newspaper Archive), form part of the Biblioteca Digital Hispánica (Hispanic Digital Library) a project of the Biblioteca Nacional and other agencies of the Spanish government, and they make possible a more in-depth examination of Spanish public opinion and perceptions of the American Civil War than has been previously easily available to historians on this side of the Atlantic. This archive is an excellent resource, but there remain gaps in the newspaper record, technical challenges with the database, and other difficulties that make this digital project as frustrating as it is rewarding. Research using these materials reveals a source that is far more useful for studying domestic Spanish politics and culture than anything relating to overseas events, but the archive is nonetheless invaluable to historians.

More broadly, the current book will augment several publications that have argued for a reinternationalization of the American Civil War. The conflict occurred in the midst of a century characterized by rising international trade, imperial growth of the European powers, the advent of widespread industrial capitalism, and the abolition of slavery and serfdom. Each of these major developments had a direct impact on the war between the South and the North—from the interests of the European powers in the war to the potential role in the world of an independent Confederacy. The South itself attempted to use global markets to its advantage, through the policy of denying its chief commodity—cotton—to its erstwhile European trading partners, unless they supported its campaign for international recognition. The failure of the King Cotton tactic, however, does not mean that it could not have succeeded or that Confederate leaders did not understand commerce or the interests of the Europeans. While they did overestimate their own importance to the Europeans, the efforts that Confederate leaders and agents made to entice the European powers—especially Britain, France, and Spain—to intervene are an essential element both in the story of this rebellion and in determining its eventual catastrophic and ultimate failure in 1865.

Chapter 1

Prewar Tensions between Spain and the American South

The fifty years before the American Civil War saw increasing tensions between Spain and the United States, with conflicts over independence movements within the Spanish empire, expansionist ambitions among Southern US politicians, and other diplomatic and military crises. Spain was arguably the least popular foreign nation with most Americans and was associated negatively with what many viewed as the least attractive elements of the Old World: Catholicism, absolutism, upper-class privilege, and hidebound tradition. Almost from the beginning of the Hispano-US relationship, the United States adopted the English image of Spain, as a nation of "irreversible decadence" that was destined to lose its remaining colonies and influence to the younger, more vibrant, Protestant nations.[1] Many Southerners, although supportive of the continued existence of slavery in Spain's colonies, looked greedily toward annexations while many Northerners and Midwesterners, exemplified by the Know-Nothing movement, held Spain as a Catholic power in great suspicion. While the Know-Nothings (officially known as the American Party) were more concerned with Irish and German Catholic immigrants, Spain was held in contempt by those who campaigned against "popery" and other Roman Catholic influences.[2]

Spain, along with France, had played a significant role in helping the American rebels gain their independence during the American Revolution, in order to gain territory (or, in the case of Gibraltar and Minorca, regain it) at the expense of the British. The collaboration did not endure for very long beyond the British surrender in 1781 and the forming of the new US government. Almost before the end of the American Revolution, it was clear that Spain and the new republic would be hemispheric competitors.[3] Unlike France, which after the sale of the Louisiana Territory directed its attentions away from the Americas (at least until the reign of Louis Napoleon, later Emperor Napoleon III, began in 1848), Spain remained focused on its territories in the Western hemisphere.[4] In Spain, as in France, however, there were concerns in the years leading to the American Civil War that there could be division of the United States, a potential hazard that could also provide opportunities for the European states to counteract the rising power of the young republic. Two American states could also pose unanticipated threats, so the coming of this expected war in 1861 was not seen as an unmitigated blessing.[5]

Spanish possession of Florida, the Louisiana Territory, and Cuba, confirmed in 1783 with the general peace settlement, set it on the road to conflicts with the American republic, once the new state began to expand to the South and West from its original thirteen colonies. Collaboration against the British and alliance with France were not common enough interests to bind Spain and the new United States, two very disparate nations, together much past the signing of the Treaty of Paris. There was not to be open warfare between Spain and the United States of America until 1898, but neither were there extended periods of peace and comity.[6] "From the start of the North American Revolutionary War in the 1770s, until the consolidation of constitutional democracy in post-Franco Spain during the 1970s, the pattern of relations between Spain and the United States could be described as consisting of long periods of disinterest and estrangement, interrupted by short bursts of mutual interaction, usually of an adversarial nature."[7] Historian Rodrigo Botero's description of these ties certainly applies to the decades immediately prior to the American Civil War. Although the US and Spanish governments did not engage in direct warfare, their citizens did, not only during the campaigns for independence by the people of Latin America but also in a series of private invasions of Cuba tolerated by the United States—the filibustering movement.

By the 1820s, diplomatic relations between Spain and the United States were characterized by mistrust, suspicion, and antipathy. Spain feared US efforts to dominate Latin America and seize Spain's remaining colonies of Cuba and Puerto Rico, and the United States disliked what were perceived as Spanish despotism and Catholicism. Cuba was the most significant area of conflict between the United States and Spain and "dominated Spanish-American relations between the 1820s and the end of the century." From the 1790s to the late 1830s, US interests in Cuba were primarily economic, although Spain's fears that the United States wanted the island prevented a commercial treaty. Offers by the United States to buy the island, beginning in the 1840s, were offensive to Madrid, which consistently refused to negotiate on the issue. For Spaniards who had lost most of their overseas colonies to rebellions supported by the United States, Cuba was the prime evidence that Spain remained an empire. At least equal to its moral and emotional significance, then, Cuba was also the essential remaining underpinning of the empire. Cuba was essential to Spain, providing funds to support the other colonies, to pay salaries of "an army of bureaucrats," and to cover Spain's national deficit. Without Cuba, it would be impossible to retain Puerto Rico, Guam, and the Philippines, not to mention even consider adding territory in North Africa and elsewhere.[8]

Spain and the United States clashed during the early nineteenth century over the independence movements in Spain's colonies, which the United States supported. US ambitions to control Florida, which included frequent incursions in the early 1800s to fight Indians, were met with Spanish hostility. In the face of continued US demands and intervention, as well as Spain's inability to defend its colony, in 1819 the United States pressured the Spanish to sign the infamous Adams-Onís Treaty. This agreement transformed Florida into a US territory in exchange for token diplomatic concessions. In return the United States promised to respect the western and southern borders with Spain's Mexican colony, a promise neglected during the Mexican War, when in fact Spain no longer controlled Mexico. Although the annexation of Florida weakened the presence of the Spanish on the North American continent and therefore averted potential military and political confrontations, it did not end the tensions that predated even the founding of the United States. Aside from the brief period of collaboration during the American Revolution, when Spain and the American colonists saw their interests align briefly in opposition to the United Kingdom, the two nations were at best neutral to each other, but more often at odds over territory in the Americas, borders, cultural values, and social systems.[9]

Continued Spanish occupation of Cuba, so close to the United States, was also a contentious issue, and at the forefront of confrontations between the two nations. Tolerance within the United States for the organization of private invasion forces—known as "filibusters," and formed to encourage an anti-Spanish uprising in Cuba—was another difficult issue in diplomatic relations. While the US federal government took some steps to prevent these groups from attacking Cuba, Southern politicians including governors, senators, and congressmen provided open endorsements and material aid to these groups, some of which reached Cuba with volunteers, weapons, and calls to arms for the local population, which they hoped would rise against Spanish occupation. Many Southern politicians felt somewhat conflicted over Spain and Cuba. Preferring to annex Cuba as a slave state or states, they still preferred that it remain under Spanish control if seizure or purchase by the United State meant abolition; in this case, sectional and economic interests outweighed nationalism or patriotism in favor of the United States of America. Better Spanish if slave, than American if free, ran this logic.[10]

During the Latin American Wars for Independence, which began soon after the Napoleonic occupation of Spain in 1808, the United States openly supported the new republics. During the decade that followed Napoleon's defeat in 1815, as Spain under the absolutist king Ferdinand VII tried unsuccessfully to reclaim its lost colonies, the United States made no secret of its enthusiasm for Simón Bolivar, José de San Martín, and other leaders of Latin American independence. The issuing of the Monroe Doctrine of 1823, which declared the hemisphere off-limits to renewed European imperialism, was aimed most especially at Spain, the country most open in its efforts to control American territory.

The 1830s and 1840s, after the failure of Spain's efforts to recapture its lost terrain, saw the economic and political rise of the United States at the same time as Spain endured the Carlist civil wars and other elements of internal political and economic instability. US ambitions to achieve its "Manifest Destiny," of a transoceanic state, led to the annexation of Texas in 1845 and the Mexican-American War that followed in 1846. The US promise to respect the border with Mexico, as pledged in the Adams-Onís Treaty, was not extended to sovereign Mexico. Not just Texas, but what would later become the territories and then states of Arizona, New Mexico, California, Colorado, and parts of Nevada and Wyoming came under the control of the United States of America. Spain, despite its own efforts to keep Mexico as its own colony in the 1820s, was outraged at what it considered blatant American aggression against Mexico. Spain supported Mexico in the Mexican-American War, arguing internationally that Mexico was the aggrieved party, although fears that the United States would use any provocation to seize Cuba meant Madrid was unable to provide material support. Even though Spain was unable to lend any direct military aid to Mexico (aid that in any case might not have been accepted), the permanent cession of almost half of Mexico to the United States in the Treaty of Guadalupe Hidalgo (1848) was seen in Spain as one more Yankee outrage against Spain's former imperial sphere of influence.[11]

While during the Mexican-American War Spain had offered to mediate between the two belligerents, its sympathies had clearly been with Mexico. Spain's preference was for Mexico either to return to Spanish control, to become an independent monarchy, or to become a protectorate of another European state. Only in this way, the Spanish government believed, would the unstable nation have a chance to resist US territorial encroachment. Some Spaniards feared that all of Mexico might be annexed by the United States. Despite having withdrawn as the colonial power in 1821 (although it did not recognize Mexican independence until 1836), Spain remained heavily invested in the Mexican economy, with extensive trade between Cuba and the Mexican port of Vera Cruz significant to both nations. During the war, the US Navy seized several Spanish ships for alleged smuggling. After the conflict, the United States refused to consider compensation for these seizures, which exacerbated feelings that already tense. Having been unable to prevent war between the United States and Mexico, Spain was relieved in 1848 that the Treaty of Guadalupe Hidalgo at least preserved Mexico as independent, albeit greatly truncated by the loss of its northwestern provinces.[12]

US and Spanish interests did converge over the issue of slavery, as Spain's colony of Cuba maintained its slave economy in the midst of a global effort by the United Kingdom to promote abolitionism in the 1840s. Along with Cuba, Brazil, the American South, and the Republic of Texas were the primary holdouts against this British campaign. President John Tyler made the defense of slavery in the United States a primary goal of his administration and foreign policy. He and his allies expressed their "ideological sympathy for Cuba and Brazil" and attempted to forestall successful emancipation there or anywhere slavery still prevailed.[13]

Spain did manage to retain its sovereignty over Cuba and Puerto Rico, however, a fact noticed by many American, especially Southern American, politicians. Many senators and congressmen wanted to annex Cuba, the "Pearl of the Antilles," but a higher priority was to prevent it from becoming a British colony or otherwise ending the practice of slavery there. Maintaining slavery on the island of Cuba was more important to most pro-slavery politicians than the actual ownership of the territory.[14] Whether it was to be independent, controlled by Spain, or annexed to the United States as one or several states (four states was a common proposal), the fundamental necessity was to preserve the institution of slavery in Cuba.[15] Should emancipation come to Cuba, it would inexorably move to the United States, following this early version of the domino theory. Absent successful abolition in Cuba, there would be less vulnerability for Southern slavery. Fears that Spain would lose control of Cuba to the British, who would allow the island to become "a black military republic" along the lines of Haiti, were pervasive. Even more frightening was the possibility that Mexico and Britain would cooperate to bring emancipation to the Republic of Texas, independent from Mexico since 1836. Emancipated slaves in Texas could then allow it to become a haven for escaped slaves as well as a base for future black rebellions in Southern states and Cuba. While the same fears applied to Brazil, its distance from the United States reduced the imminence of that threat as did its independence and larger size. The 1845 annexation of the Republic of Texas to the United States did diminish some fears of a successful British campaign for emancipation in the entire hemisphere, but Cuba remained a proximate and serious concern in the minds of many interested in defending slavery in the American South.[16]

Cuba was very important to the United States in the 1830s and 1840s, and by itself was America's third most important trading partner after the British and French. Even more than its trade significance was its role as a slave economy, in a hemisphere where abolitionism and emancipation appeared to be gaining traction. Although many US politicians wanted to gain control of Cuba, and to a lesser extent Puerto Rico, until this happened they preferred both colonies to remain in weak Spanish hands rather than become independent or the territory of Britain or France. With continued control by Spain, there was an expectation that slavery would continue. Independent, many feared Cuba would become another Haiti, with a slave revolt and massacres of white landowners. As a British colony, there was no doubt that emancipation would follow immediately after the arrival of the Union Jack, thus adding momentum to the abolition of slavery in the United States. By the 1840s, the United States was committed to using force to keep Cuba and Puerto Rico under Spanish control, with slavery and open ports to the United States, unless both could be purchased or otherwise acquired from Spain. This policy angered Britain, which had its own designs on the Caribbean and which supported abolitionism, even to the point of encouraging slave revolts.[17] Until the mid-1840s, Britain and France were willing to offer a security guarantee to ensure Spanish control over Cuba for Spain, but Spain for reasons of national pride rejected these offers. Later, during the 1850s, when Spain asked for this guarantee, Britain and France had become reluctant. Both feared conflict with the increasingly powerful United States, after the Mexican-American War showed its strength and greatly expanded its territory, population, and resources.[18]

Southern politicians made no secret of their ambition to annex Cuba as a slave state and, given the ongoing failure of diplomatic means to gain the island, mounted several military expeditions to achieve that end. The drive for the annexation of Cuba was wildly popular in the South and accelerated after Texas joined the United States, giving rise to local efforts across the region to organize armed units to cross the Caribbean and spark an anti-Spanish uprising. Secret societies and public organizations formed in major cities, and the idea gained traction among Southern congressmen and senators, especially in the aftermath of the successful Mexican War. The most notorious annexationist campaign was the August 1851 invasion of Cuba by Narciso López, a Venezuelan adventurer, and almost four hundred volunteers, supported by Southern US "filibusters." While most of López's supporters were Southerners, he also was able to generate some enthusiasm and funds from Northern commercial interests and believers in Manifest Destiny. While his goal was to annex Cuba to the United States and maintain slavery, joining Cuba to the United States was not only endorsed by those who supported slavery. Despite the enthusiasm with which it was launched, the operation had failed by early September. López was captured, his landing party was imprisoned or executed, and hostility revived between the United States and Spain. The Spanish government and its colonial administrators blamed Washington for allowing the expedition to raise money, train volunteers, and equip itself in Southern ports.[19]

Given the proximity of Spain's Caribbean possessions to the American South and the history of the region as the primary base for filibustering campaigns, it should come as no surprise that Cubans served in the Confederate army. By one estimate, at least seventy former residents of Cuba joined Southern units, including a company of Cubans organized in New Orleans. One key player within the filibustering movement was Ambrosio José Gonzáles, an émigré from Cuba and collaborator with López. Gonzáles, an American citizen, became a favorite of many Southern politicians and military figures, including P. G. T. Beauregard, John C. Calhoun, and initially, Jefferson Davis, who probably preferred to see a Cuban American face at the front of annexationist efforts in the Caribbean. A chief organizer of efforts to send filibustering expeditions to Cuba, Gonzáles became an early supporter of Southern secession and served during the American Civil War as a colonel in the Confederate army. During the war, his time was primarily in positions responsible for logistics and artillery, including in coastal defenses and as chief of artillery for General Beauregard.[20] Gonzáles later ran afoul of Jefferson Davis, perhaps over his association with Beauregard or as a result of too many requests for promotion. This personality conflict with the president of the Confederacy continued to the end of the Civil War and prevented his promotion to the rank of general, despite qualifications, contributions to the war effort, and political connections that matched or exceeded those of others who achieved this grade.[21]

The United States offered on several occasions to purchase Cuba from Spain, following the precedent of the $15 million spent on the American purchase of the Louisiana Territory and the payment of

$5 million in 1819 to acquire Florida from Spain and settle claims against it. The initial proposed price for Cuba was much higher: $100 million in 1848, offered to Spain by US minister to Spain Romulus Saunders, a Southern politician sent to Madrid even though he spoke no Spanish or French. His offer, conveyed on behalf of President James K. Polk, was rejected immediately, and he returned home in 1849. Five years later, the United States renewed the offer, this time at $130 million but in even less diplomatic terms. US diplomats in Europe—including John Mason and Pierre Soule, two ardent proslavery Southerners—collaborated with James Buchanan, who would two years later become president, to issue the draft Ostend Manifesto in October 1854. This statement demanded that Spain sell Cuba or face a war with the United States. Buchanan and others feared that, given the weakness of Spain, Cuba's slaves might revolt, following the example of Haiti. Britain and France supported Spain's vehement objection to this document, which quickly became an embarrassment to the United States. The declaration was repudiated by then secretary of state William Macy and was never formally issued, but it put an end to negotiations with Spain over the issue.[22] Before the manifesto there was a small chance that Spain's Liberal Party might have agreed to sell Cuba, but the events of 1854 ended that possibility.[23] No matter how large the purchase price offered or the accompanying commercial advantages proposed to Spain or the amount of "moderation" in the offer, no Spanish politician, especially at a time of rising national self-confidence, could entertain the idea of selling Cuba to the United States, or any other power.[24]

Some Southerners even dreamed bigger than just attaining control over Cuba and promoted the idea of annexing the entire Caribbean basin, from Cuba to the Antilles to coastal Mexico to Central America. This vast territory, open to slavery, could transform the United States and clearly tip the domestic political balance away from the free states. Plantations of sugar, cotton, rice, tobacco, and other crops could support an expanded planter class of whites and reinvigorate the slave economy. Southern politicians spoke openly of reinstituting slavery in Mexico and elsewhere where it had been banned, believing that creoles in these territories would welcome the stronger hand over the indigenous population that uniting with the United States would bring. Although there was some ambivalence among Southern politicians for annexing large sections of Mexico or beyond (with particular concern over the problematic absorption of mestizo populations), after the Mexican-American War, 1846–1848, this was at least considered a possibility. Particularly attractive was the expectation that new states would add sufficient numbers of US senators to counterbalance the rising advantage of free states in the House of Representatives.

No such ambivalence existed in the desire to gain Cuba as a state. Without a significant mestizo population and already with an economy based on slavery, the island could be integrated into the United States politically to match its close economic ties. Cuba consistently ranked in the top four trading partners with the United States, exporting sugar and other crops in exchange for US manufactured goods. Cuba was also of key importance to the United States as a potential transit point for a projected canal in Central America, and its eventual annexation by the United States would not only reflect the ongoing US ambition to implement the Monroe Doctrine fully—by driving out the last Spanish redoubts from the hemisphere—but also practically end Spanish tariffs on US sales to Cuba.[25]

Enthusiasm for annexation ran especially high among planters in the southern United States but also in Cuba itself among the landed aristocracy and plantation owners, who believed that Spain's weakness would eventually lead to emancipation or independence. It was primarily the wealthy sugar plantation owners in Cuba who supported being absorbed by the United States, and these creoles—mostly members of the influential Club de la Habana opposed to Spanish trade restrictions—had disproportionate means to support their ambitions.[26] Some Southerners even dreamed that Cuba, which had a white majority of 57 percent, could become four new slave states, balancing expected accessions by free states. There were sporadic movements by Spanish creoles in Cuba to support this effort. These efforts were fairly minimal, however, in the face of the greater fear that any unrest might lead to slave uprisings as had happened with devastating effect in Haiti in 1798, when European plantation owners had been slaughtered and a black republic established with Haiti's final independence from France coming in 1804.[27]

The Spanish government had excellent intelligence on the filibustering movement, collected from public information as well as from inside sources. With this evidence, Spanish diplomats protested vigorously to the US government, from as early as the 1840s, about the activities of the filibusters. President Taylor directed US attorneys and other officials to keep careful watch on these movements and to prosecute violations of federal law, but the widespread sympathy for the filibusterers in the South made successful prosecutions in that region difficult at best.[28] What had been difficult soon became nearly impossible with the move of most annexationist leaders from New York and Washington, DC, to New Orleans and other Southern cities after 1850. In the South, friendly governors, mayors, and other local officials could provide protection and logistical support, adding even more burdens to the federal efforts to stymie filibustering. These campaigns, which in any case had never been very vigorous, fell far short of what the Spanish government had requested of the US government. Gonzáles and López themselves, the two best-known leaders of the movement, were detained several times by US marshals, with charges brought forward by state and federal prosecutors. In each case, the Spanish government was disheartened to see these cases dismissed for lack of evidence or, as with three federal trials in New Orleans, resulting in deadlocked juries and the end of federal attempts at prosecution.[29]

The filibusters made another major landing on May 19, 1850, with just over six hundred volunteers invading the northern coastal town of Cárdenas, Cuba, before being expelled from it the same day by the local Spanish army garrisons. In order to forestall future assaults, Spain developed and used a network of espionage agents and paid informers in the United States to infiltrate the movement in the hopes of gathering intelligence or misdirecting its attacks on Cuba.[30] A final landing, conducted by Narciso López in August 1851, ended in total failure. Spanish soldiers successfully moved against the expedition, reversing its temporary gains. Instead of bringing a revolution to Cuba, the landing resulted in the death or capture of approximately 350 filibusters, including López himself, and effectively ended major operations of this type against the Spanish occupation of Cuba. Spain was hardly a military giant, but it clearly possessed sufficient means to defend its territory against poorly trained adventurers, whose strategy rested on rallying a white minority that already dominated Cuba's economy and social system.[31] The landing raised such a furor in Spain that there were public demonstrations in Madrid and other cities, nearly leading to a riot against US diplomatic offices in the capital.[32]

Despite the failure of the filibustering movement, Spain faced diplomatic pressure from Britain, in particular, to emancipate its slaves as a way to undermine Southern enthusiasm for annexation. Spain understood that the British would not intervene to protect Cuba from seizure by the United States so long as this meant defending the institution of slavery. With France in support of the British position, Spain would stand alone against renewed filibustering or even outright American military aggression. Having lost Florida as a result of US pressure and thinly veiled blackmail, Spain understood the seriousness of the Cuba situation and the attraction of British protection. The British navy could be a shield for Cuba, Lord Palmerston argued, should Madrid be willing to undertake abolition. Spain did make modest efforts to encourage manumission by individual landowners and to enhance bans on slave trading but stopped well short of what the British would have preferred: complete emancipation of all slaves in Cuba and Puerto Rico. The fear in Madrid that the white population in Cuba might see emancipation as sufficient motivation to declare independence or join with the South forestalled any serious movement in this direction by the Spanish government.[33]

Spain's naval presence in the Caribbean and its efforts to defend its colonies against smugglers and filibusters—including boarding and impounding civilian vessels—provided another grievance for anti-Spanish agitation. Expeditions had to navigate through seas patrolled by the Spanish navy, eager to sink ships filled with what Spain regarded as traitors and enemy combatants.[34] The most famous incident of this category occurred in 1854, when the Spanish colonial government seized the US-flagged merchant ship *Black Warrior* in the port of Havana. Port officials took this action after identifying that the captain had listed the cotton in the ship's cargo hold as ballast—and therefore free of tariffs—in an attempt to avoid paying Spanish duties on the commodity. Realizing that this seizure would be seen by the Americans as a provocative act against free commerce, the Spanish governor signed an order, dated prior to the event, authorizing such confiscations of illegal cargo. Technically, the Spaniards did have the authority to impose and collect duties on cotton imports and other goods, but the process followed in the case of the *Black Warrior* left them vulnerable to charges of arbitrary enforcement, given the widespread smuggling by Americans and others that was tolerated in Spanish waters.[35]

The event became a major diplomatic conflict, and US secretary of state Daniel Webster presented a report to Congress about the crisis. This official version, which included diplomatic correspondence, affidavits, police reports, and other official and private documents between US officials, Spanish diplomats, and private citizens, provided a damning account, entirely from the US perspective. Webster's information also referenced sixteen other incidents involving US-flagged vessels or American citizens in conflict with Spanish authorities, in or around Cuba, during the years 1839–1854. Included in the inventory were a wide range of offenses, including interdicted mail, unfair duties, arrests, and impounding of US-owned property by Spanish colonial representatives. Of course, left out of the inventory were US offenses against Cuba, including toleration for the filibusters, attacks on Spanish interests, and diplomatic blackmail to force the sale of Cuba. The report caused a stir in Congress and in public opinion, and the two thousand copies printed received ample coverage in the press. Some Southern senators called for war against Spain for this affront, but negotiations led to a calmer settlement in 1855 with the Spanish government paying an indemnity for its actions.[36] The initial US demand, that Spain sell Cuba in order to fund the compensation of wronged Americans, was never taken seriously by the Spanish government.[37]

US congressional support for annexation had begun to decline that very year, however, as opposition to the Kansas-Nebraska Act of 1854—which opened both territories to slavery—motivated Northern congressmen to take a stronger stand against the potential expansion of slave territories or states within the Union. The same act emboldened Southern politicians and their Northern and Western allies to aim for more annexation as rapidly as possible—further exacerbating the widening gap between North and South. These years 1854–1856 also saw heightened agitation in the United States for the annexation of Cuba, as Britain, France, and Russia were too embroiled in the Crimean War to pay much notice to events in the Western hemisphere, or so many Southerners believed.[38]

While Cuba agreed to pay for damages claimed by American merchants, who alleged that Spanish authorities damaged or impounded legal cargo in and around Cuban waters, changes in Spain made it less likely that the United States would in the future be able to bully Spain into selling Cuba on American terms or otherwise complying with US interests. Indeed, clumsy US initiatives to force a sale of Cuba by bribing officials or pressuring Spain to sell the island to make payments on Spanish debts only increased the unwillingness of Spanish officials to consider these proposals. On June 30, 1858, General Leopoldo O'Donnell became prime minister, appointing Saturnino Calderón Collantes as his foreign minister. Calderón immediately conveyed to US diplomats that Spain would never sell Cuba.[39] To demonstrate that this position was more than merely political posturing or a negotiating gambit, O'Donnell's government used the ongoing threat of US military action to pursue larger military budgets and a more aggressive foreign policy in defense of Spanish interests in the Americas and worldwide.[40]

The failures of the filibusters and the purchase offers put a temporary end to American ambitions toward Cuba. Another factor was the obvious strengthening of Spanish power in the Caribbean during the 1850s. A revived Spanish economy reduced the attractiveness of American dollars, and investments in the Spanish army and navy improved Cuba's ability to resist filibusters or even US attacks.[41] Spain increased its military forces in Cuba from nineteen thousand in 1853 to thirty thousand in 1859 and also pursued peninsularization—filling key positions in the Cuban colonial and military administration with native-born Spaniards rather than creoles born in Cuba. Although this led to resentment among the native whites, it did improve the reliability and effectiveness of the Spanish forces. While many creoles had served Spain loyally during the attacks of the filibusters, some had exhibited mixed loyalties over potential annexation to the United States. There were no such problems with regiments raised entirely from recruits from the Iberian Peninsula. As early as the mid-1850s, the strengthened Spanish military posture effectively deterred additional filibustering efforts, including a major expedition planned by former Mississippi governor John Quitman, which aborted in April 1855. For the moment, at least, Cuba was safe, at least from privately funded invasion.[42]

Other than its status as a slave territory, Cuba was attractive for its agricultural productivity and potential for seamless integration into the United States. Cuba remained an island whose economy was based on one commodity—sugar cane. Although tobacco, cotton, and subsistence crops were grown, they were increasingly dominated by this one product, so suited for growth in the Caribbean. Cuban harbors and roads and its proximity to the United States also made production of this commodity financially rewarding for landowners on the island. Sugar cane contributed 70 percent of overall agricultural production, employed just over 50 percent of the slave population, and grew on 25 percent of the available land. Just as cotton was king in the South, so sugar was king in Cuba. The overwhelming majority of this sugar (over 75 percent) went to the US market in the 1840s and 1850s, a trend that increased over time. The United States came to dominate Cuba's external trade, purchasing 89 percent of its sugar and molasses in 1858. In 1859, 41 percent of all Cuban exports went to the United States while only 12 percent went to Spain. Of this total, 84 percent of Cuba's exports were sugar or molasses. Close trade ties, however, did not necessarily lead to cordial diplomatic connections.[43]

Difficulties continued between the two countries in 1860, the last full year before the beginning of the Civil War. Under President Buchanan, the United States pressed Spain to negotiate a treaty to resolve outstanding claims by American citizens, mostly for alleged offenses against persons and property in and around Cuba. After difficult discussions, Spain and the United States agreed in March 1860 to a convention to establish a joint commission, empowered with the authority to adjudicate. Spain promised an initial $100,000 toward the $128,635.54 in total claims, with the balance depending on the commission's final evaluation. The Buchanan administration supported the agreement and sent it to the US Senate for ratification on May 3, but the Senate voted down the measure on June 27, 1860, regarding it as insufficient redress for the array of grievances against Spain. Many senators still looked to the annexation of Cuba as the final necessary adjustment. President Buchanan supported the same goal of acquisition but committing to a "fair purchase" and "upon conditions highly favorable to Spain" at a mutually agreed price. Given the absolute intransigence of Spanish political figures on the idea of ceding Cuba to the United States, it would be difficult to imagine what possible combination of price and conditions could meet this test.[44] Indeed, Spain's ministers to Washington, DC, had no higher priority than forestalling an American annexation or forcible purchase of Cuba. Fear of even more US dominance of trade with Cuba also meant that Spain deferred discussions of a commercial treaty with the United States as well, fearing that what little Hispano-Cuban trade existed would be absolutely sidelined by merchants and bankers from the economic powerhouse to the North.[45]

Even though the Cuba issue had faded somewhat as domestic politics—and the threat of secession—rose in importance in the years prior to the Civil War, it never disappeared completely. While the newly formed Republican Party did not seek foreign territory or make any mention of Cuba in its (admittedly brief) platform, both sides of the divided Democratic Party did so. The Northern Democratic faction, whose nominee was US senator Stephen Douglas of Illinois, reaffirmed the party platform of 1856, which had called for a stronger presence in the Caribbean, but then included more specific language, stating that the United States should acquire Cuba in a way that would be "honorable to ourselves and just to Spain."[46] The Southern Democrats and their nominee, Vice President John C. Breckinridge of Kentucky, adopted nearly identical language in their platform, adding only the phrase "at the earliest practicable moment." Neither the Whigs nor the Constitutional Union parties made mention of Cuba or Spain in their electoral platforms.[47]

In this environment, the position of Spanish diplomatic envoy to the United States was an unenviable position, as Gabriel García Tassara, appointed minister to Washington, DC, in 1856, was to discover. Upon arriving, presenting his credentials, and taking his post in February 1857, the young poet and politician from Seville almost immediately was confronted with an ongoing national discussion over how to annex Cuba, a territory that had been in Spanish hands since the 1490s. For American politicians it was only a question of when—not if—Cuba would become a US territory and then state or states. At the age of thirty-nine when he first arrived in the United States, Tassara was well connected in Andalusian political and economic circles. Despite his youth, his personal health was always precarious, which limited his effectiveness in the rambunctious politics of the United States. Tassara's mandate was to do what he could to limit the expansion of the United States in Latin America as well as to work to promote greater cohesion—and perhaps, at some distant point—political union with former Spanish colonies in the Americas.[48]

Given the relative weakness of Spain in contrast to the United States, Tassara's mission was a difficult one—to persuade Latin American republics, most of whom had violently expelled Spanish forces of occupation, to choose Spain over the United States, which had supported their campaigns for independence and was the economic colossus of their hemisphere. Complicating his task were the frequent changes in the Spanish Foreign Ministry. Given that it could take upward of a month for his diplomatic messages to reach Madrid, there were frequent occasions when Tassara would reply to a message from the foreign minister, only to discover months later that his answer had arrived after a change in the cabinet. Civil servants in Madrid continually had to brief new ministers, who by the time they developed an understanding for the position would be reshuffled once again. While General O'Donnell's persistence in the office of prime minister was unusual, and it did provide some consistency, he did not provide direct guidance to Spain's diplomatic representatives. Minister Tassara likely felt somewhat on his own in his mission.[49]

Minister Tassara's hopes to convince American politicians to put aside plans to annex Cuba were eventually successful, though more so out of developments in domestic US politics than from anything the Spanish diplomat was able to accomplish. In February 1859, the US Senate took up the issue of annexing Cuba as its most important order of business, with a proposed law to grant the president $30 million to initiate negotiations to purchase the island. President Buchanan had sent an envoy to Spain to negotiate in this direction, hoping that congressional action and divisions within the Spanish government might make a final sale possible. The US Senate debate foreshadowed the future struggle over Confederate diplomacy; the bill's sponsor was Democratic senator John Slidell of Louisiana, later to serve as one of the South's main emissaries to Europe. In opposition was Republican senator William Seward of New York, later to serve as President Lincoln's secretary of state. The Senate bill eventually failed, in the face of united opposition by Republicans. In the meantime a unanimous vote by the Spanish Senate against selling Cuba and the failure of Buchanan's envoy to Spain, William Preston, rendered the proposal moot.[50] Buchanan's efforts to annex Cuba had not been very popular except in the South, and his failure in the US Senate marked the final collapse of his efforts to take over the Caribbean island. President Buchanan claims that Cuba was "comparatively unimportant" to Spain, as in his speech to Congress on 6 December 1858, showed a lack of comprehension of Spain's attachment to the island as well as of its essential status in the Spanish empire.[51]

Beginning in 1860, and then during the American Civil War, Spain's primary ally in the Americas was France. While France remained dependent on the United Kingdom's tolerance for its overseas ambitions, France like Spain did push this forbearance mightily in the Americas. Intervention in Mexico, proposals to reoccupy Haiti, serious consideration of an alliance with the Confederacy, and even suggestions that this might come at the expense of territory in Texas—these were the serious actions and plans of the French emperor, Napoleon III, in the Americas. For good reason, as the Civil War was beginning, partisans of secession and of union were convinced that France would enthusiastically welcome the permanent division of the United States, even though the French position was in fact far more ambivalent, given the uncertainties that would accompany secession as well as the mercurial nature of Napoleon III.[52] The French ambassador to the United States, Henri Mercier, even became involved in a proposal during the war to mediate personally between Presidents Lincoln and Davis. Mercier wanted to avoid exposing France to retaliation after "premature recognition" of the Confederacy should the United States reassert its authority over the South, yet he did advise the French government to be prepared to offer "immediate" diplomatic ties should the survival of the rebellion seem more certain.[53] Before the Civil War began, the chance for such foreign intervention had the potential, at least in the opinion of Secretary of State William Seward, to rally Southerners against outside interference; once the war started, however, the potential for foreign recognition, even support from foreign warships and soldiers, was a cause for optimism among the Southern rebels.[54]

The tensions between Spain and the United States established a hostile climate between the two nations in the years leading up to 1861 and the beginning of the American Civil War. This climate continued even as the United States split into two nations at war with each other. Cuba remained an ambition for both the United States and the Confederacy, which explains why neither would grant an unconditional public guarantee to Spain permanently recognizing its possession of the island.[55] Once the American Civil War began, President Lincoln made little mention of Cuba. Of course, it had been primarily Democratic politicians who had publicly agitated for US control, but even Lincoln and many Republicans believed that Cuba would eventually become part of the United States.[56]

Even so, it was the military and economic power of the United States that loomed larger as a threat to Spain before, during, and after the American Civil War. Although they never were officially enemies, there was a broad context for mistrust between the United States of America and the Kingdom of Spain, especially over the issue of Cuba. There might well be more opportunity for a fresh start between Spain and the Confederacy, but Spanish politicians understood that the leaders of the rebellion, including Jefferson Davis, had been important US figures before they took positions in the Confederacy. American politicians, especially Southern politicians, had made no secret of their desire to take hold of the island, which the latter hoped would tip the balance in favor of slavery in the United States, perhaps by becoming several new slaveholding states and serving as a bridge to even more expansion in the Caribbean.

Many of these same pro-slavery politicians would become key figures in the Confederate States of America, complicating efforts to gain a sympathetic hearing from the same Spanish government that Southerners had threatened so often and even openly attacked in the preceding decades. Nonetheless, conversations in the direction of an alliance did advance surprisingly far during the first year of the American Civil War. Both Spain and the Confederacy, despite their deep misgivings, held their most hostile feelings toward a common enemy: the Union remnant of the United States of America, regarded by both as an impediment to their own survival, territory, and national sovereignty in the Western hemisphere. Over this single issue—that of a shared antipathy toward the Yankees—Southerners and Spaniards could find significant shared political ground. In the end, it would be nearly enough for both nations to look past their previous grievances.

Chapter 2

Spain in the Mid-Nineteenth Century

Even after the end of its sixteenth-century Golden Age, Spain continued to be globally significant because of the extent and importance of its territorial possessions. The country had been in relative decline for many years, and the Napoleonic years were cataclysmic, causing the loss of most of its empire, not to mention its army, navy, and national sovereignty. This debility would continue in the midst of internal weakness and civil war, even after the expulsion of the French in 1813. During the mid-nineteenth century, Spain briefly seemed to be on the rise internationally, with growing influence in Africa, Asia, Europe, and even Latin America. Forays into Southeast Asia, Morocco, and the Caribbean seemed to indicate that Spain was attempting to reclaim its seventeenth-century greatness. Spain remained focused primarily on its European affairs, yet it looked increasingly to Latin America as an arena for restoring its influence. Indeed, the French and British supported the Spanish revival, believing it could serve as a useful counterweight to the United States in the Caribbean and Pacific.[1] Some Spaniards even spoke openly of reclaiming Portugal, which had been controlled by the Spanish monarchy once before (1580–1640).[2]

Spain, which had been considered a great power as recently as the mid-eighteenth century, was by the early nineteenth century a decidedly minor state, with strength and reputation comparable to the Netherlands, Portugal, or Denmark, all of whom had overseas colonies but little influence over major European or global events. Although it did participate in the deliberations, Spain was not considered one of the five major powers at the Congress of Vienna (1814–1815) and had suffered tremendous losses, both internal and external, from the Napoleonic era to the first Carlist war (1833–1840). Spain also lacked a strong leader with experience or education in international affairs. Isabel II was inconsistent in her policies. With a few exceptions, talented Spanish politicians were not interested in foreign policy, and those interested in foreign policy were not especially talented. The Spanish army and navy were also weak, just beginning to rebuild after tremendous losses, and there was not a strong intellectual climate promoting imperial expansion. Most European states recognized Spain as a client of the British and French, and ongoing disputes over the legitimacy of Isabel II had forestalled recognition by some governments, including Austria, the Vatican and Prussia, until 1848.[3]

Spanish officials realized in the 1850s and 1860s, even as their strength was rising, that they could not confront the United States or any other major power on their own. The American Civil War was a perfect opportunity to take advantage of the temporary weakness of the United States, provided Spain could find allies in this endeavor. The most obvious choice was the Confederacy itself, which explains Spanish interest, however tentative, in supporting the fortunes of the Southern rebels. United with the Confederacy, French-controlled Mexico, and with the tacit support of France and Great Britain, Spain could have stood against the United States during this period, a possibility explored with great interest by both Confederate and Spanish officials.[4]

For a short time there seemed to be the possibility for internal domestic stability, economic growth, and a restoration of Spain to the ranks of major powers, if not quite to the level of France and Britain. This apparent internal calm was accompanied by rising external prestige, including on the fields of battle. In 1859–1860, Spain defeated Morocco and seized the territory of Tetuán, convincing the Spanish government under Queen Isabel II that it could restore the kingdom's former glory. For the first time in many years, the Spanish government was genuinely popular, a result of the Moroccan victory and general economic growth. Spain also benefited from close ties to the two principal political, commercial, and naval powers of the day, Britain and France. Unlike in previous centuries, when Spain had consistently been in conflict with one or both of these great states, from the 1830s to the late 1860s, the three states cooperated closely, albeit with Spain in a subaltern position. Spain had no love for either Great Power as it had suffered at the hands of both during the Napoleonic Wars, and under their commercial and imperial dominance thereafter. Given the strength of Paris and London, however, it was certainly less dangerous to be an ally to both than an enemy to either. Spain continued to resent the British occupation of Gibraltar and French territorial encroachment into North Africa, which provided an additional limitation on any true mutual understanding among the three nations.[5]

Underlying Spanish weaknesses—including unstable governments, high debt, peasant uprisings, civil wars, conflicts between liberals and conservatives, and dependence on Britain and France—limited its international freedom of maneuver, however, and prevented this rise from being more than ephemeral. Despite its ambitions Spain had not rebuilt its military either. Budgets and military personnel remained constant, or even slightly declined in the 1860s, despite increased overseas commitments in Asia, Africa, and the Americas. Dependent on the forbearance of the United Kingdom and to a lesser extent France, Spain had limited room to assert itself internationally, and even less means to do so.[6]

The country also lacked a strong leader with experience or education in international affairs. Spanish politicians rotated through ministries and other government positions too rapidly to have any permanent impact. The Spanish army and navy remained weak, just beginning to rebuild after tremendous losses in the Napoleonic Wars, Latin American Wars for Independence, and Carlist civil wars. Despite the historical and political context, with Spain having a long tradition of overseas engagement and now close ties to the two most powerful colonial powers, there was not a strong intellectual climate promoting imperial expansion. Even though Spain in the mid-nineteenth century had more opportunities to increase its profile as a power, it was unable to capitalize on these chances, and by the 1870s was once again below even such relatively weak states as Italy and the Ottoman empire in terms of military and economic power. After the 1860s, major European powers such as the United Kingdom, France, Germany, and Russia could in practice ignore Spain in their deliberations and actions. For a nation that still viewed itself as a Great Power, this was a humbling condition and increased the impetus to strengthen Spain's imperial image and reality. The Spanish writer Bravo Murillo remarked that Spain's attempted imperial revival was as realistic as "a very short man proclaiming himself tall."[7]

Among the many barriers to Spain's renaissance as an imperial power was the weakness of its military. A late and incomplete participant in the Industrial Revolution, the Spanish economy was unable to provide the materiel necessary for a modern army and navy. Attempting to keep pace with its European counterparts, the Spanish government began a succession of military reforms, embarked on major procurement efforts, and attempted to restructure its forces, but with very limited success. As an example, the Spanish army changed its primary infantry weapons on an average of every three years between 1802 and 1867, which led to a proliferation of rifles, muskets, carbines, pistols, and other small arms. This greatly complicated the task of supplying Spanish forces with ammunition and other necessities of war.[8]

The Spanish armed forces were also top-heavy in the officer corps. Without a mandatory retirement age, many generals and admirals never retired. The number of flag rank officers declined from 607 in 1861 to 466 in 1866, but this was still perhaps four or five times too many. Even after the creation of make-work positions for dozens of officers, 308 had no real assignments in 1862.[9] With too few actual duty positions, command posts, or other real assignments available, these senior officers were posted *de cuartel* (at the barracks), usually at 50 percent salary and with no responsibilities. Their pay continued to drain the military budget, however. As late as 1867, even after reforms to encourage retirement, there were over ninety serving generals aged seventy or older. Overall, the army had a tremendous surplus of commissioned officers. While other continental forces typically had one officer for every 50–100 soldiers, Spain's ratio was one officer for every 10–12 soldiers, and one general for every 125–150.[10] One benefit of Spain's growing foreign entanglements, however, was that it deployed more officers overseas and thereby removed them from domestic political intrigues and the temptation to participate in military *pronunciamientos* (declarations, or limited coups) or other disruptive actions against the monarchy.[11]

Given the poor conditions for troops, conscription was always a challenge for the central government. Many potential soldiers did their best to avoid service, even through leaving Spain. Emigration was a serious problem, as the families of young boys tried to send them to the colonies or encouraged them to emigrate to Latin America or the United States in order to avoid conscription. The Guardia Civil, Spain's national paramilitary police, had orders to watch the coast and port cities for young men trying to leave, and colonial governors were prohibited from issuing passports to boys who could not prove service or exemption. The government passed laws in 1856, 1861, and 1862 to enforce conscription regulations and to minimize exemptions, but filling manpower needs continued to be a struggle.[12] Even so, as late as 1865, 17 percent of recruits were able to purchase their way out of service, at a cost of eight thousand reales (two thousand pesetas) each. Wealthy families could also pay substitutes, for slightly less than a purchase, but if the substitute deserted, the original draftee would be liable for the entire term of service, making this a less attractive proposition.[13]

Spain had universal conscription obligations but selected only a certain percentage of the male population to serve the mandatory four-year terms in the army or navy. In 1860, 50,000 soldiers were drafted, with approximately 35,000 drafted during each of the following five years. Out of those initially drafted, close to 50 percent purchased or gained exemptions, causing additional rounds of conscription to fill the vacancies. The price for a substitute was between six and eight hundred pesetas. Of those who could not avoid service, approximately 45 percent went into the infantry. After exemptions and medical or physical disqualifications, in a typical year approximately 30,000 were inducted into the army, from a potential pool of 150,000 young men in each year group.[14] Each group of recruits would then be inducted into the active forces, which averaged approximately 115,000 during the 1860s, out of a total force (including reserves and paramilitaries) of just above 200,000 in most years. Organized into seventy-five regiments (forty infantry, twenty cavalry, and fifteen artillery) plus special troops, they could be assigned to Spain or the colonies, but most were based in the peninsula.[15]

Given the state of perpetual war, as well as the other conditions, many viewed the draft as a death sentence for recruits. Only those without means to avoid service put on the uniform, as demonstrated by the low numbers of volunteers (typically only two thousand annually), although this rose after the upsurge in patriotism following the Moroccan War.[16] Reenlistments also rose and avoidance decreased in the 1860s as conditions improved and Spain's army experienced a brief period of higher prestige. The reputation of Spain's troops also rose in Europe, with foreign observers noting an appreciable increase in the discipline and numbers of soldiers in the peninsula. Spanish army engineers and artillery, in particular, had greatly improved reputations, supported by their performance in Morocco, as well as numerous smaller operations in Europe, Asia, and Africa.[17]

Parallel to the increase in nationalism in the 1860s, however, there was also an economic slowdown after 1861, which proved a major factor to encourage volunteers. Disruptions in international commerce caused by the American Civil War and other conflicts and a downturn in the business cycle saw rising bankruptcies and fewer employment opportunities in Spain. The number of young men asking to join the army rose to an annual average of ten thousand by 1865, from less than five thousand in 1861. While many of these were unfit for service, nonetheless the increase was impressive.[18] The percentage of conscripts in the Spanish army remained high. In practice this meant that untested soldiers often bore the brunt of combat. Some historians have argued that this was by design; perhaps the Spanish army preferred to send recruits rather than veterans into battle, because they cost less if wounded. Veterans received higher pensions and salaries when they reenlisted, especially if they had been wounded. As Daniel Headrick wrote, "Spain wanted to have a large army and to fight wars with a small budget; in practice, this meant spending men instead of money."[19]

The navy, as well, suffered ongoing personnel shortages. Dangerous conditions onboard Spain's warships, inadequate rations, low pay for draftees, uniform shortages, and poor leadership all discouraged volunteers. The navy was so unattractive that those who found themselves drafted for sea service often tried to volunteer for the army instead.[20] Spain's navy had long suffered from neglect. Between 1796 and 1852, the navy had received not one single major new warship and only a few frigates and minor vessels. The nadir was in 1833 by which time the Spanish navy had declined to three major warships and three frigates. Spain was allied with England during most of this period and could count on the British to provide protection for its commerce, but nonetheless this was a humiliation for a nation that until the Napoleonic Wars had boasted the third largest fleet in the world, connecting Spain to its colonies in the Americas, Africa, and Asia.[21] Because of its internal instability and the first two Carlist civil wars (1833–1839 and 1846–1849), Spain lost valuable years of economic and military modernization, while the rest of western Europe was industrializing and building new navies. A major technological change left Spain even more behind its rivals, for after 1850, steam began overwhelmingly to replace sail as the primary means of propulsion in warships, although for a few years many vessels were equipped with both. Until the 1850s Spain was only able to purchase a handful of steam-powered warships and other ships of the line.[22]

During the period in question, 1861–1865, even the Spanish War Ministry was in turmoil, with nine different ministers occupying the top position—in some cases for only a few days or weeks. Many of Spain's liberal politicians, whose rotations through office were the butt of many jokes in the Spanish press, viewed ministerial positions as plums for loyalty—positions from which to dole out contracts, offices, and other perks to their allies, supporters, and relatives, rather than duties to fulfill in service to the nation.[23] The Navy Ministry, as well, saw a revolving door, with twenty-nine navy ministers in office in the fourteen years between July 1854 and September 1868. Of these, only three lasted more than one year in the position. Some of this was because of the overall instability and frequent cabinet shuffles during this period, but neither ministry was seen as particularly prestigious, at least during the 1850s.[24] The nineteenth century as a whole presented the same picture, with 129 war ministers in office (even excluding interim officeholders) between 1814 and 1899.[25]

A major military reform of 1844 strengthened the military, narrowed its focus to national defense, and created the Guardia Civil to take the internal security mission away from the army. These reforms attempted to bring reserve and active forces under the same hierarchy and established the end strength of approximately two hundred thousand. Subsequent governments devoted increasing financial resources (at least 40 percent of the national budget) to the armed forces, with generally positive results in terms of overall combat effectiveness and unity of command.[26] The army allocation remained at 16–18 percent of the national budget, with a similar amount going to the navy. This figure did not include dedicated local revenues (as in the colonies), which also provided for militias, coastal defenses, and other decentralized costs not paid by the Treasury in Madrid.[27]

The Spanish economy was not a particularly robust base from which to launch an imperial revival, but there were hopeful signs in some areas. During the 1840s and 1850s, Spain's annual growth in gross domestic product and per capita income remained around 1 percent. Figures for industrial production were much better, however, with annual rates closer to 5 percent—comparable to growth in France and some of the German states and superior to Italy, Austria-Hungary, and Russia. Exports, especially of agricultural products such as citrus, wool, and distilled spirits, contributed to a significant increase in earnings, although this was offset by even larger imports of manufactured products, especially from the United Kingdom.[28] Grain, wine, citrus and olive oil, agricultural products for which Spain had a comparative advantage in international trade, were the most significant exports, with wine alone contributing over 25 percent of the total export value.[29] The tax burden, land distribution, rural unemployment, and commodity prices remained sources of instability throughout the countryside, however, especially in the poorer south and west. Although not on a scale that threatened the national agricultural economy, there were peasant uprisings in 1856 and 1861 that interrupted the slow economic growth in many regions.[30] Resistance to conscription also played a role in this unrest, with both the army and the Guardia Civil involved in the repression.

Beyond the national picture, however, Spain saw particularly significant growth at the periphery. In Catalonia, port activities as well as industrial growth in textiles and other manufacturing contributed to a regional boom. By one measure alone, port usage, Barcelona experienced a fourfold increase between 1845 and 1862, leading one historian to call it "Spain's workshop." Textiles and shipbuilding—along with providing services to Catalonia and surrounding provinces—created the beginnings of a real middle class in Barcelona.[31] The Basque region, as well as adjacent territories in northern Spain, also experienced a period of above-average economic growth, in this case fueled by heavy industry, coal and iron ore mining from the nearby Asturias region, and other smokestack industries.[32] While still overshadowed by the dominant British economy, which by the 1850s produced half of the world's coal, iron, and textiles, Spain was growing into a minor industrial state, able to produce for domestic and foreign markets. The slow pace of revival, and the return of foreign merchants, nonetheless over time had a dramatic impact on the availability of goods and the overall prosperity of the Spanish economy.[33]

Fiscal and legal reforms during the 1850s contributed in a significant way to economic growth in Spain. The General Railway Law of 1855 provided major incentives for private capital to extend railroad lines and construct new networks and succeeded in attracting French, Belgian, and English investment. Trunk and feeder lines began to connect not just major cities but even less accessible regions throughout Spain, encouraging a stronger internal market and more opportunities for the export of cash crops, such as citrus, olive oil, and even some manufactured products. There was not yet a unified national rail system, and there would not be until the twentieth century, but Spain was beginning to enjoy the benefits of its first internal transportation infrastructure. Small communities that had previously been connected to Madrid, Barcelona, and other major cities only through a poor road network or coastal shipping lanes now found the rest of the nation increasingly accessible. Private and state-supported rail companies laid over three thousand kilometers of track in Spain between 1860 and 1870 alone, much of this financed with British and French foreign capital.[34]

After the initial wave of construction and enthusiasm over the new mode of transportation, however, by the late 1860s many lines found it hard to maintain their profitability, given the overly ambitions schedules many offered. Despite initial optimism about linking Spain's internal markets to the national economy and export opportunities, and a few years of economic growth at midcentury, the Spanish economy was still in the process of maturing to the level that it could accommodate such ambitions.[35] Although primary rail lines connected most of the major cities, the pace slowed after the completion of these main connections, as geography, difficulties in raising commercial capital, and the relatively modest size of Spanish railroad companies prevented a more widespread adoption of the new transportation technology.[36]

The broader political context was positive for a strengthening of Spain's international position. When Isabel II assumed the throne in 1843, after ten years of regency during her minority, Spain was emerging from the period of the Carlist civil wars, with major fighting having ended only in 1840. Under the queen, the Spanish government began a period of more moderate rule, with a revived Cortes, a liberal constitution, and restricted suffrage. Her reign saw the ending of aristocratic and clerical entails on land, a key in the transition to full private property. This change led to a marked increase in agricultural output, and after stagnating during the first few decades of the nineteenth century, by the 1840s the population began to grow as well. Census data is limited, but official figures from the end and the beginning of the century demonstrate the change: from 11.5 million in 1800 to 18.6 million in 1900.[37]

The Spanish market was uneven, however, with an agricultural sector laboring under inefficient land usage, an abundance of unskilled labor, low productivity, and low incomes. Large areas of potential agricultural activity, especially in the south, remained uncultivated and concentrated in large estates.[38] The available labor force was again on the increase, after the disruptions of the Napoleonic Wars and the Carlist civil wars of 1833–1839 and 1846–1849. Spain's population, growing slowly and steadily over the previous decades, reached just over 15.6 million in 1860, according to the census taken that year.[39] The restoration of normal life and the decreasing likelihood of another civil war encouraged not only investment but a return to larger families. Despite rising economic possibilities, emigration to Argentina and the United States continued in the aftermath of the Carlist wars, but by the end of this period the pace slowed somewhat. Economic growth in the mid-nineteenth century was beginning not only to convince Spaniards to remain, rather than emigrating, but also to bind the nation together politically and commercially through railroads, telegraphs, and other communications infrastructure.[40]

Although Spain's population growth in the nineteenth century was higher than in the seventeenth and eighteenth centuries, its rate of increase was far behind that of every other European state except Ireland, which suffered a dramatic famine in the 1840s, and France, which suffered disproportionately from the Napoleonic Wars and other conflicts. The areas of fastest population growth were the same areas that exhibited economic vibrancy—the peripheral regions including Catalonia, the Basque country, Asturias, and other regions outside the traditional Castilian heartland. The growth that did occur in the nineteenth century was most notable during the years from 1833 to 1860, when an absence of wars and major plagues joined with the beginnings of industrialization to cause a surge.[41] Indeed, during this period, the Spanish economy began to modernize, at least in relation to its previous experience. As Jaime Vicens Vives noted: "Almost all the century's institutions—and even some present-day ones—arose out of those years: reform of the Treasury and tax structure, establishment of the Bank of Spain (although it had existed in previous forms), definite establishment of provincial administration . . . construction of railways . . . the textile industry, and developed financial capitalism."[42]

The leading political figure in Spain's brief economic and imperial renaissance was General Leopoldo O'Donnell, the dominant political figure in Spain from 1854 to 1866, who served as prime minister from 1858 to 1863. In terms of government structure, this was one of the most stable political periods in the nineteenth century. O'Donnell, the leader of the Unión Liberal party, immediately increased military spending, first to defend against a perceived threat from Morocco but also to fulfill a more grandiose vision.[43] While O'Donnell served at the pleasure of the queen, he also benefited from a divided conservative opposition in the parliament. Initially, his position was solidified by the strengthening economy of the late 1850s and early 1860s.[44]

Planning to revive the Spanish empire in the Americas and Africa, or at least restore Spain to the ranks of the Great Powers after almost two centuries of decline, O'Donnell also hoped that a weakened United States would pose little challenge to the ongoing colonial occupation of Cuba, Puerto Rico, Guam, and the Philippines.[45] An effective prime minister with the support of the queen and, initially, the majority of the ruling elites, O'Donnell seemed poised to transform Spain. With his wars O'Donnell hoped to spark enthusiasm to create "a spirit of national enterprise" to remake Spain as a great power once again.[46] Unlike many Spanish politicians, the general was genuinely popular among the Spanish people and was also a close confidant of the queen: two factors that explain the longevity of his service.[47] Earlier in his military career, he had served as captain general of Cuba in the 1840s, when he provided sanctuary, arms, and ammunition to Dominican rebels fighting against Haiti. In 1844, these Dominican rebels successfully expelled their Haitian occupiers and reclaimed independence for their state. Later, as prime minister, General O'Donnell would once again see his career tied to events in Santo Domingo.[48]

The relationship with the rebellious American South seemed an arena where Spain could develop its own course. Prime Minister O'Donnell saw the CSA's interests coincide with Spain's resentment of the Monroe Doctrine, the US blockade of Southern ports, and "unjustifiable violence" against neutral shipping.[49] At the level of domestic Spanish politics, the prime minister hoped to change what had been a tradition of intense regional patriotism—for Castile, Catalonia, the Basque Country, Andalusia, other provinces, or even just cities and towns—into a national Spanish patriotism. Military successes, political unity, economic growth, and liberal politics would lead to a more cohesive Spain, after decades of foreign occupation, civil war, and penury.[50]

O'Donnell dominated Spanish politics during the late 1850s and early 1860s, after having earned the favor of the diffident and mercurial Queen Isabel II. While not always prime minister, he was the decisive factor in determining who else could fill the position. With his military experience in Cuba and elsewhere, he was keen to strengthen or even expand the Spanish empire. The threat of Carlism and reactionary monarchism had been defeated on the battlefields, yet the leaders of liberal Spain feared their resurgence, for the movement's values continued to be nursed in rural areas, among elements of the priesthood, and in many northern zones of Catalonia, Navarre, and Aragon. Within these communities, the centuries of the Spanish Inquisition were looked upon with nostalgia, for they were considered times of safety when Spain was protected against atheism, immorality, Protestantism, and other nefarious influences. In this context the traditional rights of certain towns and regions were seen as legitimate barriers against a centralizing and secularizing state. Just as dangerous to an increasingly assertive central state were the "sectional aspects" of Spanish politics, for many citizens judged their highest loyalty to be to their region or city rather than to national government or capital.[51]

Spain remained a mostly illiterate nation, especially in the rural areas, but there was a vibrant intellectual life in the cities. Although in theory the central government maintained tight censorship based on laws passed in 1857 and 1864, in practice a wide range of political perspectives were reflected in newspapers and other media such as illustrated weeklies, magazines, and pamphlets. There was in the 1850s and 1860s a proliferation of daily and weekly papers, with twenty-two dailies published in Madrid alone, expressing a range of political opinions from extreme rightist monarchists to conservative Catholics to moderates and liberals. There were constraints on the press (for example, none could safely call for the queen's abdication, for a secular state, or for revolution in Spain), but there was opportunity for dissent on other issues such as slavery, economic policy, and support for individual parties and figures within the liberal Isabelline political consensus.[52] While Spanish papers avoided the examination of scandals such as cases of corruption or personal moral turpitude by political figures, they did engage in "bitterly partisan" presentations of the issues of the day.[53] The popular press had little to no impact on policy, but they were read nonetheless for clues about activities within the court and government in Madrid.[54]

Spain's potential revival was strengthened during this period by its close identification with Great Britain, the most powerful nation in the world during the mid-nineteenth century. There were tensions between these two states, to be sure. After abolishing slavery in its empire in 1833, the British put increasing pressure on other states to do the same. Given Spain's dependence on the United Kingdom in trade and foreign relations, Spanish slave owners feared their government might undermine the slave economy in Cuba. Paradoxically, this was one action that could have actually strengthened international support for Madrid's Caribbean holdings, with the British and French more willing to pledge protection if free labor replaced slave. Still, there was a general alignment of policies. Given that it was the British who at key junctures—the defeat of the Spanish Armada in 1588, the destruction of the Spanish navy at Trafalgar in 1805—had raised insurmountable barriers to Spanish ambitions, gaining the British as allies was a necessary precursor to any imperial renaissance.

Spain followed the lead of the British in many cases, including accepting the 1856 maritime treaty at the Congress of Paris. By this agreement, the signatories conceded to the abolition of privateers, the principle that neutral ships with non-contraband goods were to be free from seizure in wartime, and that a blockade had to be effective to be legal—in other words, a nation declaring a blockade must be able to enforce it in order for it to receive international acceptance. This treaty, signed within a few years by every maritime power except the United States, would be significant during the American Civil War, when the neutrality of foreign commerce and the imposition of blockades would become issues of immediate relevance. Once the American Civil War began, the United States would "regret" not having acceded to the treaty, for the South did commission privateers and take advantage of neutral ships for its non-contraband cargoes. US efforts to sign the treaty after the Civil War began were deferred by the French and British, as the obvious self-interest of the United States was in gaining European collaboration against Southern privateers. Realizing this would not conform to their understanding of neutrality, the French and British rejected the US offer.[55]

The Spanish military saw a significant revival in the 1850s and 1860s. Spain's navy was the recipient of significant funds and support to rebuild its strength. During the early 1850s, Spain had only fifteen capital ships and all of them wooden sailing ships, but by 1867 it had completed six armored frigates, six smaller steam-powered warships, and twelve schooners, in addition to vessels acquired through foreign purchase.[56] The Spanish built dozens of ships, large and small, in their own dry docks and also contracted with the French and the British to build large ships. Despite tensions with the United States, Spain purchased thirty gunboats from US companies for use in the Caribbean. The new ships in the naval inventory were much better than those they replaced, with more steam, more steel, more cannons, and far greater capabilities all around.[57]

From 1856 to 1868, the Spanish navy received 170 vessels into the fleet, including armored frigates, corvettes, and other ships of the line. Almost all of these acquisitions were steamships, from British, French, and US shipyards. Only a dozen were sailing ships. The schooners and other sailing ships were built in Spanish shipyards. Naval officials understood that these craft would be outmatched and were in fact obsolete before the keel was even laid, yet the craft continued to be produced for political reasons. The Spanish government was unwilling to cede construction of its navy completely to foreign contracts, for this would have caused mass unemployment in key port cities. The Galician town of El Ferrol, for example, boasted naval construction facilities that were a point of national pride, even though it was more expensive and less efficient to build there than purchase elsewhere. With the new warships it built and purchased, by 1860 Spain had the fourth most powerful navy in the world, after Britain, France, and Italy, in terms of total firepower and displacement. Russia and the United States had more ships, but these were mostly coastal or riverine vessels. As with other contemporary navies adjusting to the new propulsion, Spain's warships still carried sails, since steam engines were weak, dependent on coal, and unreliable. Eventually steam became the exclusive mode, but initially, the boilers were typically used only for combat cruising or when speed was absolutely necessary.[58]

Along with its rising capabilities, Spain became involved in extensive overseas operations, either alone or in concert with its Great Power allies. Spain, as a partner of France and Britain, did at the request of both nations consider sending an expeditionary force of twenty thousand soldiers to fight in the Crimean War (1853–1856). The British even suggested they would heavily subsidize this effort. While the Spanish government was willing, it feared that Russia would encourage the United States to use the opportunity to seize Cuba. Indeed, Jefferson Davis, the US secretary of war at the time, was involved in discussions along these lines with the Russians. Instead of sending an expeditionary force, Spain encouraged its citizens to volunteer for the French Foreign Legion, or in the British forces—through a recruitment office in Gibraltar.[59] While the Spanish army did not participate in direct action, it did dispatch a robust observer mission to the battlefields of the Crimean War, charged with learning about new weapons and tactics and demonstrating Spain's alignment with its allies.[60]

The commander of this mission was General Juan Prim y Prats, a former captain general of Cuba (1843–1848), who in 1854 led a team of twenty-five, including five field-grade army officers, one artillery captain, two engineer captains, two infantry lieutenants, and fourteen enlisted soldiers. The expedition was escorted by two allied advisors, an Italian Piedmontese major and an English captain from India. The Spaniards were always accompanied in the Ottoman empire by a Turkish officer as well as a handful of Ottoman escorts. Prim was impressed by Ottoman military reforms as well as by the courage of their soldiers. Although officially neutral, the Spanish military engineers lent technical and tactical advice to the Ottoman army in the construction of fortifications and defenses against the Russians. Spain's mission continued to cement ties with Britain and France and also accelerated the adoption of modernizing reforms within the Spanish military.[61]

Three years later, Spain sent forces to Cochin China (Indochina) as an ally of the French. The purpose of this expedition was to punish the indigenous government for the kidnapping of a Spanish missionary bishop of Tonkin, José María Díaz, in June 1857. Spain sent six frigates and one thousand men from Manila and expected to receive control of an Indochinese port for its aid to the French. The sole beneficiary turned out to be the French, who eventually annexed Cochin China as a colony. Spain gained little from the intervention other than the right to send missionaries to Southeast Asia, but it did maintain a small force in Saigon until 1863 as a sign of its relevance to Asia.[62] Perhaps chastened by this operation, Spain did not become involved in the Italian Wars of Unification (1859–1861). Its position was somewhat awkward, given its family ties to the Bourbon dynasty in Sicily and its previous intervention, in 1849–1850, as an ally of Austria to save the pope from capture by the Italian nationalist Giuseppe Garibaldi. Indeed, in 1861, Spanish warships helped evacuate the Bourbons from Naples.[63]

The most dramatic intervention, however, one that transformed Spain's self-image, came in North Africa with the waging of open warfare against the kingdom of Morocco. A border dispute over Ceuta, which had been in Spanish control since the fifteenth century, led to rising tensions and Spanish preparations for war. Morocco had become increasingly bold in its border incursions against Spanish territory, sponsoring repeated minor raids and skirmishes against Ceuta and Melilla, Spain's two outposts in North Africa, in 1844, 1845, 1848, 1853–1855, and 1859.[64] Before launching its campaign against Morocco, however, the Spanish government consulted with its allies. Portugal and Piedmont-Sardinia supported Spain, while the French and British were indifferent so long as Spain did not permanently occupy the city of Tangier. With this international backing, Spain's Cortes declared war on October 22, 1859, sending thirty-five thousand soldiers and three thousand horses against Morocco. This campaign, which required dozens of transport and cargo ships and incorporated naval gunfire and a blockade, was the first use of joint forces—army and navy—in a successful operation in many decades. After Spanish victories over the outgunned Moroccans, the two nations signed a ceasefire on April 26, 1860. The eventual treaty ceded Sidi Ifni and other territory to Spain, recognized Ceuta and Melilla as Spanish in perpetuity, and forced Morocco to pay an indemnity of one hundred million pesetas. This first clear victory by Spanish troops against a foreign opponent in many decades led to a wave of national pride in Spain.[65] While it came at the cost of two thousand Spanish battlefield deaths and an additional five thousand deaths from disease and other non-battle causes, the victory was nonetheless welcomed in Spain as a reversal of years of defeats and losses to foreign armies, both at home and overseas.[66]

Spain began to expand its presence elsewhere in Africa as well. In May 1858, it occupied the islands of Fernando Póo, Corisco, and Annobon off the coast of what would later become its colony of Equatorial Guinea, although it did not maintain a permanent presence there for some years. In 1860 Spain used its navy in an attempt—albeit unsuccessful—to protect its ally the Kingdom of Naples against the forces of Italian unification.[67] These relatively modest operations, even when unsuccessful, demonstrated Spain's ability to manage expeditionary and colonial operations at some distance from the Iberian Peninsula, experience that would prove vital as the country initiated efforts soon after to return to its previous role as a major power in the Americas. The year 1861 would see two significant operations along these lines: a joint deployment with Britain and France into Mexico and a unilateral operation in Santo Domingo to restore that nation's colonial status.

Spanish confidence had risen dramatically, so that with the new year of 1861 came declarations that 1860, which had included the victory over Morocco and other operations, had been "one of the most beautiful registered in the history of modern Spain," which had demonstrated "the heroism of our brave troops" and "immortalized the name of our army." These triumphs were expected to "fortify the decayed public spirit, and to open new horizons for the patriotic ambitions of the country, the parties and the government" and to demonstrate to Europe that Spain had overcome its legendary "lethargy" on the road to "regeneration and progress."[68]

Mexico was one area where Spain demonstrated the end of its "lethargy." In the midst of revolution and civil war, Mexico had fallen into arrears with the international community, and the debt issue concerned Spain, which could hardly tolerate a complete suspension of payments.[69] In late 1861, Spain sent sixty-two hundred soldiers under the command of General Juan Prim y Prats, alongside seven hundred British and two thousand French soldiers and with dozens of warships, to force Mexico to pay its debts to the European powers. This operation had been many years coming. In 1857, after years of frustration at the unwillingness or inability of Mexico to pay its debts, Spain had closed its legation in Mexico City and withdrawn its minister. The triumph of the liberal Benito Juárez in July 1861 had led to an official abrogation of this same debt to Spain, Britain, France, and other nations. Mexico announced it was suspending payments for two years and expelled Spain's remaining diplomats, accusing them (with some justification) of having supported Juárez's conservative rivals. The occupation of Veracruz, Mexico's primary port, was intended to force Juárez to reverse course and resume payments. Soon after the trilateral force had landed, however, General Prim recognized that the French had more far-reaching goals, including the incorporation of Mexico into the French empire. After consulting with the British, who also had decided to end their involvement in the operation, General Prim withdrew Spain's forces. This action angered the French, who had counted on Spanish collaboration in Mexico to help dampen resistance to their plans. In Spain, conservatives were furious at what they saw as General Prim's abandoning of a former colony, fellow monarchists in Mexico, and for having left behind two key allies. The British evacuated their forces at the same time as the Spanish, and there was a perception that it had been Spain that caused the collapse of the joint operation. Just as important, some were upset that Spain had forsaken the prestige of being considered equal to France and the United Kingdom in the debt-collection expedition against Mexico.[70]

Spain—which had taken the lead in organizing the expedition and contributed the largest forces, drawn principally from its garrisons in Cuba—had abandoned the French to their machinations in Mexico. The Spanish and British evacuation came as a relief to the United States, which had supported Juárez from the beginning and was concerned that the three-party intervention might lead to a permanent occupation. Even with the withdrawal, Spanish participation in the expedition had been successful from a financial perspective; initially, the Mexican government not only negotiated openly with the European powers but agreed to devote 80 percent of customs revenues passing through Veracruz to settling its debts with Britain, France, Spain, and other nations. Spain had also managed to overcome British hesitation about participation, demonstrating both competence and skill in its organization of the effort. Spain and Britain also coordinated policies as they began to consider ending their efforts.

Only with the French attempts to install Archduke Maximilian, which accelerated in late 1862, did the elected Mexican government cease compliance with this accord. Spanish support for French ambitions might have been possible had Napoleon III approached his allies in Spain and Britain more openly. Isabel II might have supported a Bourbon king in Mexico—especially a Spanish one, for example—but did not want to give a blank check to the French or to see Habsburg rule in Mexico City. Prime Minister O'Donnell was more ambivalent about the withdrawal of Spanish forces, because he did not want to embarrass the French, who recognized Spain as an ally, but also did not want to support an Austrian monarch as the new sovereign of Mexico. Austria-Hungary had been one of the key supporters, after all, of the rival Carlist dynasty in Spain and one of the last European states to recognize Isabel II's reign. While France was an ally, Austria-Hungary was not.[71]

While Prime Minister O'Donnell was upset at this precipitous initiative, taken without consulting him or their French allies, Queen Isabel II was pleased by the disentanglement and so prohibited O'Donnell from taking any punitive action against General Prim for his unauthorized actions.[72] Perhaps the queen should have followed her chief minister's advice, however. In a surprise move in 1864, Prim resigned his commission and taking advantage of his new popularity became the leader of the Progressive opposition to the Liberal Union. In this capacity, he lent his military and intellectual prestige to multiple attempts to overthrow the government through military coup, parliamentary maneuvers, or dynastic politics. The liberal leader was eventually successful—albeit temporarily—in his antimonarchist efforts. In 1869, General Prim became regent after the overthrow of Queen Isabel II. This personal victory for the general did not endure, however, and Prim was himself assassinated in 1870.[73]

The end result of these overseas operations and others—including the tripartite intervention in Mexico—was an increase in experience and popularity for the navy, unparalleled since the early decades of the Golden Age of Spain, prior to the defeat of the Spanish Armada in 1588. Unlike the army, which rose in rebellion frequently in the nineteenth century and continued to be riven with political factions, the Spanish navy was more disciplined and loyal to the central state, considering itself apolitical and "the best representative of the nation to the outside world." Its performance in the 1860s, not only in the Caribbean but also in the Pacific, added to its reputation. It would be too much to consider the Spanish navy a global force, for this was a status really only achieved by the British in the nineteenth century. The other naval powers—principally France, the United States, and Russia,. but also Italy, and Austria-Hungary—were just as limited in their ability to conduct continuous or simultaneous worldwide operations.[74]

Even after almost two decades of reconstruction and reconstitution and the experience gained through interventions in the 1840s and 1850s, the Spanish navy continued to struggle as an expeditionary force. Inferior cannons, a shortage of engineers and other skilled personnel, and a social bias in the officer corps against technical skills other than gunnery and navigation continued to hinder the combat effectiveness of the navy. Still, compared to where the fleet had been in the five decades since Trafalgar, when it had been eliminated by the British in one day, the Spanish navy was tremendously more capable and popular as an extension of the state. It had real warships, using both sail and steam, with trained crews. Spain also could boast of its fleet's having a global reach (albeit on a limited scale), something only Britain, and to a lesser extent France, had before the 1850s. From a position of weakness for many years, Spain now had "a powerful and efficient naval force capable of operating for long periods of time in distant waters." For missions of great duration, the Spanish navy did remain dependent on neutral states or allies for the use of coaling stations, but Britain and France were helpful in this regard.[75]

With this fleet at its disposal, Spain was arguably more attractive to potential allies—including the Confederacy—than at any time since before Napoleon Bonaparte first put on a French uniform. This new potential, and attractiveness, would be tested during the American Civil War, when both the United States and the Confederacy made genuine efforts to win Spain to their cause. In the case of the United States, this meant maintaining Madrid's initial position, that of

Spanish neutrality in the conflict. For the Southern rebels, however, Spain was a potential ally of significance, especially as it was expected to act in conjunction with France, and with the consent of Great Britain. At several key points in time, Spain nearly did extend recognition and more tangible measures of assistance to the Confederacy.

Chapter 3

The First Year of War

Flirtation with Alliance

During the first phase of the Civil War, when Confederate optimism in battlefield victories rode high, Southern leaders put little faith and fewer resources in diplomacy. "King Cotton Diplomacy," the conviction that the South held the upper hand in relations with cotton-dependent foreign powers, dominated conceptions of the international arena. By 1860, after five years of debate, articles, and books on King Cotton, "the belief in the power of cotton to force European intervention was almost universal."[1] The leaders of the rebellion expected Great Britain, France, Spain, and other nations immediately to extend recognition, welcome the Confederacy into the family of nations, and resume normal commerce to Southern ports, despite the Union declaration of a blockade, and all of these actions to be motivated by European industrial demand for raw cotton. Europe was also divided, however, with partisans for each of the two American republics: "German revolutionaries, French socialists and radicals, and English liberals and Abolitionists, from John Bright and Victor Hugo to Garibaldi and Marx, supported the North in the war against slavery and for republican democracy. Napoleon III and Eugénie, Pope Pius IX, Spanish Catholic reactionaries, and English Tories supported the South and were delighted to see the United States fall apart."[2] While the American Civil War was of interest in Europe, it often received far less attention in Spain and other European states than events closer to home such as the ongoing unification of Italy, an uprising in Poland, or the vagaries of domestic politics. Given the delays in receiving news from the Western hemisphere (it would not be until 1866 that the final transatlantic cable was in use), events in North America could seem even more distant that they were by geography. Despite the brewing conflict, which soon broke out into open warfare, some editions of leading Spanish newspapers provided no coverage at all of the Confederate rebellion in early 1861 or gave just a brief account of a major battle, buried under news of dynastic marriages, the latest debate over Italian unification, or the ongoing struggles over Russian occupation of Poland.[3] Instead of focus on the conflict between the United States and the Confederacy, it was "the two overseas republics . . . Mexico and Santo Domingo which are the focus of daily conversations and absorb all the attentions of the government . . . and of the two states, one (Mexico) hates us and one (Santo Domingo) loves us." At times, the minor items reported on the American Civil War were misleading, as when one newspaper suggested that there would be an amicable division of territory between the Union and the Confederacy—a seriously mistaken analysis of conditions in North America.[4]

As the euphoria of the first few months faded into the grim reality of bloody warfare, and the commitment to a long struggle began in earnest, President Jefferson Davis and other leaders began to understand the importance of making genuine efforts to involve outside powers in the struggle. Given the imperatives of the ongoing war, however, these same leaders were unable to devote the financial resources, deliberate policy, and skilled personnel that might have gained success in this area of operations.[5] Without an adequate stable of experienced and capable diplomats, with only limited financial assets to conduct public diplomacy, and with little to offer in terms of trade or territorial concessions, agents of the South were unable to achieve a great deal during this initial period. Overall, in contrast to US representatives such as Charles Francis Adams in London and William Dayton in Paris, CSA agents sent to Europe were "inept diplomats and ill-equipped to deal with the problems and frustrations they encountered there."[6]

William Seward, Lincoln's secretary of state, was a skilled politician who was far more successful at managing his—admittedly more substantial—resources of diplomats and funding. In 1861, however, there was deep concern in the United States that the South would be triumphant in its expectation of foreign intervention, which made Seward's maneuvering with Britain, France, Russia, and Spain (at the time perhaps seeming somewhat desperate) all the more necessary for the survival of the Union. The international position of the United States in mid-1861 was fragile at best. A full-scale rebellion in the South, Spanish occupation of Santo Domingo, European intervention in Mexico, and a sense across Europe that the young American republic might be on the verge of collapse meant that diplomacy rose to the level of critical necessity. The British government's dispatch of three additional army regiments to Canada in mid-1861—some ten thousand soldiers, plus artillery and engineers—could not have been reassuring to Lincoln and Seward in the midst of full-scale war and increasing European garrisons throughout the hemisphere.[7] Canadian authorities including the governor general made clear their intent to be prepared for "serious eventualities" and stressed to the British garrisons and Canadian militia alike that the government was counting on their loyalty.[8] Given how difficult the situation of the United States was, Lincoln and Seward even put aside long-standing US priorities such as the annexation of Cuba—although admittedly this was consistent with the 1860 national platform of their own Republican Party.[9]

There were some possibilities for the Confederacy, especially with Spain and France, for attracting foreign recognition, mediation, or even intervention. Even without formal diplomatic achievements, for example, Spain was willing to enable Confederate blockade running through its Cuban ports, building goodwill and financial benefits to the day when the Southern government would achieve sufficient battlefield successes so as to establish its independence from Washington, DC. More than this the Spanish government was unwilling to offer, until it saw proof not only of battlefield success but also of competence in the Confederate government and the representatives charged with implementing its foreign policy.

Even before the American Civil War began in April 1861, Southern leaders had written two constitutions, elected a congress, a president, and a vice-president, and established the broad outlines of key policies, including foreign affairs. The Constitution of the Confederate States of America paralleled that of the United States in foreign policy; the president remained vested with overall responsibility, and states were strictly prohibited from conducting their own diplomatic affairs. In the military sphere, the Confederacy struggled to overcome the local interests of each state and was unable to bring all armed forces, including militias, under one command. The same could not be said of foreign policy, where by constitution and the precedent of the US experience, President Jefferson Davis had significant autonomy. Also unlike in military affairs, the constituent states of the Confederacy did not attempt to assert their own influence over the conduct of foreign relations. While some Confederate generals, especially Edmund Kirby Smith, did make modest attempts to improve ties with foreign nations in their respective theaters of command, these were minor in impact.[10]

Despite his free hand, however, President Davis did not initially seem particularly interested in the possible benefits of foreign entanglements. In his inaugural speech and other comments at the time, President Davis mentioned his responsibility for conducting "foreign intercourse, finance, military affairs, and the postal service," but he did not lay out any foreign policy other than the promotion of free trade, friendly relations with all nations, and a settlement with the United States, allowing both nations to divorce peacefully.[11] Although his initial comments on foreign policy were vague, he did include emissaries among his first appointments, naming three men to represent the Confederacy "as a commission to proceed to Europe" in February 1861. Those chosen were William L. Yancey, Pierre Rost, and A. Dudley Mann.[12] Yancey would be the most significant of these agents, and the most identified with the "arrogant demands" made of the Europeans, relying on the misguided belief in the indispensability of King Cotton to Britain, France, Spain, and other nations.[13] As an adviser to these commissioners, Davis appointed Edwin DeLeon, a figure who would soon become the key Confederate propagandist in Europe, especially in Paris and London. DeLeon served initially from May 1861 to January 1862, a time when support for the rebels was at a high point in western Europe.[14]

Once fighting began in earnest, the major European powers recognized the belligerent rights of both the Confederacy and the Union: Britain on May 13, France on June 10, and Spain (appropriately, given its sympathies) one week later.[15] At the same time, each nation also declared its neutrality in the conflict, hoping to avoid entanglements and expressing the hope for a negotiated settlement. Opinion concerning the two warring sides was still mixed in European public opinion and in the halls of government. Many in Britain, for example, sympathized with the North but nonetheless hoped for a diplomatic solution that would allow the Confederacy to remain free and independent.[16]

The majority of European states—without significant trade, cultural affinity, or political interest in the conflict—were indifferent to the American Civil War. Most of Europe deferred to Britain, the only real global power at the time, and only France and Spain had any significant interests of their own in the Americas. Aside from some of the landed aristocracy and military, who (as might have been expected) identified with the Confederacy, European public opinion sided mostly with the Union. Russia was a perhaps unexpected exception to this divide. For most of its history, Russia had been an empire in which serfdom—in many ways similar to slavery—had prevailed. Unfortunately for the Confederacy, this changed the year the American Civil War began, when Tsar Alexander II emancipated Russia's serfs. The tsar then became, from 1861 onward, the most prominent and clear foreign supporter of the Union and also advocated for the future emancipation of all slaves throughout the world, including not only the Confederate States but also Brazil and Cuba. Official Russian opinion was very friendly to the United States, with the Russian fleets visiting US ports in a show of solidarity. The arrival of a significant Russian naval presence in San Francisco in October 1863—a flotilla that would remain based in California until late spring 1864—was a major morale boost for the Union. Fears of a French-dominated Mexico, which might make common cause with the Confederacy, concerned many people in the thinly populated West. Russia's show of force was meant to reinforce Russia's commitment to the United States, a cooperation that continued after the Civil War through the sale of Alaska to the United States in 1867. Unlike other governments, which received Southern agents unofficially, the Russian government rebuffed the efforts in 1864 by a Confederate agent, L. Q. C. Lamar, to visit the tsar in St. Petersburg.[17]

While there was pro-Confederate sentiment in Belgium and Portugal, Spain was the primary middle power with significant sympathy toward the CSA. Many Spanish aristocrats, military leaders, and slave-owning colonial creoles supported the South, although the government preference was to remain neutral until the war's end was clear—even if the fighting had not yet ended. A clear majority of Spanish officials and creoles in Cuba sided with the South. Among Spain's middle and lower classes and within the Liberal party, there was a rising pro-Union sentiment, a feeling accelerated by the Emancipation Proclamation of January 1863, but these elements were not significant in the government, dominated as it was by General Leopoldo O'Donnell and the queen's other favorites. Spain was open to involvement, in the early stages of the war, in the midst of overall optimism about Spain's overseas potential and in 1861 or 1862 would have followed French recognition of the Confederacy without hesitation. Although in March 1861, Spain's foreign minister Saturnino Calderón Collantes informed Pierre Rost, the Confederacy's agent in Madrid, that Spain would not initiate recognition on its own, he did not rule this out in concert with other powers. At a minimum, Spain would need the approval of France and Britain, if not their active collaboration, in any undertaking of this great a magnitude. Defeating Morocco alone was one thing, taking on the United States, even as an ally of the Confederacy, was a task beyond the capacity of Spain in 1861.[18]

This private and unofficial meeting proved the high point of Rost's engagement with Calderón, however. The Spanish foreign minister held off meeting with Rost again, indefinitely, despite frequent requests from the Confederate agent, until the war situation was clarified. Such clarification as did occur, of course, did not indicate that a Confederate victory seemed imminent. While the Spanish government would engage in serious discussions with France and Britain over recognizing the rebellion, these conferences did not directly involve Confederate agents. Absent decisive strategic Southern victories as well as the CSA's demonstrated viability as an independent state, Spain and the Confederacy would have nothing to discuss under the tenure of Calderón.[19]

Even so, Spain made every effort to appear correct in its diplomatic relations with the United States. Despite some initial, unofficial meetings with Confederate representatives, Spain made it clear fairly early on that it would not grant de facto recognition by receiving diplomats from the South. The United States made some missteps early in its wartime diplomacy toward Spain, most notably through the naming of Carl Schurz as the US minister in early 1861. This naming came after Lincoln's first choice—Cassius Clay, an abolitionist from Kentucky—rejected the position in favor of becoming minister to Russia. Like Clay, Schurz was an ardent abolitionist. Before emigrating to the United States, Schurz had been active in the republican revolution of 1848 in Germany. Lincoln's appointment of Carl Schurz was a sign of the importance he placed on the position of minister to Spain as the well-connected activist was close to the new president. Schurz himself believed it was the most important diplomatic position after Mexico. His instructions in late April 1861 from Lincoln and Seward were to block Spanish recognition of the CSA, improve commercial ties, and remind Spain that it had always been Southerners who encouraged the annexation of Cuba. With his republican background, however, Schurz was not received well in monarchist and pro-slavery Madrid; his appointment even led to a formal protest by the Spanish embassy in Washington. The Spanish government was even more upset to learn that the governments of Portugal and Brazil had successfully rejected the possibility he might be named to those states.[20]

Schurz did go to Spain, but his tenure there was short-lived. He despised Spain almost as much as the Spanish despised him and did everything he could to return home as soon as possible.[21] After several months of sending dispatches hinting that the Spanish government would soon recognize the Confederacy, he resigned his position in order to join the Union army. With his political status as an outspoken antimonarchist, he had not served US interests in Spain, but the brevity of his position prevented him from causing significant damage. By the end of 1861, to the pleasure of all concerned, Schurz was on his way home to fight in the Civil War, leaving legation secretary Horatio Perry as chargé d'affaires until a new ambassador could be named. Reaching the United States by early February after visiting family in Prussia, Schurz was appointed to the rank of brigadier general in the Union army in March 1862. On arriving in the United States, he passed along to the US State Department his belief that Britain, France, and Spain would soon recognize the CSA if Union forces did not gain more battlefield successes and if the United States did not move more aggressively forward to the emancipation of all slaves on both sides of the Mason-Dixon line.[22]

The United States also introduced strict visa requirements for visiting foreigners, which caused inconveniences, delays, and complaints from Spanish merchants and other visitors.[23] On the positive side, Spain agreed to allow the US Navy to contract for a coaling station near Cádiz—an accommodation to the increasing dependence of all major navies on coal, which was rapidly replacing wind as the primary fuel for propulsion. The United States offered reciprocity on this, and Spain was authorized to establish its own stations on American soil. The proposal was not pursued, given Spain's modest needs at the time for coal replenishment because most of its fleet were still driven by sails.[24] Seward was forthright in his responses to Spanish questions, such as when Foreign Minister Calderón Collantes inquired, through the Spanish minister to the United States Gabriel García Tassara, about the expected duration of the Civil War. Seward's prediction in April 1862—that the war would be over in two years—was incorrect, of course, but his willingness to indicate that the conflict would not be over quickly gained him credibility with Spanish authorities. At the same time, Seward made clear that the patience of the United States with nations tempted toward recognition of the Confederacy was somewhat limited: "The American people have found that the reserve practiced in some quarters might be deemed indicative of a disposition, if not to aid the insurgents, at least to sympathize with and encourage them. The country has not been able to reconcile such tendencies with a generous and liberal spirit." Lest his comment be taken as a deliberate provocation, Seward added: "Spain however has been eminently just and generous."[25]

In early June, Foreign Minister Calderón promised to Horatio Perry, secretary of the US legation, that he would not receive the Confederates. Perry regarded his meeting with Calderón to have been "decisive." The American's account was unambiguous. It was widely publicized in the American press: "The Minister of State not only renewed to me the assurance given to Mr. Preston, but amplified it by stating absolutely that if any commissioners or other negotiators should appear in behalf of the so-called Confederate States, the government would not see them or recognize them in any capacity. That Spain would have nothing to do with the rebel party in the United States in any sense."[26] Spain did, however, make gestures that worked on more than one level. In November 1861, Prime Minister O'Donnell made a gift to the US legation of two complete sets of Spanish small arms—those currently in use by the Spanish army—expressed as a gesture of gratitude for the treatment of Spaniards in the United

States by the Union. The choice of gift, however, belied another image. Modern weapons, including those comparable to US equipment, showed that Spain was prepared for any contingency.[27]

Spain noted preparedness on the other side, as well, with the Spanish embassy in Washington, DC, sending back newspaper clippings and reports to the Spanish Foreign Ministry concerning the size of and major movements by the Union army and navy. Reports about the growth and strength of the US Navy were particularly important, as these had a direct bearing not only on the blockade of the Confederacy but as a potential future threat to Spanish control of Cuba. New weapons, changes in the conscription laws, recruiting for state militias, and the employment of major units against the Confederacy —all details were compiled and sent to the Spanish Foreign Ministry by the Spanish legation in Washington, DC. It was primarily the US press that provided this information, but Spain's diplomats also were in close contact with US officials, including Seward, who no doubt wanted to continue influencing Spain to remain uninvolved in the Civil War.[28]

In late 1861, Britain, France, and Spain, angry over the failure of Mexico to pay its debts, dispatched forces to seize Mexican ports. The three states had initialed a joint agreement on October 31, committing to the intervention in order to collect debts and protect their citizens and property. All three also agreed to cooperate to prevent the United States from seizing Mexican lands and also to forswear their own territorial acquisition. The United States had been invited to participate but declined to join the operation.[29] The choice of Spanish commander in chief—General Juan Prim—was unusual. Prim, who also had power as minister plenipotentiary to negotiate with the Mexican government, had family ties to the Juárez government, was fairly open in his opposition to monarchy, and had previously spoken out against intervention in Mexico. However, he was considered the most capable general on active duty for this most important mission, with previous experience as governor of Puerto Rico, as observer in the Crimean War, had been successful in command in the Moroccan War, and also had friendly connections to the French emperor, Napoleon III. Prim, appointed on November 12, sailed from Madrid with instructions to avoid territorial conquest and interference in Mexican affairs, ensure the protection of Spanish citizens and property, and reestablish the collection of debt from

Mexican government. Meeting up with Spanish army units in Cuba, which would form the bulk of his forces, Prim also conferred with General Serrano, captain general in Cuba, before departing for Mexico to take command of his expedition.[30]

The intervention, which began on December 17, 1861, with the Spanish occupation of Veracruz, came despite US proposals to assume most responsibilities (other than fiduciary) for collecting Mexican debts. The European occupation—at a time of US weakness during the Civil War—caused fear in Washington, as Seward and others were concerned this foray was a test to see how far European imperialism could go. Was this a precursor to European efforts to "gain permanent political footing in Mexico," perhaps even to lend direct aid to the Confederacy? By early 1862, the threat of foreign intervention suddenly became more realistic, with the forces in Mexico added to bolstered British garrisons in Canada and the Spanish army of occupation in Santo Domingo. Lacking the means to do more than issue feeble protests, the United States could do little more than look on with frustration as British, French, and Spanish troops occupied Mexican soil.[31]

By early 1862, however, General Prim began to be concerned about French imperial ambitions. While Emperor Napoleon III upheld the letter of his agreement and did not claim Mexico as a French colony, it became clear that the French did intend to control Mexico, even to the point of imposing an Austrian archduke as emperor. The allied commissioners who began negotiations with Mexican authorities beginning in early January 1862 soon came into conflict with each other. The French hoped the discussions would fail, thus justifying a campaign to take Mexico City. The Spanish, led by General Prim, aligned with the British, who hoped for a fair settlement for all concerned and continuation of the principle of non-intervention in domestic Mexican politics. There is some evidence that the Spanish government in Madrid had expected to offer its own candidates for the throne of Mexico, an idea that had already been proposed by Mexican conservatives in the 1840s. With developments heading in another direction, however, Spanish monarchists were no doubt disappointed at French disinterest on this possibility. Prim was a liberal republican and thus personally not interested in any course that would support placing a king or emperor, whether Mexican, Spanish, or any other nationality, on the throne in Mexico City.[32]

On April 9, 1862, after consulting with the British who had reached the same conclusion, Prim ordered a withdrawal. The three powers —France, Britain, and Spain—agreed to dissolve their partnership in Mexico. Adding impetus to this dissolution were strong words by Secretary of State Seward, stating that the United States found monarchy absolutely unacceptable in the Western hemisphere. Unwilling to sacrifice Spanish lives to defend French imperial plans, Prim had by mid-1862 withdrawn Spain's forces. In Cuba, General Serrano made clear his disagreement with this move, even initially refusing to send Spanish naval vessels to aid in the evacuation. The British had no such hesitation and allowed the first wave of retreating Spaniards passage on their warships. Although Prim initiated this withdrawal without orders from Madrid, a point that upset Prime Minister O'Donnell, troubles in Santo Domingo quickly proved the merits of this decision to abandon Mexico.[33]

Southern agents in Madrid, Paris, and London failed to press their advantages early in the American Civil War and failed to promote the successful treaty between the Confederacy and the Five Civilized Tribes in Oklahoma as a potential precedent in Europe. The CSA also failed to establish relations with Mexico, primarily because of the bumbling of its emissary, Colonel John T. Pickett, who among his failings spoke openly of supporting independence for the city of Veracruz, plotted the seizure of northern Mexico, alternatively promised to return New Mexico and California to Mexico or to annex it to the Confederacy, earned a reputation as a drunk and a brawler, was arrested for assault, and had to bribe his way out of a Mexican jail. The collapse of Pickett's mission (he left Mexico ignominiously in December 1861) was soon followed by that of the Mexican government itself, which soon had to endure landings by Britain, Spain, and France to force debt repayment and, at the hands of the French, occupation until 1867.[34]

Complicating already tricky Confederate diplomacy was the difficulty in maintaining secure and timely communications between Richmond and its agents in Europe. With little in the way of a navy and the CSA's vulnerability to Union naval forces, Southern emissaries had to depend on neutral ships, principally those of Great Britain, which proved not the most efficient method of travel. Repeated failures to maintain Confederate operational security meant that Northern warships could interrupt these vessels, particularly given the rapid losses of Southern coastal cities to Union forces. With a decreasing number of possible ports of departure, it became increasingly difficult to guarantee the security of these agents and of the secret papers and financial instruments they carried to attempt purchases and other commercial activities in Europe. Southern representatives also labored without accurate updates about the impact of the blockade on cotton exports, trade balances, or genuine bottlenecks in the European textile industry, other than what they could surmise from newspaper coverage of statements by government officials and European companies.[35] While 80 percent of British cotton imports did come from the US South, and 20 percent of British workers did depend, directly or indirectly, on cotton industries, British merchants in anticipation of the Civil War had been stockpiling the commodity for months and had also begun to plan acquisitions elsewhere, such as from Brazil, Egypt, and India, factors not considered by the government in Richmond. Indeed, with careful management, some British experts predicted it might be as much as a year before genuine shortages in raw cotton might emerge in the global markets.[36] While there is some evidence that a reduction in cotton exports, rather than a complete embargo, might have caused a greater impact on Europe, the total cessation of the cotton trade forced Britain and France to find alternatives rather than give their attention to increasing the flow from the Confederacy. The South, which before the Civil War had accounted for 85 percent of European cotton exports, quickly went from this dominant position to providing 0 percent of the crop. How could this not have a direct impact?[37]

Initially, the Confederate representatives could count on a favorable environment, which by the end of 1861 seemed headed toward not only international diplomatic recognition for the Southern rebels but perhaps even a military response against the Union by the United Kingdom and its French and Spanish allies. One infamous incident, the *Trent* Affair, threatened in 1861 to bring Britain into the war against the Union. The *Trent* was a British mail ship, which on November 7 sailed from Havana en route to London. On board were two Confederate agents, James Mason and John Slidell, commissioned by Jefferson Davis to advocate for Southern recognition in Europe. On November 8, the USS *Jacinto* stopped the ship and its captain ordered the seizure of Mason and Slidell, despite the protests from the British captain and crew that this was a violation of maritime law and the rights of neutral nations. This became known as the *Trent* Affair, causing great tensions between the United States and the United Kingdom, but it perhaps surprisingly did not become a serious issue in Madrid. Even though the *Trent* had sailed from Havana, the capture occurred outside Cuban territorial waters, which left Spain without any legal entanglement or significant political interest in a resolution.[38]

Spain did not get involved, but the affair did become an international crisis between the United States and Great Britain. The British increased their military preparedness in Canada (with eleven thousand additional soldiers) and, in the Caribbean, demanded an apology from the United States, as well as the release of the Confederate operatives into the custody of the United Kingdom.[39] Members of the Confederate government rejoiced at the rising tensions and hoped the crisis would drag the British and French into the war. Faced with the imminent threat of foreign intervention, President Lincoln and Secretary of State Seward backed down. Mason and Slidell were released at the end of December 1861, yet the United States did not apologize for the act nor forswear similar seizures later. The United Kingdom considered the episode closed, nonetheless, and the war scare subsided.[40] The British, who took some satisfaction in seeing the difficulties the Civil War was causing the Americans, were not looking for a reason to go to war.[41]

The end of this incident dealt a serious blow to Confederate diplomatic efforts, for Yancey had made a dramatic show of highlighting the crisis, even demanding European recognition as a consequence of American behavior. The peaceful diplomatic conclusion of the *Trent* Affair thus undermined what had been the main thrust of Southern diplomacy—that President Lincoln was an international rogue, bent on destroying European commerce.[42] Not only had the United States and Britain avoided war, they had successfully navigated through a major crisis, arriving at a calm negotiated settlement, and Britain in late 1861 also counted on its alliances with France and Spain, so an Anglo-American settlement protected the United States from conflict with these two states as well. At the same time, two key Confederate diplomats had been detained by the United States for critical months, during which time they could have been strong advocates for European intervention in support of the South. By the time they finally arrived in London, the emphasis of Confederate diplomacy had shifted from demands for recognition to denunciations of the blockade, a less effective issue for encouraging international intervention on behalf of the Confederacy. The advantage of this new approach, however, was that it played to European self-interest; even those advocating neutrality or a pro-Union position had to concede that by 1862 the blockade of Southern ports was having a negative impact on British and French textile industries. Even so, slow communications between Confederate agents and the South, as well as a lack of real insight into British and French public opinion, led to other failures. One example was the missed opportunity to capitalize on the Union blocking of Charleston in December 1861 by a fleet of old whaling ships, sunk in the harbor after being filled with stones. The Confederacy was slow to exploit this clear violation of international maritime law, losing valuable time and allowing the United States to calm the British and French with explanations.[43]

The South believed it could count on a friendly France and Britain. The British prime minister in 1861, and for the duration of the conflict, was Lord Palmerston. Not only was he sympathetic to the aristocratic leaders of the Confederacy, he was a bitter enemy of the United States. Although they refused to receive the credentials of Confederate agents, thereby granting de facto recognition of the independence of the South, Lord Palmerston and his foreign secretary, Lord Russell, did meet with William Yancey and Dudley Mann in their capacities as private citizens. Although both British leaders made clear their hopes that the Confederacy would succeed in becoming a permanent state, they also insisted that the South had to achieve more battlefield success against the North if it hoped to receive international recognition. The increasingly effective Union blockade, for example, would have to be broken, and Southern armies would have to expel Northern forces from New Orleans and other key locations.[44]

France was led by Emperor Napoleon III, nephew of Napoleon Bonaparte, who also made no secret of his support for the rebels. Like Palmerston and Russell, the French emperor met with Southern agents, encouraged them to return when they had more concrete victories to trumpet, but refused to commit to open recognition or other forms of support to the Confederacy. The emperor, too, was an early disappointment to the Confederacy, most notably with his speech on January 27, 1862, that opened the French parliament meeting. Despite rumors that Napoleon III would denounce the blockade of Confederate ports, he confined himself to complaining that war was "ravaging America . . . and our commercial interests," limiting his commitment to action to that of "praying ardently that these dissensions may soon come to an end."[45]

While it would be an exaggeration to say, as did Confederate agent Edwin DeLeon, that only "the ranks of the Revolutionary party . . . Radicals and Chartists" initially hoped for a Union victory, there does seem to have been an ample base of potential support for the rebels in European capitals in 1861 and 1862, at least enough to make recognition of the Confederacy a real possibility.[46] Of the European powers, only Russia was openly supportive of the Union in the first year of war. This unequivocal support was in some ways ironic, given the long-standing Russian institution of serfdom, a system only ended with Tsar Alexander's emancipation of the serfs in1861.[47]

There were Southern sympathizers and commercial interests in both Britain and France that viewed breaking the blockade and recognition of the Confederacy as necessary, but they failed to make significant headway in the British Parliament. Prime Minister Lord Palmerston sympathized with the South, to be sure, but also insisted on avoiding actions that might precipitously draw the United Kingdom into conflict with the United States. Given US threats to declare war on any nation that recognized the Confederacy, this put long odds on British intervention, absent dramatic Southern victories over Union armies. Palmerston's maneuvers in Parliament gained time to await developments, gradually undermining what had been significant support for the Confederacy in public opinion and especially in the House of Commons.[48]

Some Confederate leaders understood the importance of Spain and Cuba. In the prewar South and Southwest and even in Northern states, secret societies such as the Knights of the Golden Circle led by the adventurer George W. L. Bickley dreamed of annexing Mexico, Cuba, and other areas.[49] In the case of Cuban Americans, this direct interest had been expressed through the filibustering movement of the 1840s and 1850s. While Cubans fought on both sides of the war, the physical proximity of Cuba, the identification of the Southern rebellion with the cause of Cuban independence, and the possible involvement of Spain in the American Civil War provided an outsized importance to those who wore gray. More Cubans, for example, served in units from Florida than from any other state, with the other

Southeastern states—Georgia and South Carolina—also overrepresented in terms of numbers in uniform. It was also in the armies of the Confederacy that Cuban Americans from the émigré community rose to the highest ranks such as lieutenant colonel and colonel in state militias and in the national army of the CSA.[50]

One of Secretary Hunter's first appointments in July 1861 was Charles J. Helm as emissary to Havana. In his first meeting with General Serrano, Spain's Captain General in Cuba, Helm disavowed any efforts to seize Cuba or any other Spanish territories, realizing that this would be a question in the minds of Spanish officials. After all, Southern politicians had made no secret of their desire for Cuba, even supporting private invading parties in the 1840s and 1850s.[51] On the contrary, Helm argued that Spain should fear Union attempts to seize Cuba. Although the Spaniards were noncommittal, Helm was encouraged by their sympathetic comments and obvious disdain for the United States. Spain was, after all, the European state with the most common interest with the South and the most similar social and economic system, at least in its Caribbean colonies. According to Helm, the Confederacy hoped to be a close collaborator with Spain, and he even offered to begin negotiations toward a defensive alliance. The new CSA was willing to abandon all claims on Cuba, recognize the Spanish occupation of Santo Domingo, and give a fresh start to what had been strained relations between North Americans and Spain, all in the greater interest of collaboration against the United States. Although the meeting was cordial, Serrano later denied it had even taken place, perhaps in response to vigorous protests from the US consul general in Havana. In any case, Serrano promised to both men that Spain would continue to follow a "strict and severe neutrality (as it had) . . . from the beginning of the current conflict."[52]

Even meeting with a Confederate agent and pledging neutrality in the struggle between the United States and what the American government considered illegitimate and criminal rebels constituted a significant recognition of the genuine state of war between the two sides. Not surprisingly, the United States denounced the meetings and demanded an explanation from Spain's ambassador in Washington, DC.[53] Even if Spain suspected that the South harbored secret ambitions to take over Cuba, in contrast to what Helm had stated, opinion in Madrid and Havana considered that the Confederacy, if it tried to fulfill this dream, would be "weak and easier to stop than the previous giant had been."[54]

The concerns of some Spaniards that the South had not recanted its desire to annex Cuba were well founded. Secessionist politicians in 1860–1861 frequently mentioned that after the South broke from the Union, Cuba, Mexico, and Central America would naturally join or be joined to the new Confederacy as slave states, creating a "slave empire in the tropics." While these types of comments nearly disappeared after the Civil War began, they and the previous experience of filibustering remained a concern in the background as Spain considered its options in managing relations with the upstart Confederate States of America. Although Southern newspapers such as the *New Orleans Delta* did declare that "Spain has nothing to fear from the South," it would take time for Spanish authorities to see the sincerity of these comments—primarily through evidence from the war itself that perhaps even the Union had little to fear from the South.[55]

In his report to the Foreign Ministry about his encounters with Helm, General Serrano indicated that he had expressed Spain's "strict and severe neutrality," but also his belief that this was an issue to be resolved in Madrid rather than Havana. The general forwarded all the materials presented by Helm on every occasion, awaiting word from the Foreign Ministry should Spain's neutrality change. The US consul general in Havana, R. W. Shuffelt, protested vigorously at General Serrano's meetings with Helm, even on the occasions when the captain general merely accepted documents from the Confederate emissary. Not only did Shuffelt demand an explanation from Serrano, he also reminded him that US ships had so far left Spanish shipping and warships alone near Cuba, despite the presence of Confederate blockade runners and a powerful US Navy flotilla in pursuit of them. Serrano was angered by this barely veiled threat and responded that, if there was a point at which Spain became no longer neutral, it would become immediately obvious to the United States. As a Spanish gentleman, he would at that time act in accordance with Spanish honor—a promise and a warning from the military governor of Spain's most important territory outside of Iberia itself. The Spanish foreign minister approved both General Serrano's meetings with and comments to Helm and his terse note to Shuffelt.[56]

Confederate hopes in Spain were high. Unrealistic expectations often characterized Southern ambitions during the first year of the war, but in the case of Spain, there was at least some correspondence to reality. An editorial in the *Richmond Dispatch* from early 1862 reflected the opinion of many Southern leaders that Spain was the most enthusiastic foreign state and the most likely to align with the rebel cause.[57] While this optimism did not prove well placed, it did reflect widespread Confederate opinion at the time.

In August 1861, Hunter ordered CSA representatives in Europe to focus on Spain, "to hurry to Madrid, to inform Spain that since secession the South no longer desired Cuba; to represent that mutual interests seemed to invite a close and mutual alliance, and to ask for recognition. . . . the growth of Spanish power and resources could never be a cause for Confederate jealousy." The South did gain some initial diplomatic success: the granting of belligerent rights by Britain, France, and Spain, which enabled Confederate ships to use these nations' ports. While Prussia, the Netherlands, and other states also granted this form of recognition, in practice it was the Spanish, British, and French whose geographic, political, and economic significance was relevant to the war.[58] Opinion in the North turned particularly against Spain as a result of these actions, as indicated by an anti-Spanish editorial in the *New York Times* from the summer of 1861

> We have already an account accumulating against Spain, which will be brought to a settlement very early after the close of this civil war. . . . When the struggle shall be over, we shall possess a Navy of truly formidable proportions and armament, and an Army of five hundred thousand experienced fighting men. These will not be disused and disbanded until all outstanding difficulties in our foreign relations shall have been adjusted. Spain, at once craven and presumptuous, will have a severe reckoning; and it will be found, generally, that the Monroe Doctrine, which, through the long period of our military weakness, has been nothing more than a phrase, will in that period of strength become and remain a fact.[59]

Articles such as this one—dutifully sent to the Spanish Foreign Ministry by the Spanish legation in Washington, DC, could not have done much to encourage Spain to maintain its neutrality. If it was already receiving the enmity of the American people, why not support the CSA explicitly and at least have the enthusiastic friendship of some in North America? The shift in military conditions in early 1862 put this possibility aside for the moment, however, anticipating future shifts in the fortunes of war.[60]

In the case of Spain, a declaration of neutrality in the conflict was included in its announcement of June 17, 1861. By this decree, Spanish citizens could not serve in either the US or CSA army or navy, warships from either side could dock in Spanish or colonial ports for twenty-four hours or less in order to take on supplies or make minor repairs, there would be no weapons sales to either side, but merchant ships from either side could trade in Spanish ports. The North was angered by this announcement, since Seward and Lincoln had asked that the European states should regard the Confederates as illegitimate criminals and pirates. Southerners welcomed the granting of belligerent rights, viewing it as a step preliminary to recognition. While many did expect it to be a temporary and preliminary measure, until either the war ended or the European states extended full diplomatic recognition to the Confederacy, in practice it provided Spain and the other European states with sufficient flexibility to provide benefits to whichever side—initially the CSA, and later the USA—it made the most sense to support during each phase of the war.[61]

The extension of belligerent rights proved to be not the beginning but the end of Southern diplomatic achievements. Perhaps events might have developed differently with more effective representation, but from the perspective of Richmond the expenditures of effort and resources in foreign capitals seemed almost a total waste. By early 1862, many rebel leaders were so frustrated with the lack of diplomatic progress that Confederate Vice President Alexander H. Stephens suggested withdrawing all Southern agents and representatives from abroad, in order to concentrate resources on the battlefield. After expected triumphs of arms, these same agents could then return to their overseas posts from a position of strength, able to demand Confederate rights and recognitions in ways not possible without victories over Union armies and the blockade.[62]

Instead, Jefferson Davis appointed Judah Benjamin, who had served as attorney general and secretary of war, to the position of secretary of state. Although unpopular for his perceived failures in leading the Confederate military effort, Benjamin was an intelligent and trusted advisor to Davis. Uniquely suited to hold the position, with his knowledge of the world and fluency in several languages, he was limited by having only a small staff and budget and constrained by communication delays with his agents in Europe. The new leader of Southern diplomatic efforts recognized that he needed to promote a more nuanced policy to gain support abroad, especially given the deterioration of the Confederate military position. Among his objectives were to forge a special relationship with France, through selling cotton at "remarkably low prices," and also to engage in arms purchases from French and British suppliers, again to link both nations' commercial interests more closely with those in the South.[63]

Instead, Davis and Secretary Benjamin sent back Edwin DeLeon, along with $25,000, to bolster Confederate propaganda efforts in Europe, especially in print. Almost immediately coming into conflict with Confederate commissioners Slidell and Mason, who reached Europe in January 1862, DeLeon's mission to improve the visibility and popularity of the Confederates had limited success. Even more of a factor than incompetence within the ranks of Southern agents in Paris and London, however, was the failure of Southern forces to achieve significant battlefield victories against the Union. With such victories, Confederate agents could expect doors to open; without them, all the propaganda and alleged sympathy toward the South would dissipate without result.[64]

On the question of the Civil War, the rest of Europe deferred to Britain, and only France and Spain had any significant interests in the Americas. France retained control over several small islands; Spain's territory in Puerto Rico and Cuba was much greater. Only Britain, with its powerful navy, global empire, and trading interests, had the means to lead a major intervention, whether diplomatic or military, in the American conflict. With most Europeans other than some elements of the military and landed aristocracy supportive of the Union, the presumption was that Britain, France, and other powers would let the Civil War run its course, so long as it did not interfere with vital European interests in the Atlantic or Caribbean. Spain had no such luxury, given how close the American conflict was to its Cuban colony. The kingdom could not stand by and observe, given that warships from the Union and Confederacy passed through its colonial waters and docked in its harbors, and that both sides included leaders who had proposed seizing Cuba from Spain.[65]

However, as one Spanish diplomat, Francisco de Zea Bermúdez, noted: "Cuando Francia e Inglaterra marchen de acuerdo, secundarlas; cuando no, abstenerse" (When France and England march in step, we second them; when not, we abstain). In other words, Spain could not afford to antagonize either power, needing at least the tolerance of both to execute major policies such as an alliance with the Confederacy. This de facto permission from France and Britain seemed close at several points during the war—with several opportunities—had several factors converged. When there were Confederate battlefield victories, effective Southern diplomatic efforts, errors made by the United States, and Spanish receptiveness, an alliance seemed possible. There were times when one or two of these elements were in place, but never enough to lead to a real political and military alignment between Spain and the Southern rebels.[66]

Recognizing the critical importance of the Civil War to his nation's interests, Minister Tassara advocated in April 1862 that Spain should dispatch a warship from Cuba to American waters to be ready for any eventuality. Tassara did not see any immediate problems such as any need to evacuate Spanish citizens but advised it would be a good expedient nonetheless. France, Britain, Russia, even the newly formed Kingdom of Italy had vessels in US waters, so Spain needed one, too, in order to be considered a serious state. Previous port calls by new Spanish warships to New York harbor had greatly improved the image of Spain in the United States, Tassara argued, and this request would demonstrate that Spain was a revived power in the world. This was the minister's third recommendation of this type, but this one was also rejected by the Spanish government.[67]

During the Civil War, Spain was willing to join proposals to recognize the Confederacy, mediate between the Union and the South, or support other joint European interventions to end the war in a way that preserved two states instead of one. In 1861 and 1862, Spain would have followed French or British leadership in recognizing the Confederacy but was not yet in a position, despite the ambitions of Prime Minister O'Donnell, to take such as initiative on its own. In 1862, there was even some sentiment in monarchist circles for redeploying the army units that had been withdrawn from Mexico, particularly if this could occur in the context of clearer security guarantees for the Spanish empire.[68] In 1862 and 1863, Spain joined French proposals for mediation and an armistice, while allowing the French to take the lead.[69] While in practice Spain did not initiate any actions that were strictly illegal under international law, in the United States many perceived that it strongly favored the Confederacy. Typical was a newspaper article from the *New York Herald Tribune*, the headline of which read: "Spain, The Only Friend of the Rebels."[70]

The Spanish government did provide limited sanctuary for Confederate warships in its ports, although the watchful eyes of American diplomats limited the possibilities for this form of collaboration. For example, on January 4, 1862, the cruiser CSS *Sumter* arrived in Cádiz, after destroying six Union ships and bonding ten others carrying neutral cargo. The port authorities initially were willing to let the ship's captain make repairs, but thanks to shortages of funds and the vigorous diplomatic efforts of the US government, the *Sumter* was forced to leave after two days. The captain, Raphael Semmes (later to gain even more fame with the CSS *Alabama*), was surprised at this treatment by Spain, given his expectations of favorable treatment, but the US diplomatic presence in Cádiz made any accommodations to the Confederacy awkward. The short time horizon afforded to Semmes provided only enough time to release the ship's Union prisoners, make some urgent repairs, and steam away without even taking on coal. Forced to dock in Gibraltar, while being pursued by Union ships, the *Sumter* remained there disabled from April to December 1862, when it was sold to British cotton merchants—soon to reenter service to the Confederacy as a blockade runner.[71]

During the summer of 1863, before the Confederate defeat at Gettysburg, Spain seemed favorably inclined to support mediation or foreign intervention, which would have been of direct aid to the South. The Southern invasions of Maryland and Pennsylvania accelerated this interest, especially given the letters sent to Cuba and Spain by Tassara. In late June 1863, the diplomat was so panicked at what he saw as an imminent Southern occupation that he demanded the Spanish navy send a warship from Havana to cruise up the Potomac River to rescue him and his diplomatic staff. While the Spanish government demurred and the immediate danger subsided (along with Tassara's panic), Spain continued to watch the conflict closely. Cuba remained the primary station for many of Spain's newest warships, as well as the base for some of its best army regiments, against any eventuality.[72]

Despite these moments, correct if not cordial Spanish relations with the United States continued. Confederate missteps, such as CSA Secretary of State Benjamin's June 1863 ban on contact between foreign nationals and their resident diplomats in Washington, did not contribute to positive feelings toward the South. The expulsion of foreign representatives that followed immediately thereafter, which included Spanish diplomats, soured feelings in London, Paris, and Madrid.[73] While the summer of 1863 seemed a dismal time for Confederate diplomacy and even propagandist DeLeon called for the recall of all Southern agents from Europe, there was progress made in Madrid and Paris toward possible international intervention. This progress, however, awaited a significant and strategic battlefield victory by General Robert E. Lee, something that seemed consistently on the verge of happening during the first two years of war. The Confederates won tactical military victories at Fredericksburg in December 1862 and Chancellorsville in May 1863, but these were battles fought on Southern territory, and they did not reverse the growing Union strength.[74] The growing Union advantage in manpower and materiel also meant that time was against the Confederacy. Unrest in the North, including draft riots and calls for a negotiated settlement, began to rise in 1862 and 1863, yet these events never approached the level of an overall threat to the Union's war efforts.[75]

Of the European powers, France under Emperor Napoleon III seemed most enthusiastic about the Confederacy. Striking textile workers, over three hundred thousand of whom were forced into unemployment by cotton shortages in 1861, caused the emperor to consider recognizing the Confederate States in early 1862. Support for a diplomatic settlement to the American Civil War was particularly strong in French regions such as Normandy, Alsace, and the northeast, which depended heavily on the textile industry. Manufacturers and bankers dependent on the cotton trade urged French mediation and leadership in favor of the Confederacy, and with a few battlefield victories this could very well have occurred. Spain and the United Kingdom were likely to have extended parallel diplomatic recognitions of the government of President Jefferson Davis. The Union capture of the key Southern city of New Orleans on May 1, 1862, however, caused the French emperor to hesitate, and instead he proposed mediation and a truce. New Orleans not only had importance as a primary Southern port but also held even greater significance as a former French colony. France had to be cautious also because, in addition to its cotton imports, it also relied on imported Union wheat to feed its people—agricultural sales, primarily from the Unionist American Midwest that could be severely curtailed if Napoleon III demonstrated excessive advocacy for the Confederacy.[76]

While France had to cope with rising unemployment in its textile industry, the broader French economy would have experienced even greater damage from the cessation of trade with the United States. Even recognition of the CSA carried with it the possibility of a US embargo of France and associated economic risks. No other economy was as dependent on cotton for its livelihood as the CSA, so the greatest impact of the cessation or revival of trade in this commodity would always accrue to the South. King Cotton was really only King in the Confederacy; everywhere else he was only one prince among many vying for attention in the royal courts and parliaments of Europe.[77]

Spain seemed more favorable terrain for the Confederacy, at least during the initial stages of the war. Spain's Foreign Minister, Saturnino Calderón Collantes, even described Spain to Confederate agent Pierre Rost as the "natural ally and friend" of the CSA.[78] This statement, which unfortunately for Spain made its way into newspapers in the United States, was an accurate description of the two states. However, the relative strengths of the Union and the Confederacy made it incumbent on Spain to tread carefully in this direction. The Spanish might agree to joint diplomatic efforts if France or Britain led, but they were limited in their ability to launch independent initiatives, an ironic situation given the rising overall strength of the Spanish economy and military.[79]

Overall, the South had great hopes that its diplomatic efforts in Madrid would eventually come to fruition. As the Confederacy's first secretary of state, R. M. T. Hunter observed in his guidance to Pierre Rost, the Confederate representative in Madrid, in August 1861, "Of all the great powers of Europe Spain alone is interested through her colonies in the same social system which pervades the Confederate States."[80] Many leading members of the Spanish aristocracy, especially those with property, familial ties, or experience in Spain's Caribbean colonies, believed that the Confederate government was only one major victory away from international recognition and would have been enthusiastic advocates for this. Despite delays in communications, news from the battlefields of the American Civil War did eventually reach Europe, so there was a correspondence, albeit a delayed one, between the fortunes of Southern armies and Southern diplomacy.[81]

Confederate representatives might have used the good offices of Spain to gain recognition from Portugal as well. Portugal was even smaller than Spain, of course, and of less international significance and military potential. Despite this weak position, it was a nation that boasted not only an African empire in Angola, Mozambique, and elsewhere but an outsized role in the illegal slave trade that continued to the Americas throughout the nineteenth century, despite British naval and diplomatic efforts to destroy this commerce in human cargo. Some of the slaves transported by the Portuguese came surreptitiously to Brazil or Cuba, while others were purchased within the Ottoman empire. A traditional ally of Britain, Portugal nonetheless resisted entreaties from London to put a stop to this practice among its merchantmen and shipping companies. Like Belgium, another small nation with outsized territory in Africa, Portugal nonetheless could have played a role in a coalition of states, which might have also included Brazil, to buttress the Confederacy. These states, of course, relied upon the toleration of the British empire—the only power with an effective veto over major operations by these minor countries.[82]

Madrid was far weaker than France in terms of its economic, military, and political power, and even more so in comparison to Great Britain. Even in its strengthened position in the early 1860s, after the economic revival, arms buildup, and creation of what seemed a more stable government, Spain had not yet overcome its image of decadence and internal strife. Consequently, Spain received less attention from the Confederacy, which also realized that Spain's freedom of maneuver in the American Civil War was very restricted.[83] On the issue of slavery, where there seemed to be a convergence of positions between the slaveholding Southern states and slaveholding Spain, there were actually some differences. While Spaniards in Cuba were enthusiastic supporters of a renewed slave trade and of closer commercial ties with the Confederacy, hoping for a weaker United States, in metropolitan Spain these sentiments were not the same. Abolitionism was rising in Madrid among Spanish liberals and even within some conservative circles, this mitigating against pro-Southern sentiment. Even among those predisposed to look favorably on a division of the United States, there was also the fear of a strong South, having gained its survival. Who was to say that the Confederacy would not emerge from war just as intent on annexing Cuba? Would Spain really be in a stronger position if the South survived? The fear that Spain would cast its fortunes with an independent CSA and other areas with slave-based economies such as Brazil was prevalent especially in liberal political circles. Was it really wise to do so when the economic future of Europe and the globe appeared to be in the hands of Britain, the world's only superpower at midcentury?[84]

When pressed by Britain and the United States, however, Spain did collaborate in repressing the slave trade. Although the country was not enthusiastic about pursuing merchant ships, given its hopes to encourage shipping through its ports, in some cases the actions of the slave traders were so blatant that Spain would have been hard-pressed to deny the US request for assistance. It was rare for a slave ship to make port calls in Spain, in fact, as the far more permissive Portugal provided a more convenient stop before or after crossing from Africa. The long coastline of Brazil as well as minor ports throughout the Caribbean welcomed the trade in human cargo. Without a market or a source for slaves in Spain, it was only other needs of commercial business or emergencies that would bring a slaving captain to Spain or France, or even less to Britain, the global crusader against the nefarious business.[85] Spain had outlawed the trade as early as 1845 but was less effective in implementation than the British would have liked—no surprise given the overall weakness of the Spanish central government. Illicit trade, especially to colonial markets in Cuba, continued well into the 1850s.[86]

Spanish cooperation with American diplomats on the issue of the slave trade was rare, but it did occur. For example, in spring 1862, the United States provided Spain with information that a Southern-based American merchant ship, the *Falmouth*, was probably participating in slaving from Africa. The two states worked closely together from March to May 1862, eventually detaining the ship and its crew in Cádiz as it docked there. In an unusual set of circumstances, Spain complained about the incompetence of E. S. Eggleston, the US Consul in Cádiz, in the investigation. Both the Spanish captain general for Cádiz and the Spanish Foreign Ministry were upset over Eggleston's slow responses to their requests for information. There was some suspicion that the US consul might have been personally involved in the trade, or receiving bribes from those who were, yet his political connections included a direct appointment from Seward and made it problematic to push this too far. Perry did upbraid Eggleston, warning him that his "easy-going, somewhat careless disposition" might end him up "in very serious trouble" and might cause major problems for the US government in the middle of a war.[87]

Still, even Spain's chief diplomat in the United States was in the summer of 1862 advising his foreign minister that the time had come to consider recognition and the imposition of mediation on the two warring sides. Of the four great powers with significant influence in the Americas (Britain, France, Spain, and Russia), only Russia was too identified with the United States to be unsuitable for intervention. If Britain and France would lead, Spain could and should ally in this effort to bring the American Civil War to a close, with permanent status for both the Union and the Confederacy. The interests of three of the four major nations in the Americas supported a negotiated settlement to the war. The Confederacy, too, would be expected to support nearly any solution that guaranteed it survival. The most difficult challenge would be to approach the Union and its intractable foreign policy team of Lincoln and Seward, at a time of weakness, perhaps in the aftermath of a major battlefield loss by the Union army. Should there come a moment when Confederate arms seemed poised to overrun Washington, DC, or to crush the armies of General Ulysses S. Grant, the time would be opportune for an imposed settlement. In this eventuality, Spain would have enthusiastically aligned with France and Great Britain to force the United States to accept a foreign-brokered accord that recognized the Confederacy and permanently hobbled the Yankees.[88]

Spain depended on France and Britain for leadership in its foreign policy. Many Spanish aristocrats, military leaders, and slave-owning colonial creoles supported the South, but the government wanted to remain neutral until the war's end was clearly determined. Clearly sympathetic to the social system of the Confederacy and hopeful that the conflict would weaken and perhaps permanently divide the United States, Spanish leaders, including Prime Minister Leopold O'Donnell, nonetheless remembered that it had been primarily Southern politicians who had plotted to annex Cuba. For most of 1861 and 1862, there was rising support in Spain for the Confederacy, coupled with plans to establish a formal alliance with France to provide indirect support to the Southern rebels. On their own initiative, Spanish officials in Cuba initiated contacts with Confederate agents and facilitated blockade running and other naval activities that supported the economy of both the Spanish colonial empire and the Confederacy. Southern diplomatic and commercial agents operated freely in Havana, encouraging Confederate leaders to make use of Cuban facilities for blockade running and other smuggling operations.[89] Financial interests, local ties, and the logic of geography encouraged collaboration between Spain and the Confederacy in the Caribbean. However, the weakening of the government of O'Donnell in Madrid and Confederate battle losses diminished the attractiveness and wisdom of these forms of cooperation, as the United States began to put pressure on the Spanish government for their cessation.[90]

Even though Spain was an "ideological soul-mate" to the Confederacy, its international weakness and Southern efforts to exploit the potential relationship did not develop into a diplomatic breakthrough between the two states. The potential for tangible benefits for both Spain and the South, from territorial gains to a weakened United States, were not realized, and in the end the explorations of a relationship ended without providing any gains for either Madrid or the CSA. Less powerful than France or the United Kingdom, Spain was at the same time better situated in terms of geography and proven enmity to the United States to provide tangible assistance to the South. While the British controlled Canada, and the French retained some Caribbean possessions, Spain's colonies of Cuba and Puerto Rico were already serving Confederate ships as safe harbors against the Union fleet.[91]

Even had Spain been more willing to support the Confederacy openly through diplomatic or military measures, it had little means to do so. With ongoing difficulties in its remaining colonies and its increasingly limited resources in the midst of expanding overseas commitments, Spain was in no position to seek additional burdens by getting involved in the American Civil War. Its garrisons in Cuba and Puerto Rico lacked sufficient arms and its naval forces in the Caribbean barely sufficed for coastal protection against smugglers, much less a serious engagement at sea against a determined and well-equipped enemy. More important, in 1861 Spain took on a new overseas commitment, by occupying the eastern half of the island of Hispaniola: its former Caribbean colony of Santo Domingo.[92]

This unilateral move by Spain was its boldest campaign yet to revive its imperial ambitions, but it also accelerated tensions with the United States. There is clear evidence, for example, that Spain deliberately slow-walked the annexation in order to ensure that the United States would be fully occupied by its own struggles in its civil war and therefore unable to organize any effective resistance to the Spanish recolonization. The reoccupation of Santo Domingo was welcomed by the Confederacy as one more signal of growing opportunities to drive a wedge between the Union and the European powers. In the end, this military action by Spain did not prove sufficient to cause an open conflict with the United States, although it might have. Britain and France supported the annexation, primarily because Spain's weak and probably temporary control was preferable to the strong influence of the United States on the island. They knew that Madrid would probably lose the colony, as it had done previously, whereas the United States would never leave Hispaniola should its forces arrive as the protecting power over Santo Domingo. The occupation of former British, French, and Spanish territory by the United States, as well as its ambitions on other lands, gave sufficient proof of the permanence of conquests by the North American republic.

In the end, British and French expectations were fulfilled but not before Spain endured a hard season of bitter war and nightmare losses in what was intended to be the crowning achievement of a revived Spanish empire—the reclaiming of a colony and perhaps the first step toward the reestablishment of dominion over Latin America. If events in Santo Domingo went well, with a peaceful occupation and smooth assimilation into the Spanish empire, the Spanish government could hope for more. Under this scenario might not the other republics in the hemisphere, which so recently had been governed by Madrid, abandon their failed republican experiments? After seeing the magnanimity and efficiency of the reoccupation of Santo Domingo, would they not ask to be brought back under the efficient, benevolent rule of the Kingdom of Spain and its monarch, Queen Isabel II? Spain's annexation of this small and relatively unimportant republic could presage a rise in sympathy for the old colonial period, with conservatives and monarchists throughout Latin America encouraged to follow the example of Dominican president Pedro Santana, who had invited Spain to return, ostensibly with the enthusiastic support of his people.[93]

Events did not go well, however, and Spain's imperial dream died in a cascade of international hubris, violent insurgency, and the affliction of yellow fever. Coming as it did during the American Civil War and with opposition from the United States, the Spanish occupation of Santo Domingo had the potential to encourage closer ties with the Confederacy. Although neither additional annexations nor an alliance with the South emerged from the Spanish campaign in Santo Domingo, they were nonetheless active possibilities at the time and weighed as factors in the diplomacy of other nations, including the United States of America.

Chapter 4

Spain's Dominican Enterprise

Spain's most spectacular attempt to revive its imperial glory came in March 1861 when it annexed the Caribbean state of Santo Domingo, allegedly to protect the Dominicans from potential invasion from Haiti. Santo Domingo, the eastern two-thirds of the island of Hispaniola, had been a Spanish colony before 1822, when it was occupied by neighboring Haiti, an occupation that ended only in 1844. Ostensibly to prevent a recurrence of Haitian incursions as well as to promote economic development, Dominican president Pedro Santana invited the Spanish occupation, believing it would strengthen his rule. Santana and Spanish colonial officials from Cuba agreed on the terms of the annexation: no reinstitution of slavery, no changes in Dominican laws, the continuation of local officials and priests in their positions, and no change to local currency or property ownership. The accord, implemented without direct involvement by the Madrid government, was announced in Santo Domingo on March 18, 1861, by Santana and Spanish military officials who had negotiated the reinstallation of colonial forces from Spain's main Caribbean base in Havana.[1]

This was not the first time Dominican leaders had invited foreign occupation in order to buttress their hold on power and forestall the Haitian threat. As early as 1809, the white creole population rebelled against French and Haitian occupation and invited Spain to return as the colonial power.[2] After Santo Domingo's independence in 1821, the next two decades featured repeated Haitian invasions and Dominican rebellions, leading to an understandable fear of Haiti and the identification of the elite—a mostly white or biracial class—with Europe and its civilization. Even blacks with some property or status would sometimes refer to themselves as *blancos de la tierra* (whites of the earth) to differentiate themselves from the "barbarian" Haitians.[3]

Indeed, the first Haitian occupation began in February 1822—just two months after Dominican independence in December 1821. Even at this early stage, the Dominican elite had looked to outside aid as the only remedy against their large neighbor. In this case, the provisional Dominican government sent a request to Simón Bolívar, president of Gran Colombia, asking to be absorbed into the larger state. Bolívar was himself still fighting to expel Spanish forces from South America and was unable to consider the request. Under Haitian occupation, slavery ended and creole land was expropriated, to be redistributed mostly to Haitians. Fearing persecution by the Haitians, the majority of Europeans fled, as did any creoles with the opportunity to do so. The corruption and incompetence of the Haitian occupation led to a successful revolt in 1844 and the restoration of Dominican independence. Haiti continued to loom as a threat, however, even after this expulsion.[4]

In the mid-1840s Dominican president Pedro Santana encouraged the French to consider a protectorate—an offer declined by Paris. Santana was even unable to gain full diplomatic recognition by the United States and Britain, France, and Spain, the three principal European states with holdings in the Caribbean, given the obvious weakness of the Dominican Republic and its vulnerability to a Haitian attack.[5] Santana's fears were prescient, as Haiti invaded again in early March 1849, leading to panic in the Dominican capital and entreaties to Britain and France to extend a protectorate. By late April 1849, the Dominicans, led by Santana in his triumphant return from retirement, had repelled the incursion. Santana used the prestige gained through this victory to seize power again, receiving the title "Liberator" from a grateful Dominican Congress and being confirmed as commander in chief of the army. The threat from neighboring Haiti continued, however, with sporadic fighting until 1855, when the two nations agreed to peace terms. Santana, apart from brief episodes in exile or disfavor, continued to dominate the political system. In 1859 he was again elected to the presidency, for the third time in the short history of the Dominican Republic.[6]

In early 1859, as well, a new Haitian government committed itself to living at peace with the Dominican Republic, promising to end the warfare that had plagued Hispaniola since the western half successfully broke from Port au Prince in 1844. Despite these new conditions, Santana continued to seek a foreign benefactor and settled on Spain only after being rejected by France. The absolute penury of the Dominican government after less than fifteen years of independence, caused primarily by wars and revolutions, was greatly exacerbated by the endemic corruption among the ruling elites, including Santana and his allies.[7] Spanish recognition of Santo Domingo's independence in 1855 in some ways actually weakened the political and economic stability of the young republic, as a provision of the treaty allowed the white creole population to emigrate to Spain—which the majority of them did.[8]

In 1850 the United States, France, and Britain gave Santo Domingo a security guarantee, promising support should Haiti invade. Even with this bolstering of Dominican defenses, its economy continued to weaken. The Haitians had tried to promote cash crops at the expense of subsistence farming, but this transition remained incomplete, leaving the nation's agricultural lands in even worse condition. By the end of thc 1850s, with civil wars, corruption, inflation, economic instability, and fears of Haiti endemic, total collapse seemed imminent. The Dominican currency was worthless and the national bank was in bankruptcy. Illiteracy was nearly universal, internal commerce stagnant, and the rudimentary financial system was plagued by capital flight and permanent trade deficits.[9]

Santo Domingo signed two key treaties in an attempt to strengthen itself both domestically and internationally. In 1854 the United States and the Dominican government signed the Treaty of Friendship, Commerce, and Navigation, and in 1855 Spain and Santo Domingo signed the Treaty of Peace, Friendship, Commerce, Navigation, and Extradition. The accord with the United States was revised in 1856, adding sections on extradition and navigation. These agreements envisioned a burgeoning of trade and other exchanges between the Caribbean nation and more powerful nations, but the poor state of Dominican agriculture and the overall economy meant it had little to offer for export and even less ability to pay for imports.[10] Despite Santo Domingo's history as a previous colony of Spain, France, and even Haiti, only France remained a major trading partner during its independence period. The top five nations—in terms of their exports to and imports from Santo Domingo in 1850—were the United States, Great Britain, France, Denmark, and the Netherlands. Spain was in a distant seventh place, even considering trade between Santo Domingo and the nearby Spanish colonies of Cuba and Puerto Rico.[11]

As early as 1858, Santana had suggested that Spain should consider annexing Santo Domingo, and in April 1860 he wrote a personal letter to Isabel II to this effect.[12] Santana's extraordinary envoy and minister plenipotentiary to the court of Queen Isabel II, General Felipe Benecio Alfau Bustamente, had raised this issue during his initial meeting with the queen, when he presented his diplomatic credentials in February 1860. Alfau conveyed informal hints of what Santana would later ask formally; that the Dominican Republic would request to be annexed as an overseas province of Spain, with full rights and representation in the Cortes.[13] Other requested provisions included a promise that Spain would not reimpose slavery, that the administration would employ the maximum number of creoles possible, that Spain would convert circulating paper money at favorable rates and validate all actions of the Dominican government from 1844 to the present.[14] While the queen and her government did not express any initial interest in this proposal, Prime Minister O'Donnell did dispatch a military mission to help train the Dominican armed forces and also to explore the strategic position and its possibilities for Spain.[15]

Faced with some reluctance in Madrid to take on the burdens of Santo Domingo, Santana turned to the captain general of Cuba, General Francisco Serrano, who had received instructions from Madrid to discuss the issue with the Dominicans but not to move precipitously for fear of angering the United States. Only with the clear and overwhelming support of the population of Santo Domingo should Spain consider the proposal. Santana encouraged the colonial official to advocate a return of Spanish troops, allegedly forestalling any occupation by the United States or possibly even the emerging Southern Confederacy. Fears of these dangers were baseless, as the United States and the Southern rebels in 1860–1861 obviously had other concerns.[16] But this was enough to prompt Serrano, along with the Spanish government, to take up Santana's offer and thus begin one of the most disastrous Spanish foreign policy adventures—what one historian called "one of the unhappiest periods in Dominican history" and what another characterized as a military operation that, at least from the Spanish side, was "attempted with very little conviction."[17] With the United States focused on its own civil war, there was at least less of a concern in Madrid that Washington, DC, might take active measures to prevent the occupation or even attempt to substitute its own forces for those of Spain. By late 1860 and early 1861, there was little chance that Abraham Lincoln's incoming administration would divert any political and military resources away from the immediate defense of the Union. Prime Minister O'Donnell, anticipating a war between the South and the North, believed that Spain would eventually align with the South.[18]

Santana hoped to encourage Spain to move by demonstrating it would be welcomed by the Dominican population. Frustrated by his slow negotiations with Spain, Santana decided to force the issue by unilaterally creating a show of public opinion. In order to do so, he organized a faux plebiscite in March 1861, allegedly showing mass support for annexation. In fact, the vote was anything but popular, with participation limited to the wealthy, powerful, and those allied to Santana. Only 4,000 out of a population of 280,000 actually signed the petitions, representing a mere 1.4 percent of the nation.[19] Many of the "votes" were cast in the private homes or government-controlled facilities. Nonetheless, on March 18, 1861, Santana announced the results of the vote and declared a restoration of Spanish rule in a speech in the Plaza de Armas in the capital of Santo Domingo. In his comments, Santana declared that the popular will of the people demanded Spanish annexation.[20] The Spanish government and General Serrano were upset, feeling outmaneuvered by Santana and with little choice but to proceed with the occupation. In early April, some three thousand Spanish soldiers in Cuba were given orders by General Serrano to prepare for deployment to Santo Domingo, to begin a provisional occupation, subject to ratification by the Spanish government. Prime Minister O'Donnell was angry that the first news of the plebiscite came to him through the newspaper rather than through diplomatic or military channels.[21] Only after determining that the United States would not go to war over Santo Domingo did Isabel II accept the annexation, in a decree of May 19. A few days later, two more battalions arrived from Cuba. These soldiers, sent by General Serrano, were unprepared for their mission. They had no maps, no information about the island, or instructions about what they should do upon arrival.[22]

The reaction of the international community was fairly muted. The United States protested, and Seward presented war as an option to President Lincoln, but the new president was too engaged with his own civil war to enforce the Monroe Doctrine. Britain tolerated the occupation, with what one historian described as "reluctant acquiescence," following the understanding that Spain would not reimpose slavery. France supported Spain, seeing "no menace to French interests," and perhaps hoping for the same endorsement of its imperial ambitions in Mexico and elsewhere. Haiti was adamantly against the occupation, still hoping to retake Santo Domingo for itself, but was unable to provide any substantial resistance to Spanish military activities, even though it was repeatedly accused of doing so.[23]

The Spanish Cortes was out of session for most of 1861, from March to November, and so was not able to consider the matter formally until months after the annexation had begun. After a limited debate, the parliament ratified the actions of the government, including the annexation, on December 16, 1861, by a vote of two hundred to eighty. Opponents included members of the liberal opposition, who feared the imposition of slavery, as well as political rivals to Prime Minister O'Donnell. Support for the retaking of Santo Domingo was strongest among the "propertied classes, aristocrats, Catalan industrialists, urban landowners, military and religious leaders" who believed this campaign would revitalize Spain's image and economy, restore Catholicism to the colony, and protect Cuba.[24]

The Spanish navy imposed a cordon around Santo Domingo and other ports to prevent external interference, a flotilla that rose to include as many as twenty warships at the height of the Spanish landings. Concerns for the safety of newly arriving troop reinforcements or when rumors of Haitian or US involvement concerned local Spanish commanders provided the justification for larger deployments of the fleet. Given the history of filibustering from the United States, invasion from Haiti, and the movement of volunteers and smuggled arms within Latin America and the Caribbean during those regions' struggles for independence from Europe, this self-blockade of Dominican ports was a prudent move.[25]

Santo Domingo in 1861 was a poor, isolated, and thinly populated nation. Aside from the capital, subsistence agriculture and livestock management predominated throughout the countryside. Despite making up approximately two-thirds of the island of Hispaniola, there were at most two hundred thousand inhabitants according to the official census of 1863, a figure that the US government considered inflated by at least 20 percent.[26] The capital city, also called Santo Domingo, had a population of approximately five thousand.[27] Flanked to its west by the nation of Haiti and in the midst of a Caribbean dominated by the British and US navies, Santo Domingo had few prospects for generating revenue, raising living standards, or achieving progress, especially given the ongoing bitter conflicts within its domestic political class of petty landowners and merchants. Perhaps an outside force such as Spain could provide the stability and incentives for development that most Dominicans recognized were desperately needed. Given the failures to gain interest in this possibility by the United States and France, the former colonial power was a final external alternative.

With over twenty thousand soldiers and some support from the Dominican ruling class, the occupation of 1861 at first seemed a successful effort, but initial acceptance of the annexation gradually declined. Dominicans were forced out of office and the military in favor of Spaniards; the American Civil War weakened commerce; Spain delayed redeeming Dominican paper money for gold and silver, contrary to its promises; and harsh Spanish laws were reimposed. Even the Catholic clergy became angry as Spanish priests replaced native Dominicans in key remunerative positions. Most of Santo Domingo was Catholic but of a very local variety, mixed with traditional religions and heavily influenced by Haitian practices, especially along the border. There were also many Protestant churches as well as many Freemason lodges, which immediately came under attack from the Catholic Church. Another issue that caused controversy was that many Dominican couples lived together in common law marriages, having not received the sacrament in the church. Spanish clergy, with no understanding of local traditions, denounced these arrangements as sinful and demanded that couples marry in the church after confession and penance.[28]

The naming of a Spaniard, Archbishop Bienvenido de Monzón y Martín, as prelate in Santo Domingo contributed to the difficulties.

The episcopal see had been vacant since the death of Archbship Antonio Cerezano in July 1860, and Cerezano and his predecessors since independence had all been natives of Santo Domingo. Having the highest position within the Catholic Church go to a priest from Spain was a clear signal to the local clergy of the absolute dominance expected by the Spanish leaders of the church. Although the new archbishop was young for a bishop (he was in his early forties), his youth was not accompanied by flexibility. His pastoral letter of January 1, 1863, condemned the cohabitation practiced by Dominicans, which had been common for centuries in the territory. Common law marriages were widespread, especially in rural areas where there was a shortage of priests able to perform the sacrament of marriage, and were a commonly accepted part of Dominican culture. For the leading religious figure to insist that these relationships be normalized with marriage vows when it was the deficit of priests and churches that had caused the issue in the first place showed a lack of comprehension of local conditions by the peninsular leaders. Monzón's decree that any children resulting from cohabitation would be considered illegitimate understandably upset the population as well. His insistence on Roman Catholic religious orthodoxy and that all Freemason lodges and Protestant churches be closed immediately was not well received by a population known for its religious tolerance not only of these practices but also of Haitian folk religions.[29]

Spain's European soldiers were not prepared for the circumstances of the occupation. One major challenge was the threat from yellow fever and other tropical diseases, which routinely felled more soldiers than did combat operations.[30] The Spanish conscripts who made up the bulk of the army were not culturally prepared for long-term residence among the Dominicans, who were far less acculturated into Spanish civilization than Cubans or Puerto Ricans. Those Spaniards with experience in the Caribbean had acquired it mostly in Cuba, but in translating this to Santo Domingo many of them brought along their perception of blacks as slaves. These opinions, while usually accurate in Cuba, were disastrous in Santo Domingo, especially when Spanish soldiers shared these prejudices with the local population. Fears that Spain would reimpose slavery, despite official assurances from the colonial administration, were widespread in Santo Domingo, a fear that attained more credence given the behavior of the Spanish soldiers. The common practice by the Spanish army of confiscating local animals—especially mules and horses—for military use, typically without compensation, was another contributory factor to indigenous resentment of the foreign occupation.[31]

Early in the occupation, the Spanish lost their strongest ally—in fact, the one most directly responsible for the renewed European presence in Santo Domingo. In January 1862, just a few months after the arrival of the first Spanish soldiers, Governor General Pedro Santana, who also held the honorary rank of captain general in the Spanish army, resigned from the office of governor. He did, however, retain his military rank, later adding to it that of senator. As president, he had considered Spanish occupation to be the panacea for Santo Domingo's problems as well as a way to outmaneuver his rivals. With the reality of the occupation and its increasing unpopularity, and feeling sidelined by the Spanish authorities, he broke with his erstwhile European patrons. Santana did not take a position in support of the rebellion, but neither did he see Spanish occupation in the same light. He died in 1864 in the capital of Santo Domingo, shortly after being named a Spanish marquis.[32]

By 1862, the Spaniards were contending with a limited insurgency and losing hundreds of soldiers to guerrillas and the devastation of yellow fever. The occupation—described by one historian as "incredibly inept"—was a massive and humiliating failure for the Spanish government.[33] By 1863, Santo Domingo, which had been considered a minor operation when it began in 1861, became the most important foreign policy issue for Spain, of far more significance than the American Civil War, the conflict in Mexico, or anything beyond the immediate defense of the homeland and other colonies.[34] Discontent with the occupation in the parliament and court was a major contributing factor in the collapse of the government of Prime Minister O'Donnell in February 1863. By early 1864, the rebellion had become a nationwide uprising in Santo Dominigo, and in Spain became common knowledge, with public unhappiness beginning to cause major domestic problems for the queen. Discussion within the ruling classes was not so much about how to win the war but how to extricate Spain with the least amount of damage to its reputation and the fewest losses among its soldiers.[35] By the end of the conflict in 1865, Spain had suffered more than five hundred deaths to enemy action, almost seven thousand deaths from disease, and almost two thousand men seriously injured.[36]

President Lincoln and Secretary of State Seward protested the Spanish occupation in 1861, a position echoed in the Northern press, which warned that Santo Domingo would see the reintroduction of slavery and that Spain would then move on to conquer Haiti.[37] The United States even briefly considered declaring war on Spain to show their displeasure at this violation of the Monroe Doctrine.[38] On April 1, Seward's initial instructions to his emissary to Santo Domingo, as well as messages sent to the Spanish embassy in Washington and Spanish Foreign Ministry in Madrid, hinted darkly of "effective resistance" should Spain attempt to annex the Dominican Republic. Within a day, however, Seward had reconsidered this hard line and did not even break diplomatic relations. Given the conflict looming with the South and the necessity of retaining ties with all significant nations, Seward instead referred the issue to the US Congress, where it was likely to be subsumed under greater issues.[39] Instead of declaring war, US diplomats reminded Spain of the former annexationist ideas of Confederate leaders Jefferson Davis and other Southerners, who had supported filibusters and demanded Cuba and Puerto Rico.[40] Public opinion in the United States was clearly against the Spanish occupation, and editorials asserted not only that Haiti would come to the aid of the Dominicans against the "comedy" of Santana's treason but that indigenous resistance would swiftly rise up and drive out the foreign aggressors. In fact Haiti remained neutral, despite its previous occupation of Santo Domingo, but editorial predictions of internal rebellion by the Dominican population were to prove prescient.[41]

Even after the Dominican rebellion began, the United States did not support the insurgents, fearing this might encourage Spain to recognize the Confederacy or even declare war.[42] While the United States, along with Haiti and Peru, issued diplomatic protests, this was as far as Washington was willing to push Spain, given the context of the American Civil War.[43] Although Spanish colonial officials believed American smugglers were selling arms to the rebels and heard rumors of impending US landings or invasions in alliance with Haiti, they had little evidence of actual or planned intervention. Spanish fears that hundreds, perhaps thousands, of American soldiers and marines were offshore waiting for the opportune time to join the rebels proved inaccurate.[44] Newspaper editorials in Spain denounced alleged US conspiracies to arm the blacks in Haiti, seize

Cuba and Puerto Rico, or invade Santo Domingo. One issue of *Novedades*, a Spanish newspaper published in Madrid, included articles confirming that the United States was supporting the rebellion as a precursor to uprisings in Cuba and Puerto Rico, and annexation of all three to the United States.[45]

While the Spanish press and educated public opinion did not initially demonstrate great enthusiasm for the occupation, the press did present the dangers of a rising United States, emphasized the importance of Santo Domingo in protecting Cuba, and highlighted the shared cultural and religious heritage between Spain and its restored colony. Although there was not a wave of patriotic sentiment, as had accompanied the victory over Morocco, neither was there significant opposition to the occupation in Spain. The operation was seen by most as a logical continuation of Spain's return to great power status, and perhaps a first step to restoring lost regions of its Latin American empire.[46]

In the face of this coverage in the Spanish press and repeated inquiries for clarification by the Spanish ambassador, Secretary of State Seward made every effort to convince Spanish officials that the Union had no immediate interest in the Caribbean.[47] In return, the Spanish Foreign Ministry promised that "if any commissioners or other negotiators should appear in behalf of the so-called Confederate States, the government of Queen Isabel II would not see them or recognize them in any capacity, whether official or unofficial."[48]

Pro-Confederate Spanish diplomats in New Orleans, Paris, and other locations employed spies to investigate accusations of Union plots to support the rebellion in Santo Domingo, possibly as a future dumping ground for freed black slaves, but found no proof.[49] The United States continued to worry about upsetting the Spanish and refused to enter into any negotiations with the rebel Dominicans. Seward issued orders banning any contacts between American diplomats and representatives of the provisional government in Santo Domingo, a ban that continued even in late 1864, when Spain itself had already begun to negotiate the terms of its withdrawal from the island. The United States was concerned to avoid anything that might appear favorable treatment toward the Dominicans, as this might reopen the issue of Spanish recognition of the Confederacy—an ongoing possibility as late as mid-1864.[50]

Far from supplying arms to the Dominican rebels, in spring 1861 the United States hosted a small delegation of Spanish army officers, with a mandate to investigate possible weapons purchases for the colonial administration in Cuba and Puerto Rico. General Serrano was concerned that the arms and ammunition at his disposal were insufficient on both islands to combat potential internal and external threats. To aid Serrano in his defense of the island, the Spanish government authorized the dispatch of a team of three artillery officers to the United States. Although the Spanish army would have preferred to procure weapons from domestic producers, there was an insufficient supply available, given the necessity of equipping forces in Morocco, the Philippines, and the Spanish peninsula. Their visit was inconclusive, as the United States was focused on equipping its own forces to fight the Southern rebellion, but the hospitality afforded the delegation by American officials and arms manufacturers built positive feelings on both sides—unusual for the Hispano-US relationship.[51]

Although rumors of American intervention proved incorrect, the potential for Santo Domingo or Haiti to be areas of resettlement for emancipated American slaves was a real one. In 1858, the government of Haiti invited potential emigrants from the United States to consider their nation as a potential home. In 1861, the prominent African American leader and abolitionist Frederick Douglass even visited Haiti and spoke favorably of the possibility of the Caribbean as a site for emigration of former slaves.[52] With the beginning of the Civil War, however, emigration advocates took pause, as the potential for being attacked by Confederate warships or being caught up in a war between Haiti and Spanish-occupied Santo Domingo intruded on these possibilities. The thousand or so who did emigrate to Haiti found conditions much worse than any had anticipated, and most of those who survived the smallpox, yellow fever, and other epidemics and were able to do so, returned permanently to the United States. Over the course of the early nineteenth century, several thousand more free blacks immigrated to Haiti and were distinct from this later group. By every measure, however, mass immigration failed to materialize.[53]

There was also some effort made by the government of Santo Domingo to encourage emigration from the United States. An ordinance passed in June 1860 established a board of immigration in each province, to support "the cheapest and easiest ways of bringing immigrants to the country," especially those of "the agricultural class, or those following some craft, profession, or useful form of labor."[54] Despite some pro-immigration effort by publicists in the United States, only a handful of free blacks undertook this journey at the time, establishing a community of a few dozen near Puerto Plata. As many as thirteen thousand free blacks had immigrated to Santo Domingo in previous decades, mostly organized by private Wesleyan and Methodist religious groups. This community, who arrived during the latter decades of Haitian occupation, concentrated in districts around the capital city, as well as in the towns of Puerto Plata and Samaná, and resisted linguistic and religious assimilation for many years.[55]

During the Spanish occupation, there were even proposals to bring Southern whites to Santo Domingo, in order to increase the percentage of those with European origin among the population. These proposals were intended to make Santo Domingo as unlike Haiti as possible, through adding a substantial non-black component to the population and taking advantage of large sections of fertile but unused agricultural land. A group of investors in early 1863 proposed arranging the immigration of between two and three thousand white settlers to the island, with the expectation that they would bolster the occupation, as well as bringing with them more advanced agricultural techniques. Many of these families had lost their livelihoods due to disruptions from the American Civil War and the collapse of the cotton export market and could be expected to prefer the chance for a new start, especially given the land grants and other privileges proposed by the Spanish occupation authorities. This scheme collapsed because of shaky financing and Union control over the Caribbean, yet it did receive initially favorable hearings from Spanish judicial and administrative authorities. Other proposals from New York City and elsewhere to bring skilled workers and others to Santo Domingo led toward finalizing formal rules for immigration and the operations of resettlement companies, but by the end of 1863 the rising insecurity in the colony had led to the abandonment of these initiatives.[56]

Even Tassara believed that the Union was remaining strictly neutral in regards to the insurrection.[57] The United States wanted to discourage Spain from entering the American Civil War and made clear the price the Spanish government would pay. Beginning in early 1863, the United States invited the Spanish ambassador, military attachés, and other agents from Madrid to visit construction sites, dry docks, and navy bases that hosted the new ironclads, such as the new *Monitor*. Spanish officers concluded that their own navy would be no match against the new armored vessels, realizing "the incontestable superiority of the Monitors against every class of armored ship known to this point."[58] Even though Spain had begun a major naval building program in the mid-1850s, its vessels, living conditions, and organization were so weak that even during the horrific war in Santo Domingo conscripts tried to volunteer or bribe officials to get into the army instead of the navy.[59] Spain's ambassador in Washington concluded that "Wooden warships will end up being useless," which served as a warning in Madrid to avoid naval confrontations with the United States at sea.[60]

The US government also hosted Spanish army officers as observers during the Civil War in order to impress them with the capabilities of Union forces. One visitor might have been Lieutenant Colonel Valeriano Weyler (there is inconclusive information about this), who served as a military attaché in Washington, DC, after surviving a harrowing year leading combat forces in Santo Domingo. Weyler would later become infamous as the commanding general of Spanish troops in Cuba just before the Spanish-American War (1898). Some historians have speculated that he was an admirer of Union general William T. Sherman, particularly his scorched earth tactics in the campaign for Atlanta, and may have been inspired by this for his harsh tactics used against Cuban rebels in 1897. As an educated officer and military academy graduate, however, he could also have developed these ideas by studying the Russian response to Napoleon's invasion of Russia in 1812.[61]

As with Cuba, Santo Domingo was used as a safe zone by Confederate warships and blockade runners, with the full consent of Spanish colonial officials. One example of this occurred in January 1863, when the CSS *Alabama* landed in the port of Santo Domingo. An impressive ship under its captain, Raphael Semmes, it displaced nine hundred tons and boasted eight large cannons. In Santo Domingo, the vessel took on coal and other provisions and released seventeen US prisoners before steaming back into the Caribbean to sink more US ships.

While this was technically within the limits allowed by the belligerent rights Spain had granted to the Confederacy, the United States nonetheless complained about the privileges granted to Confederate ships, arguing that they were practicing piracy and were in violation of international law. Not wanting to push too hard, however, for fear of causing international incidents, the United States confined itself to delivering diplomatic notes of protest to Spanish officials and dispatching ever larger fleets in pursuit of the few remaining Confederate warships at sea, such as the CSS *Alabama*.[62]

Whatever their concern for the naval balance with the United States in the Caribbean and elsewhere, Spanish officials were consumed by the rising crisis in Santo Domingo. After Santana's stage-managed plebiscite ratified the annexation, the hard work of assimilating the territory began painfully. Spain's occupation soon became a bitter war of counterinsurgency as Dominicans realized that the occupying nation had "substituted a popular dictator with a complicated and burdensome bureaucracy."[63] Although there was sporadic resistance as early as 1862, the first declaration of resistance came on February 21, 1863, when a Dominican general, Lucas Evangelista de Peña, declared the restoration of the republic and called on his countrymen to rise against the foreign occupation. He was quickly arrested and imprisoned by the Spanish governor, and this initial phase of the rebellion had ended by early March.[64]

A major uprising began in earnest in August 1863, motivated by the Spanish government's attempts to impose strict Catholicism and the Hispanization of most government and military positions. What Dominicans would call the "War of Restoration" began in a modest way near the border town of Capotillo and was strongest in the northern and western regions, away from the central authority and main garrisons in the capital. A small group of officers, including those who had been forced into retirement by Spanish authorities, lent their names to the rebellion. On September 14, 1863, a provisional government led by General José Antonio Salcedo formed in Santiago, dedicated to the expulsion of the Spanish presence. Adding to the enthusiasm for the rebellion were fears that Spain planned to reintroduce slavery in Santo Domingo, given its continued existence in the Cuban and Puerto Rican colonies. This fear, although apparently without basis, aided the provisional army significantly in its recruiting efforts. Despite the absence of Spanish plans to implement such a policy, the fear also transformed the uprising into an increasingly racial conflict—a conflict the Europeans could not win, given the overwhelming black majority.[65]

The mostly black insurgents burned and looted property and raped and murdered whites; the Spanish shot or hung those they suspected of being or helping the rebels. The Spanish troops in fact were not very effective as they were suffering from yellow fever, did not know the territory, and were dependent on local allies who were not always reliable. As the initial reports reached Spain about the insurgency, the press described it as a limited rebellion by blacks, perhaps those encouraged by President Lincoln and the Union cause in the American Civil War. Spanish reports also linked the rebellion even more directly with the United States, accusing Lincoln's administration of sending aid to the insurgents. This aid—which the United States never sent—was reported as fact in Spanish newspapers, with Lincoln being blamed for the continuation of the rebellion despite Spain's efforts to squash it.[66] The Spanish press did not take the rebels seriously, caricaturing them as ragged, shoeless, and undisciplined—hardly a threat to Spain's army.[67]

For the first two years of the occupation, Spain had managed with fewer than five thousand soldiers in Santo Domingo, although this final number was an increase over the three thousand who initially arrived in 1861. At the end of 1862, Spain decided to send reinforcements from Cuba, and from other colonies and mainland Spain in 1863. The total number of soldiers rose quickly in early 1863 to twenty thousand, eventually reaching twenty-five thousand. Santo Domingo had difficult terrain of jungles and forests and a small but hostile population. From late 1863 to early 1865, the Spanish government maintained a force of approximately twenty-five thousand in Santo Domingo, a large number in a nation of approximately two hundred thousand. Through the various rotation of troops, which had to be continually reinforced from Spain and elsewhere in the empire, the forces of occupation suffered seven thousand dead from disease, with additional thousands incapacitated from disease.[68]

Although Spain had been welcomed to Santo Domingo by that nation's president and governing class, these proved to be allies unequal to the task of marshalling their fellow citizens. Despite having overthrown Haitian rule in 1844, and resisted a subsequent incursion launched from Port au Prince in 1849, the Dominican military was barely worthy of the name as it lacked an organized force, arsenal of weapons, disciplined troops, and professional leadership. The honor guard for the capital city, as recently as 1860, consisted of thirteen "ragamuffin boys" with no uniforms and a mishmash of weapons.[69] President Santana anticipated acceptance of Spanish occupation by most Dominicans, but the behavior of the occupiers made this increasingly unlikely. Even though the Dominican army on paper consisted of as many as ten thousand soldiers, in practice its efficiency and organization had declined dramatically since the last major Haitian invasion. Mandatory military service for all able-bodied Dominican men, instituted in 1845 but continued by the Spanish, did not yield expected results in terms of numbers and especially quality. When units began to rebel against the Spanish occupation, the local Dominican soldiers who were often the first to confront the insurgents were armed "some with lances, others with old rifles; several with blunderbusses, others with pistols of every kind, the rest with their machetes, and not a few with clubs." The same tactics that had been used successfully against the Haitians, as well as in the conduct of internal fighting among Dominicans, were then employed against the erstwhile foreign protectors of Santo Domingo. This guerrilla practice was in keeping with the means available to the rebels—avoiding direct military confrontation and taking advantage of the terrain and the supportive population to wear down the enemy with numerous small attacks.[70]

The "War of Restoration" was waged by poorly armed and untrained rebels, fighting unconventionally against European soldiers. Hit-and-run tactics, raids on Spanish outposts, night attacks, and sniping at supply lines and rear areas were the favored tactics of the small clusters of insurgents that made up the initial resistance. The rebels did not differentiate between military and civilian targets but instead aimed their campaign not only at defeating the Spanish army but also at demoralizing civilian Dominicans who had supported the occupation or who worked for the Spanish government. Military or civilian collaborators could find themselves subject to violent rebel justice, finding their homes burned down or family members murdered in retaliation for their identification with the foreign power. Spanish infantry and other regular units were not prepared for this type of warfare, having instead organized their forces to fight the set-piece battles of the Napoleonic era. This was ironic, given Spain's own history as originator of the term *guerrilla* (meaning little war), a term that had emerged during Spanish resistance to the imposition of José Napoleon—brother of the French emperor—as an unwanted foreign monarch. The Corsican king, although he did have some support initially, could be maintained on the throne only through a massive French military presence from 1808 to 1813. Spanish senior commanders had even less excuse for their troops' lack of preparedness, as most men at the rank of lieutenant colonel and above had even more recent experience with the harsh rural and mountain combat conditions encountered in Spain's internal Carlist civil wars of the 1830s.[71]

The Spanish government was confident it could win the war against the indigenous and poorly armed rebels of Santo Domingo, having defeated Morocco in 1859–1860 and rebuilt its military capability after decades of decline and civil war. The occupation of half of a small island in the Caribbean seemed manageable. Indeed, Don Carlos de Vargas, who in September 1863 was appointed as governor of Santo Domingo, wrote to colonial officials in Madrid that even though the territory was temporarily in a complete state of war, he was optimistic Spain could win this conflict. He also began to lay out plans that would contribute to the economic development of the colony to the benefit of the home country. The governor's distribution of encouraging propaganda posters among Dominican soldiers and citizens in October 1863, urging them to come together under "the generous and blessed rule of Queen Isabel II" speak to this optimism about the former republic's future as a Spanish colony. The Spanish government did not initially expect to face resistance since their presence, after all, had been invited by the Dominicans themselves (or at least some of their leaders), but neither was it prepared to abandon its reclaimed territory easily. Its dedication of personnel and financial resources provide evidence of Spain's commitment to its reclaimed colony, and its expectations for a permanent and successful presence.[72]

In their budgets for Santo Domingo in 1862–1863 and 1863–1864, Spanish colonial authorities devoted the largest amount for military operations, dwarfing the second- and third-largest categories, the central administration and the financial operations (including the collection of taxes and tariffs). Smaller amounts went to the coastal navy, interior, and investment. A comparison of the two yearly budgets is instructive, showing a more than 50 percent increase in military spending from the first to the second year and a decline in spending on the administrative system (which included government salaries) and on internal investment, as the counterinsurgency campaign took on the elements of a total war. Amounts are in pesos.

		1862	1863	Difference
Sección 1:	Gracia y justicia	194,585	158,926	–35,659
Sección 2:	Guerra	1,246,521	1,887,690	+641,169
Sección 3:	Hacienda	166,802	265,036	+98,234
Sección 4:	Marina	9,506	62,245	+52,739
Sección 5:	Gobernación	75,726	85,192	+9,466
Sección 6:	Fomento	66,192	65,270	–922
Sección 7:	Atenciones de la Peninsula	——	313	+313
Total		1,759,332	2,524,672	+765,340

Revenues, insufficient even prior to the occupation, did not keep pace with the explosive increase in expenses. The deficit grew from just over 1 million pesos in 1862–1863 to 1.7 million in 1863–1864.[73]

The occupation of Santo Domingo and the rebellion this action sparked soon proved too costly for Spain to bear. By the end of 1864, the colony had a deficit of approximately four million pesos, as expenses for just the army in Santo Domingo increased to almost seven million pesos, and tax collections plummeted. The guerrilla tactics of 1862 had by 1864 become major military disruptions, with increasingly effective rebel actions against the economy and government administration.[74] Tax revenues and other payments collected by the Dominican government—which had risen as high as US $478,768 in 1861—had collapsed by 1863. The bulk of this income (approximately 85 percent) had been collected through import and export tariffs, which declined dramatically as domestic unrest crippled internal markets and isolated the island from external trade.[75]

By late 1863, the Spanish public had lost enthusiasm for the enterprise and was beginning to see it as a mistake. Many in Spain believed that their government had been duped by a minority of officials around Prime Minister O'Donnell who supported Santana and wanted to guarantee he remained in power. There was little evidence for this suspicion, but O'Donnell's fall from power in 1863, partly as a result of the Dominican debacle, made him an easy target. Nationalist Spaniards, however, insisted that Spain could only withdraw after it had achieved a clear military victory, so it would not be seen that Spain had been defeated or expelled by force of guerrilla arms. By fall 1864, even many senior military officials were convinced they could not defeat the rebellion and began to propose ways to extricate the Spanish army from Santo Domingo.[76]

While there remained some resistance to withdrawal among those who still nursed the idea of a Spanish imperial revival, their influence was rapidly fading in the midst of yellow fever, rising debt, and opposition within the military to the costly campaign. One Spanish politician declared that withdrawal would lead to immediate Haitian occupation, sponsored by the United States. Such a humiliating annexation by the combined Francophone and Anglophone forces, conservative Spaniards argued, would be a tremendous blow to the entire Spanish-speaking world.[77] Even so, by late 1864 and early 1865 even monarchist opinion such as that reflected in the conservative newspaper *La Esperanza* was referring to the "desperate situation" in Santo Domingo, with Spanish and rebel forces in a constant struggle to control key terrain and cities.[78]

Adding to Spain's difficulties was the willingness of Haiti to take advantage of the struggle in Santo Domingo. Although the Haitian and Dominican governments had temporarily resolved their differences by agreement in 1855, the Spanish occupation provided Port au Prince with opportunities to cause mischief. Spain's colonial officials were mindful that Haiti would take any potential chances to support unrest, and indeed it did on occasion provide a safe haven for insurgents. In mid-1864, the Spanish administration in Cuba received multiple reports that between two and three hundred armed volunteers were preparing to cross into Santo Domingo from Haiti, pledging to join their Dominican brothers in the insurrection to expel the Europeans. This force never materialized, but a general fear of Haitian intervention motivated Spain to attempt a rapid resolution of its Dominican problem. Haiti's leaders were more than happy to watch the increasingly bitter insurgency take its toll on the Spanish occupation, without risking Spanish retaliation on Haitian commerce and other interests should Port au Prince take an active role in supporting the rebellion. In the end it was Dominicans, and only Dominicans, who defeated Spain's imperial designs and the ambitions of Hispanophile elites who had welcomed the return of the Europeans.[79]

By late 1864, Spain had finally recognized that its venture in Santo Domingo was a failure and began to make preparations for a dignified end to the adventure. Despite the glowing reports from some military sources, which as late as December 1864 boasted of a "glorious campaign" in which the rebels remained "morally dead" through "the triumph of our arms," even the army general staff understood that Spain had few options left.[80] By early 1865, with the American Civil War coming to a close, there was great fear in Madrid that the forbearance of the United States would soon come to an end and there would be support for the rebels from Washington, DC. Given the obvious defeat of its occupation, one of the government's first necessities was to dispatch a new governor, General José de la Gándara, with the express task of negotiating an honorable settlement that would enable the peaceful withdrawal of Spanish forces. After some difficulties in conducting these negotiations, in large part because of bitter infighting among the Dominican rebels, the queen and the Cortes in May 1865 officially approved abandoning the occupation. The queen's initial decree of March 3 authorized the withdrawal, with approval by the Cortes on April 1 by a vote of 157 to 68, and the Spanish Senate on April 29 by 93 to 39. Ardent Catholics, military hardliners, and those with investments in Santo Domingo remained the least willing to consider withdrawal and voted against the measure.[81]

The debate in the Spanish parliament had been fierce, with supporters of the government's proposed withdrawal opposed by those concerned with Spain's honor, focused on Spain's commitments to its Dominican allies. Other opponents were minority opponents of the current government. With a tentative armistice in place to allow Spain's military to leave their garrisons and outposts without being attacked, the defeated army began its repatriation to Cuba, Puerto Rico, and Spain. The final Spanish soldiers had withdrawn from Santo Domingo by the end of July, most of them to garrisons in Cuba or Puerto Rico, from whence the initial annexation force had come in 1861. The occupation was over.[82]

Among the soldiers in the final units to withdraw was a young officer, Valeriano Weyler, who opposed the retreat. Promoted to *comandante* (major), in the Spanish general staff, he argued that Spain could have won the war in Santo Domingo. Regarding the defeat as a humiliation for Spain, which could ill deal with this "unhappy result," Weyler observed that the Spanish government was at fault for this loss, not the brave soldiers who endured yellow fever and a bitter insurgency. Spain's failures to supply adequate equipment, support its forces in the fight, and communicate with its commanders, were all lessons Weyler learned from this operation. Some thirty years later, as a senior officer and later commander of Spanish forces in Cuba during the Ten Years' War (1868–1878) and immediately prior to the Spanish-American War, General Weyler would wage a counterinsurgency campaign of his own, implementing the lessons he had learned in Santo Domingo with ruthless efficiency. In the US press, his unofficial nickname, "Butcher Weyler," testified to his image.[83]

By the end of the conflict, Spain had spent over 33 million pesetas (or 392 million reales), and had suffered sixteen thousand casualties, among which were approximately seven thousand deaths. While disease, and not the insurgents, had caused the greatest number of deaths in the Spanish army, it was nonetheless a defeat for the European forces of occupation. Spain's global standing was once again very low, after withdrawing or abandoning military forces in Mexico, Cochin China, and Santo Domingo, all without tangible gains. The Spanish army, in particular, lost the prestige it had gained from the Moroccan War, although its combat power in the Iberian Peninsula and remaining colonies remained intact. Adding to this reserve of strength was the continuing alliance with Britain and France, who saw it in their interests to maintain the Spanish empire and a strong Spain. Still, Spain's international prestige and willingness to engage in overseas operations did decline during the decades following the defeat in Santo Domingo.[84] Also as a consequence of this operation, Spain became once again the most hated Great Power in the Americas, with opinion in the Latin American republics turning sharply against it as a result of the harsh counterinsurgency in Santo Domingo. French operations in Mexico would provide a rival for this disaffection, but in 1863–1864 Spain bore this dubious honor.[85]

Despite its own losses in these campaigns, Spain would continue to possess a strengthening navy, a force that would achieve many victories in a conflict with Peru, later known as the Chincha Islands War (1864–1866). Spain's army, however, would from the mid-1860s onward be consumed by difficult counterinsurgency operations in

Cuba. On that island, as had been the case in Santo Domingo, the Spanish government found itself embroiled in a difficult campaign against an indigenous rebellion. Unlike in Santo Domingo, however, Spain would initially win this struggle, the Ten Years' War (1868–1878), having learned the lessons of guerrilla warfare well enough to defeat this rebellion. The pacification of the island was temporary, however, as the conflict revived in 1895 and ended in ignominious defeat at the hands of the United States in the Spanish-American War of 1898. Spain's rise to the middle in the mid-nineteenth century, and its pretentions that it might return to Great Power status, had come to a bitter end. Unlike Britain, France, Meiji Japan, and the United States, Spain in the late nineteenth century would be on the retreat internationally with its mid-century surge having failed.[86] While it would be going too far to rest responsibility for this descent on the country's misadventure in Santo Domingo, this failed operation had at least as much impact on Spain's self-image and military capabilities as the victory in Morocco had five years previous. Both conflicts were emblematic of the limits of Spanish military and political power, being at the same time both much more and much less than they initially seemed.

Chapter 5

King Cotton, the French Temptation, and Spain First

During the American Civil War, it was France that seemed most likely to lend aid to the Confederate cause, given the open sympathy toward the South expressed by Napoleon III and his ability to direct his own foreign policy without much deference to the legislature. In the United Kingdom, there were not only two houses of Parliament but also powerful lobbying interests on both sides of the debate. France, as well, was deeply involved in the Americas with its occupation and ongoing counterinsurgency in Mexico. A friendly, even allied, Confederacy could shore up the northern border and prevent the use of Texas or other areas by anti-French Mexican rebels. Even so, Southern agents were disappointed early in the war with French inaction, a disappointment that came out of an unrealistic evaluation of their own indispensability to European trade, finance, and industry.

The Confederacy tried in earnest, from late 1862 onward, to capitalize on what it saw as new possibilities with the French, given the disappointment over British inaction. Even with the greater tacit support in Paris and Madrid for the rebellion, meager Confederate resources and poor communications and nimble opposition from the United States prevented any major diplomatic breakthrough such as recognition or foreign intervention.[1] At several points, the Confederacy also attempted to encourage Spain to lead the other European powers in recognition and intervention, but Spanish indecision and, most important, Confederate battlefield failures made this option moot almost before a more active role for a rising Spain could be fully developed.[2]

Spain was tied to France through geography, economic interests, and joint inferiority to Britain in their tripartite alliance, and the country would have joined any effort made by the French to intervene in the American Civil War. Many conservative Spaniards identified with France, seeing it as an inspiring example. As a Catholic monarchy, France was more closely aligned in terms of religion and political philosophy than Britain.[3] The French economy, although industrialized, was also more of a cognate to that of Spain, with its dependence on agriculture and state intervention. Spanish politicians, until the dismissal of Prime Minister O'Donnell in late 1863, looked for opportunities to join France in an international effort to offer recognition, mediation, or even intervention in the war. As late as May 1863, just before O'Donnell left office, Spanish diplomats received Confederate agents in Paris with sympathy, albeit unofficially, and promised that Spain would recognize the rebellion should France do so, and Britain permit the action. This was hardly a guarantee, of course, but it did reflect both the constraints on Spain and its natural inclination to support the Confederacy.[4]

The CSA did score some victories: establishing secure contact with its agents in Europe, acquiring warships and some military materiel from France and Britain, preserving a base of support in public opinion, and maintaining the belligerent rights that had been granted in the opening weeks of the war, despite US pressure on London and Paris to rescind this. The South could not survive on tactical victories alone, however. At war and in diplomacy, it needed a strategic success to guarantee its survival, neither of which was forthcoming in late 1862 or 1863. Indeed, as bad news continued to emanate from the battlefields of North America, it was in some ways helpful that there was not yet a system for rapid delivery of news to Europe. Complete and immediate accounts of Vicksburg, Gettysburg, and Chattanooga would not have been helpful.[5] In some cases, it took two weeks or even more for important dispatches of political and military news from the American Civil War to arrive in Madrid from New York, even assuming this information was not delayed by bad weather or other issues along the way.[6]

Antebellum Southerners believed that Europe and the world were so dependent on cotton that the South could force intervention on their behalf through denying this commodity to European consumers. During the first year or so of the war, Southern planters and merchants made a visible demonstration of their belief in King Cotton by destroying warehouses full of raw cotton. The two major western European powers, France and Great Britain, were dependent on raw cotton from the Confederacy, but not as much as the Southern leadership believed. Of these two states, France, led by Emperor Napoleon III, was the more sympathetic to the Confederacy, and at several key points seemed on the verge of recognizing the CSA and even providing substantial assistance to the rebels. Even more than sympathy, however, was Napoleon's belief that a permanent division of the United States would reduce obstacles to a revived French presence in the Americas. While the Monroe Doctrine was not yet a policy with any real enforcement mechanism, it was obvious to the European powers that the United States was a rising force and could soon prove an obstacle to European imperialism.

By 1863, however, the chances for European recognition of the CSA or even intervention in the war seemed to have faded, especially in Britain. Even with the obvious repudiation of their efforts by the British, Confederate agents still saw some hope in France, and in its weaker ally, Spain, for external involvement in the war, albeit most likely at a more covert level. Both nations seemed willing to aid in the equipping and maintenance of Confederate warships and blockade runners, an indispensable element of Southern naval strategy in the final two years of the war. King Cotton had become the Pirate Prince, with the Confederates able to gain French and Spanish (especially Cuban) aid through financial enticement, where appeals to international law had failed in 1861 and 1862. Key to this arrangement would be the new flexibility on cotton exports, which developed after the initial failure of the self-imposed Confederate embargo on shipments to Europe. Southern agents in Europe, however, struggled to implement this new policy due to the difficulties of communication between the Confederate government and its representatives, as both lacked the means to dispatch timely, secure letters and other documents across the Atlantic. It could take as long as six months for a dispatch from Europe to reach Richmond, by which time the international diplomatic context, not to mention battlefield conditions, would have changed substantially. Not until mid-1863 did the Confederacy successfully arrange for secure and timely communications, contracting with a private blockade running company in the Bahamas. Diplomats from the United States, who at the same time possessed formal recognition and far greater resources, were able to communicate quickly with Washington from the beginning of the war, via their own secure naval and merchant vessels. Consequently they were able to respond more nimbly to foreign policy and military developments in both Europe and at home.[7]

Europe had noted with alarm the support provided by the United States to the successful independence campaigns in Spain's colonies in the hemisphere. Even earlier, American material and moral support to France's former colony of Haiti continued to be resented in Paris; the prospect of weakening the upstart Americans through supporting the rebellious Southern section of the Union was therefore attractive. Because of Confederate military and diplomatic failures, however, these moments passed without any action taken by the French emperor, which might have also led to similar actions by the British and Spanish governments. Sympathy for the Southern cause might well have been a factor for the French, but more important was a desire to weaken the United States and make room for Napoleon's vision of expanded influence in Mexico and throughout Latin America.[8]

The most significant example of Napoleon III's American agenda took shape a few months after the Civil War began, just south of the United States, when French, British, and Spanish troops arrived in Mexico in early 1862 to collect debts owed to the European powers and ostensibly also to protect Europeans during a period of significant instability. The British and Spanish forces withdrew within a year, satisfied with the commitments made by the Mexican government, but the French remained in force even after the other European troops completed their repatriation in early 1863. Many Southerners hoped this intervention could presage a first step toward a broader intervention by the Europeans, so they welcomed the presence of France and the other states so close to their Southern border. The French military intervention, coupled with the Spanish occupation of Santo Domingo, had greatly augmented available European forces in the Americas. Both incursions were worrisome to the Union, which already had in the interests of expediency ignored its own Monroe Doctrine against European imperialism in the Western hemisphere.

Although the CSA immediately recognized the French occupation, it was not possible to parley this into a reciprocal French recognition.

The French had broader ambitions, which were to impose the Austrian Archduke Maximilian as the new emperor of Mexico in 1864. Emperor Napoleon III hoped to revive French global influence, repairing the losses incurred by his uncle Napoleon Bonaparte, though this time as an ally of Britain. Mexico was to be the base for a revived strategic, commercial, and political presence throughout the hemisphere, made possible because of the diversion of Washington's focus on internal matters. France's Austrian client, however, proved unsuccessful in his assigned task. Maximilian proved unable to gain popular support in Mexico, despite liberal intentions and the force of French arms. A popular rebellion arose, uniting most of the active population against foreign troops. Deprived of support except for a decreasing slice of the upper classes, Maximilian was unable to rule effectively. French troops remained as an increasingly unpopular army of occupation, supporting his reign until the Europeans were overthrown by the Mexicans in 1867.[9]

The high point of possibilities for foreign intervention in the American Civil War came in the summer and fall of 1862 when the British prime minister, Lord Palmerston, and other key politicians proposed that the European states should mediate between the Union and the Confederacy. This move posed grave dangers for the United States, and perhaps the only hope for the survival of the Confederacy. The United States could threaten war should any outside power intervene, but in practice the Union would not have been able to fight against Britain or France, much less the two in coalition, while at the same time maintaining its field armies in battle against the Confederacy. The initiative from Paris and London came after a summer during which French representatives had openly discussed the possibility of using the French fleet to force an end to the blockade of Southern ports, in exchange for a free trade agreement and one hundred thousand bales of cotton—with a market value of more than $12 million in 1862. Emperor Napoleon III had even discussed this possibility openly with Confederate agent Slidell on July 16, and the French monarch had seemed open to making common cause against the United States, perhaps exchanging Southern cotton for French arms and naval support to break the blockade. In the end the French avoided making this agreement, which would have entailed an immediate confrontation with the United States, but they did not dismiss it immediately.[10] Slidell's meeting with the emperor on July 25, 1862, at the resort town of Vichy was inconclusive; however, in contrast to the British prime minister and foreign minister, Napoleon III had no compunction about meeting with Confederate agents, regarding his interests as more closely supported by a strengthened rebel cause.[11] Facing shortages of raw cotton and other industrial disruptions, French business leaders, including the "chambers of commerce from Lyon, Rouen, and Mulhouse, petitioned the emperor for 'an immediate recognition of the Confederate States, and the raising of the blockade.'"[12]

It was during September and October 1862 that the French and the British moved simultaneously toward intervention (in the case of Britain, without any significant prior involvement of Confederate agents). A series of Union defeats, accounts of dissent in the North, and other news led the British government, led by Prime Minister Palmerston, to consider an international coalition to force a mediated end to the war with a permanent Confederacy as the result. This proposal failed, however, because of the opposition of French foreign minister Antoine Thouvenel (dismissed in early October for this action and for others that undermined the emperor) and also because of the Confederate agents' ineffectual support. James Mason was unable to influence the debate within the British government because he lacked solid intelligence concerning the idea. The British proposal was that an international mediation effort involving the United Kingdom, France, Austria, Russia, and Prussia would be offered to the two warring sides. If either side refused (most probably the Union), the other powers would immediately recognize the Confederacy, which would provide it with access to arms, trade, and support against the blockade. The Russians, however, refused to join, and American diplomats argued successfully that the measure would have been unequivocally of military, economic, and political benefit to the Southern rebels.[13]

On October 30, Napoleon III elaborated on the suggestion for international intervention, proposing to Russia and the United Kingdom that the European powers should not just offer to mediate but "formally propose a six-month armistice, during which time the Union blockage would be withdrawn," in the hopes of forcing a settlement. The French emperor's hope was that this would lead to a permanently divided United States with the Confederacy indebted to him and a weaker Union less able to confront revived French influence in the Americas. He even at one point proposed a four-way division of North America—not just South and North but also a new Western confederation along the Pacific and an expanded Mexico, with parts of Texas and the Southwest under French control. From Mexico, France could then extend its political, commercial, and military reach deeper into Central and South America, as well as the Caribbean. Neither the British nor the French envisioned a large-scale intervention or imposing a peace through force of arms, but both preferred a chastened United States, which a permanently divided American republic would certainly achieve.[14] Emperor Napoleon granted Slidell another interview on November 4, 1862, in a meeting that subsequently received a great deal of newspaper attention but that again did not produce any concrete results.[15]

On November 13, a divided British cabinet voted down the proposal. The British government—and more important, the course of military events in the American Civil War—rendered these efforts moot, but they had been serious proposals, and both received the support of Spain, as well. Had France and Britain intervened, they would have brought along their Spanish ally, as had been the case with the initial intervention in Mexico in late 1861 and early 1862, launched by the three powers to force Mexico to honor its international debt burden.[16] Although these proposals for international mediation in late 1862 failed, the general environment for the Confederacy remained strong, allowing the South to raise $16 million in cotton bonds in March 1863. Had actual Southern cotton been available in European warehouses to support these financial instruments, many more millions in bonds could have been sold to European investors, providing essential financing for the war effort. Once again, King Cotton diplomacy—which had held cotton back from exports in 1861 and 1862 when shipping it overseas would have been possible—continued to yield negative results for the South.[17]

Spain was prepared to join France and Britain in 1862 and also into 1863. For Spain, the issue was not cotton but the security of its interests in the Antilles. The permanent survival of two separate American states was clearly in the interests of Spanish power in the Caribbean, as made explicit in a communiqué from the Foreign Ministry to Minister Tassara in the Washington, DC, legation: "If through any circumstance one of the two great powers would recognize the division of the

Union, that is, the Confederacy of the South, the primary reason for this war, Spain could not help but gain by this through the division of interests and principles between the two republics, and the conflicts between that would invalidate each others' efforts, and would not allow them much time to focus on domestic issues."[18] The survival of two independent nations in North America, out of the wreckage that had been the United States, was to Spain's benefit, but it remained a question to what extent Spain was willing to contribute to this positive end.

Pursuing security for Cuba and Puerto Rico continued along other lines, for example with an agreement with the United States to settle through arbitration any disputes over the extent of territorial waters surrounding Cuba.[19] Rumors persisted that Spain was engaged in covert discussions with the Confederacy, which would bring Spanish recognition of the rebellion and possibly a defensive alliance in exchange for a Confederate security guarantee of Cuba. There is little evidence of such negotiations in the Spanish archives, but it is not inconceivable that, given the frequent ministerial changes in the Spanish government under O'Donnell and other prime ministers, informal discussions in this direction could have taken place.[20] If the Spanish had sent their fleet to the Americas, based in Havana, this would have added an additional layer of difficulty to the Union blockade, weakening its effectiveness and therefore its international legitimacy. Confederate promises of a guarantee for Cuba might have been insufficient to entice Spain into the conflict, but they were a serious gesture considered worthy of consideration by both the Spanish and the French governments.[21]

Although the British plan to force an armistice on the Union had ended by late 1862, the French and Spanish continued to press for mediation. On February 3, 1863, the French minister to the United States, Henri Mercier, met with US secretary of state William Seward to offer French mediation in the conflict. Mercier indicated that Spain would also collaborate in this effort, which should begin with an armistice and then move forward toward a final settlement. Seward refused to discuss this proposal and did not encourage Mercier's offer to proceed to Richmond to begin discussions. Mercier refused to be dissuaded, however, and did travel to the Confederate capital after meeting with Seward, which enraged the US leader. Disputing press reports that he had given his endorsement to the French mission, Secretary Seward denied any willingness to begin talks with "insurrectionist agents." The Union, according to Seward, was not interested in discussing anything relating to the Confederacy except repressing the illegal rebellion. Mercier's conduct created a major scandal, was debated in the US Senate, and received extensive overseas coverage. US officials denounced his actions, while foreign observers noted a more benign intent behind them.[22]

While engaging in this dispute with France, Seward moved to bolster ties with the United Kingdom, amplifying an 1862 treaty on the suppression of the slave trade with an additional article. These agreements promoted collaboration at sea between US and British warships, especially in the vicinity of the African coastline and routes from it. The Confederate constitution banned the importation of foreign slaves, and Southern leaders made no efforts to reverse this during the Civil War, but nonetheless, these treaties were another accommodation between the United States and United Kingdom and so could not have been welcome in Richmond. The US and British governments shared the same perspective on "that inhuman and odious traffic," as Lincoln described it. While banning the trade, there is little evidence that the Confederacy took serious measures against the importation of slaves, and obviously the practice of slavery itself continued to the end of the war.[23]

Not only did the institution of slavery continue in the Confederacy and in Cuba, but the slave trade did, as well, despite official agreement by all nations that it should end. Perhaps 750,000 slaves were brought to Cuba from the 1820s to the 1860s, despite Spanish law and treaties that banned the trade in human cargo. The Dominicans feared that Spain hoped to reconstitute this practice in Hispaniola, and with good reason. Even free blacks in Cuba often slipped back into forced labor through debt servitude or indenturing to landowners or even the colonial administration. Protesting against these policies after 1864, as well as the institution of slavery itself, was a new organization in Spain, the Sociedad Abolicionista (Abolitionist Society), but its activities were declared illegal in Cuba and Puerto Rico. The slave trade was less extensive in the Confederacy than in Portuguese and Spanish colonies, this was probably more because of the growing effectiveness of the Union blockade than any moral hesitance on the part of plantation owners or government officials to tolerate these purchases.[24]

By late 1863, even Napoleon III had nearly lost hope in the Confederacy. President Davis and Secretary Benjamin, at the same time, had lost faith in their chief European propagandist, Edwin DeLeon, whose exaggerated self-promotion, inability to maintain secret correspondence or maintain good relations with other Confederate agents, and patent failure to influence European opinion toward the rebels made his dismissal in December 1863 an obvious decision. By this point in the war, however, even the most brilliant, well-connected, and diplomatic press agent would have been hard-pressed to portray the Confederacy as a success worthy of European support. The war on the North American continent continued, and so did Confederate efforts to bring European strength into the conflict against the Union, which, though "an impossible task," were pursued with vigor, if not effectiveness, until the end of the American Civil War.[25]

In Britain, the United States benefited from effective diplomatic representation and successful pursuit of its goals through dedicated use of the British courts and legal system. The American minister to the United Kingdom, Charles Francis Adams, was well suited to the position, with a "calm disposition and dignified manner," appropriate to dealing with British elites. The consul in Liverpool, Thomas Haines Dudley, had the aggressive personality necessary to manage not only legal cases in the British courts but also dealings with British shipbuilders and local officials. In London and in England's shipyards, the two Americans fought a long-running and ultimately successful struggle to deprive the Confederacy of opportunities to build and outfit its warships and blockade runners in Britain. In Liverpool, a pro-Southern port city dependent on trade with the American South, Consul Dudley faced long odds. With over 80 percent of American cotton exports passing through the city before the war, Liverpudlians were naturally supportive of the Southern cause, and these sentiments endured to the end of the conflict. Despite support within the broader British population and among significant elements of the ruling class as well, the Confederacy failed to achieve its diplomatic objectives in Britain—recognition, friendly neutrality, and open opposition to the Union blockade of Southern ports—because it was London, not Liverpool, that made policy for the United Kingdom.[26]

While British shipyards were more capable of building the warships, surface raiders, and blockade runners desperately needed by the Confederacy, by early 1863 it was clear that the legal and political obstacles for Confederate acquisition agents were increasing in Britain. Ships built were blocked from leaving through American legal action, and the course of the war disheartened previous supporters in the commercial and political communities. The CSA preferred now to avoid debates in the House of Commons on recognition, as a defeat there could have threatened an end even to belligerent rights, the sole major diplomatic victory gained since the beginning of the war. One such debate, in mid-July 1863, led to a stinging parliamentary defeat for partisans of the Confederacy, with a lopsided vote against recognition.[27]

Southern agents therefore shifted their meager resources and attention to France, where Emperor Napoleon III and many of his advisers were still openly sympathetic to their rebellion. More important, the French monarch was willing to tolerate a wider scale of shipbuilding and outfitting of war materiel, so long as it did not become a point of public embarrassment. The construction of warships in France continued in earnest into late 1864, but soon even the French government became reluctant to allow armed vessels—now openly known to be destined for the South—to sail from its ports in an obvious breach of its declared neutrality. The French could not risk alienating the British, on whose alliance the French depended in their overseas engagement in Mexico and elsewhere.[28]

The United States was very active in its diplomatic efforts to keep the European powers out of the American Civil War. Most of this attention focused on Great Britain and France, but the United States did not neglect Spain. Indeed, given the proximity of Cuba to the United States and the efforts by the South to entice Spanish collaboration, it would have been surprising had Secretary of State Seward not kept Spain in mind. One key tactic used by the United States in its relationship with Spain was intimidation. After more than fifty years of rising US strength in comparison to the stagnation of Spain, this argument had been successful in the past, as in 1819 when the United States imposed Spain's cession of Florida and in the 1850s, when Spain had to tolerate raids by filibusters launched from American soil against the backdrop of US offers to purchase Cuba—thereby sparing Spain from further attacks.

During the Civil War, however, the United States was more subtle in applying pressure. In early 1863, for example, the US Navy invited the Spanish embassy in Washington to send a naval attaché to New

York to observe some new construction at the Brooklyn Navy Yard. The naval officer dispatched, José de Olañeta of the Real Cuerpo de Ingenieros (Royal Corps of Engineers), prepared an extensive report on what he had seen, which was the building of several ironclad warships. His comments included schematics and details about the program and information about the strength of the armor plating, capacity of the boilers, and planned armaments. Subsequent reports, again highly detailed, showed that the United States had built more than twenty of these vessels and that there were more scheduled. As Spain and the United States were hardly allied, the overall effect of this must have been telling. In his final report, Olañeta made clear that nothing in the inventory of the Spanish navy, especially on station in Caribbean waters, could take on an American ironclad, much less a fleet of them. The potential costs of intervention were made clear to Spain through this observation mission; the entirety of the Spanish fleet based in Cuba would be immediately vulnerable should Madrid ally with Richmond. The Union's ironclads might not be sent entirely against Spain, but even one or two could threaten the entire flotilla at Havana.[29] Before the Civil War the US Navy had not built a single ironclad, but the new weapon—authorized by an act of Congress in August 1861—now allowed it to intimidate a major European state, despite the strengthening of the Spanish fleet over the previous decade.[30]

As early as 1862 Spain had heard disturbing reports about the power of these new ships, an obvious concern to a state attempting to rebuild its naval strength.[31] While the United States was not building the ironclads for foreign export, Spain and the United States did agree that US shipyards would build four steam-powered gunboats for use against contraband smugglers and illegal slave traders in Cuba. The US War and Navy Departments did not object to the order, which achieved final approval from the US government on May 8, 1863.[32] Spain continued to send army and navy officers to the United States until the end of the war, not only to report on progress toward fulfilling this contract but also to provide the Spanish government with updated reports on US defenses, port facilities, production of munitions, and technological innovations, such as the *Monitor*-class vessels. The United States allowed these military representatives nearly complete access to American facilities—not out of friendship but for the deterrent value. As long as Spain knew the severe risk of defeat at the hands of the United States, it would be less likely to consider intervention, even in alliance with the major powers France and Great Britain.[33] An arms race with the United States would have debilitated the Spanish economy, which was already beginning to decline in 1863 after several years of strong growth. Disruption of Spain's Caribbean trade because of the American Civil War was one factor, along with the costs of the Santo Domingo campaign. Economic growth had made possible Spain's revived imperial ambitions, so the end of positive fiscal news caused a major disruption in these efforts, not to mention a rise in domestic political dissent and intrigue within the political class, a campaign that would see the overthrow of the queen in 1868.[34]

A new Spanish foreign minister, General Francisco Serrano, took office in January 1863 and seemed a likely candidate to endorse Confederate requests. Serrano had been captain general in Cuba immediately before assuming this office and had done much to aid the Confederacy. His fall from office two months later, in early March, undid some progress toward recognition, however.[35] As late as 1863–1864, the CSA relied on the leverage of cotton to convince the Europeans to grant recognition, although this campaign had become secondary to other diplomatic efforts. In any case, the failure of King Cotton came principally because the British were able to find other sources for the raw material, especially in Egypt, and did not yield to economic blackmail. France was less able to replace cotton imports and in mid-1863 seemed to be moving toward surrender to King Cotton. Despite opposition from key advisers, who feared this would entangle France in another war just as Mexico was becoming restive to French occupation, Napoleon III agreed in June 1863 to recognize the CSA if Spain did, too. He was even able to enlist Spain in this proposal—but only if France extended formal recognition first. Napoleon favored simultaneous diplomatic gestures, so this initiative failed over issues of protocol.[36]

The attempt to create a Franco-Hispano axis that would move toward recognition and intervention even if the British remained aloof did gain some momentum in mid-1863 but was soon made irrelevant by Confederate battlefield losses and Napeoleon III's focus elsewhere —such as Italy, Poland, and his own domestic troubles. The collapse of Prime Minister Leopoldo O'Donnell's government in February 1863, partly as a result of the failure of the Santo Domingo occupation, also removed from the Spanish monarchy the most ardent advocate for increased Spanish overseas involvement.[37]

The American press was aware that the European powers had been considering recognition and intervention. In 1861–1862, the press thought Britain was most likely to intervene, but by 1863 it suspected France would be the first to interject itself into the conflict. Napoleon III's occupation of Mexico, in particular, enhanced the image of France as most willing to get involved in North America. By late 1863, however, there was growing confidence in the United States that foreign intervention would not be decisive. In 1861, the United Kingdom and France might have ended the war and preserved the Confederacy, but rising Union strength two years later made this outcome far less likely. After the Confederate defeats at Gettysburg and the loss of key ports such as New Orleans, the South was in a far weaker state, and the decline seemed likely to continue. European intervention in 1863 would have hurt US overseas trade, as the British and French navies were capable of imposing their own blockade of US and captured Confederate ports, but even a combination of the major powers would have been hard-pressed to match the ground strength of the Union army. Short of a widespread mobilization by France, Spain, and Britain and the dispatch of large armies directly to North America, it would have been difficult for the European powers to control the final outcome of the American Civil War if the United States refused to submit to mediation. The threat alone of European intervention might have convinced the United States to negotiate, however, as the perception of European power in the United States was greater than the reality.[38] While it would go too far to say the European powers were not paying sufficient attention to the American Civil War, this war was not the most important issue for leaders in Paris, London, and Madrid.[39] Despite the confidence of the *New York Times*, for Spain the resolution of the war was far from a certainty. As late as mid-1864, Minister Tassara expressed doubts about the ability of the Union to bring the war to a final victory. His battlefield accounts, gleaned from newspapers and reports from both sides, were generally accurate but did reflect this sentiment of uncertainty.[40]

Minister Tassara also reported to the Foreign Ministry in Madrid about ongoing tensions between the US and European diplomats. One major complaint focused on the Union naval bombardment of

Charleston, South Carolina, that began in earnest in the summer of 1863. The US Navy had not initiated the deadly assault in August, but it continued to pound the harbor and city for months. European states understood that there would be casualties in war. The Spanish, French, and British consuls protested, through their legations in Washington, DC, that the United States had not given advance warning to the diplomats, so that they could evacuate their families and property from the city. Given the close personal and commercial connections between Spanish officials and Confederate leaders, this petition seems unrealistic. Another major complaint came from Spanish officials and diplomats in the city of New Orleans, which had been captured by Union forces in April 1862. The foreign diplomats did not object to the Union's military occupation, which in any event would have done little more than show their sympathies, but they were upset that the Union would not exchange Confederate money—accepted in good faith by Spanish businessmen during 1861 and 1862—for US dollars. By accepting this currency, Union officials could argue, these same merchants had accepted the legitimacy of the Southern rebellion and therefore also accepted the risks inherent in relying on the good faith and credit of the Confederate Treasury. In neither case did Minister Tassara indicate that these matters were critical to relations between Spain and the United States, but they were points of contention and conflict during the Civil War. Each incident was far short of becoming a causus belli for Spain or any other nation against the United States, but these events did illustrate the ongoing tensions between the two nations, predisposed as both Spain and the United Stateswere by decades of mistrust.[41]

After the aborted effort to impose external mediation on the warring American factions, Emperor Napoleon III lost interest in recognition of the Confederate states, although he did allow Southern agents to commission the construction of blockade running ships in French ports, albeit only in secret to avoid angering the United States or Britain at this obvious violation of neutrality. These shipbuilding efforts did not go entirely as the Confederates hoped, but in 1863 this construction program seemed poised to provide real combat power to the South's naval capabilities. Absent an unexpected reversal of Southern battlefield fortunes, there seemed little chance of regaining the support of the French emperor. With the French economy improving by early 1864 and a rebellion in Poland drawing the attention of many Europeans, the emperor was no longer a strong advocate for what was beginning to be seen in Europe as a lost cause.

The French were now focused more on their own troubles with Mexico, trying to prop up Emperor Maximilian in his fight against an ever more active republican insurgency. Another adventure in North America did not seem so attractive now, with French soldiers dying in Mexico to defend the soil of another nation. Involvement on behalf of the Confederacy, if opposed by the United States, could very well lead to another war for France. So soon after seeming to be on the cusp of international recognition and even foreign intervention, the Confederacy had lost the possibility for a rescue by a coalition of foreign powers. From early 1864 onward, Southern leaders could only attempt to delay the outcome that seemed increasingly probable on the battlefield and in European public opinion: the end of the Confederate States of America.[42]

Chapter 6

Collaboration in the Caribbean

The Caribbean Sea was an area of great concern for the United States during the American Civil War. Confederate blockade runners and surface raiders carried the war through coastal waters and into the Atlantic. Especially during 1861 and 1862, when the US Navy was still small and its declared blockade of Southern ports highly permeable, the Caribbean continued to see significant traffic between the CSA and Europe, relying not only on Southern ships but especially on European-flagged vessels to conduct trade across the Atlantic. By some estimates, the US Navy had as few as four warships available in American waters to enforce the blockade of the Confederacy at the moment when President Lincoln decreed its imposition, on April 19, 1861. While this number increased dramatically, to almost two hundred available vessels, by the end of 1861, the fleet was inexperienced, undermanned, unskilled, and charged with policing over three thousand miles of coastline, "from Virginia to the Rio Grande," in addition to thousands of islands.[1] At the same time, the Confederacy was also making efforts in what became a naval arms race, building and buying warships, commissioning merchant vessels as smugglers and blockade runners, and issuing letters of marquee and reprisal, essentially reviving privateering in the Caribbean. While the British colonies of Bermuda and the Bahamas were key intermediate links in the tenuous Confederate supply chains, Confederate agents pursued their major purchasing efforts in Europe.[2]

It was a deadly race between the two belligerents. Could the Confederacy import enough weapons, ammunition, and war materiel for its forces to win on the battlefield before the US Navy choked off all seaborne trade and made effective the blockade declared in 1861? At what point would Confederate raiders and blockade runners reach the point of diminishing returns, when their losses would exceed the prizes they seized and US Navy ships they sank? Would the European states ever intervene? Or would they leave the North Americans to settle their differences alone, on land and at sea, including in the Caribbean? In the end, both Great Britain and Spain profited from the actions of the blockade runners but also lost significant revenue from the US Navy's growing pressure on normal commerce. In aiming to cripple the Confederacy with its blockade, the United States also did significant damage to the Spanish, French, and British economies—an unintended but tactically useful consequence of the conflict. Given the potential for foreign intervention, the United States had every interest in weakening the European powers that could potentially align with the Southern rebels but also wanted to avoid being the cause of such an intervention.[3]

The European powers including Britain and France and even smaller states such as Spain, Austria, and Belgium "challenged the US vision" for the Caribbean basin.[4] Although Spain delayed granting diplomatic recognition, building a defensive alliance, or undertaking an even more direct intervention on behalf of the Confederate States unless led by Britain or France, during the Civil War it provided more enabling support to the Confederates than any other power. Through tolerating port calls by Confederate ships, the Spanish government, especially in its Cuban colony but also in peninsular Spain, was an indispensable de facto ally of the Southern cause. Confederate ships used Havana and other Cuban ports extensively to make repairs, exchange cargo, and take on supplies. Both the US and Confederate navies had the right to make use of Spanish facilities, but in practice this benefited the Confederacy much more. The US Navy had use of extensive port facilities in the North, and it could also take advantage of a growing number of captured Southern ports. Southern ships, on the contrary, had fewer safe harbors, and those that remained in Confederate hands during the early phases of the war, such as Charleston, soon came under more effective blockade and barrage. Spanish officials argued to US diplomats that they could not block these ships, since to do otherwise would be to grant full belligerent rights to the Confederacy, something the United States said it did not want.[5]

Confederate blockade runners numbered between five and seven hundred and as many as 20 percent of these used Cuban ports, a percentage that increased during the war as more Southern ports fell to Union armies. Along with Bermuda (another frequent safe harbor for Southern shipping), Spain's Caribbean territories helped the CSA to avoid the increasingly effective power of the US Navy.[6] Bermuda and the Bahamas had the advantage of being under British control, and therefore protected by naval forces initially stronger than the US Navy. Cuba had other advantages, including harbor officials who were more susceptible to bribes and generally more sympathetic to the South.[7] Spanish ports in Cuba, especially Havana, provided invaluable service to Confederate shipping during the war, providing repairs and safe harbors.[8] CSA ships, and especially commercial ones, frequented Spanish colonial harbors. Officially, only merchant vessels could dock, but occasionally Southern warships or armed commercial ships took advantage of these Spanish facilities. Under the terms of the Spanish concession of belligerent rights to the Confederacy, Southern ships could remain in Spanish ports for no more than twenty-four hours, but in practice this period was often extended, especially when there were no Union ships or official personnel in the area to report such violations to US consular officials.[9] For good reason, one historian has described Confederate blockade running in the Caribbean as "the most successful, large-scale campaign attempted by the South."[10]

Havana, the colonial capital and largest city, was one of the busiest ports in the Caribbean, with over two thousand visits by commercial and cargo vessels in 1860, the last full year of peace. In addition to being a market for Southern cotton and cattle, Cuba also provided other goods for the Confederacy, including tobacco, lead, coffee, small arms, ammunition, and additional supplies. Havana's merchants, slave-owning planter class, and colonial officials clearly sympathized with the slave-holding Confederacy, even if their government in Madrid was officially neutral.[11] With the coming of the war, the Confederacy's agent in Havana, Charles J. Helm, saw Havana as the great warehouse, storing goods purchased in Cuba as well as Europe before these cargoes were dispatched to New Orleans, Mobile, or other ports. The city could also serve as a staging area for cotton and tobacco shipments to Europe, should the policy of King Cotton be abandoned. While Spain did not boast major production facilities for arms or ammunition in Cuba, the Spanish colony was capable of serving as a relatively safe intermediary for the delivery of military goods to Confederate ships, rather than forcing blockade runners to cross the Atlantic, and presumably by this method encountering fewer US Navy sea patrols. With few exceptions, such as the famous *Trent* incident, the United States did not search neutral shipping unless it had intelligence that a vessel's particular cargo included contraband of war.[12] Cuba was such a fruitful area for Confederate blockade runners and purchasing agents that Helm frequently complained there were so many representatives in Havana he could not keep track of them nor prevent duplication of effort. His requests for all Southern agents to come under his supervision were not answered to his satisfaction, however. In addition to official buyers affiliated with various different Confederate departments, there were also many entrepreneurs, ships' captains of dubious provenance, shady commodity brokers, and opportunistic commercial operators.[13]

Typical of the experience of blockade runners was the career of Captain James McKay, who operated out of Key West and Tampa Bay, Florida. Prior to the war he sold Florida beef in Cuba, shipping as many as four hundred head of cattle per month to Havana. With the coming of the war, he first tried to continue his operations. At times smuggling cattle from the Confederacy to Havana, with return cargoes of pistols and ammunition, he also took on Union contracts to lease out his small steamship, the *Salvor*. He was arrested several times and charged with treason by both the Union and the Confederacy, and even while on parole granted by President Lincoln himself, he continued to steam between Florida and Cuba, delivering beef and cotton to the Spanish and returning with his hold full of critical weapons for the armies of the Confederacy. After it became too dangerous to test the blockade, beginning in late 1863, McKay served as a commissary agent for the South, purchasing beef in Florida for the Confederate army of General P. G. T. Beauregard. What had been an export commodity, with sales of several hundred head each month to the Cuban market, now became far more essential for domestic consumption. Only cotton remained in a condition of such surplus as to be available for external markets after 1863. Of course, by then the South had little means to deliver King Cotton to its intended purchasers, who in any case had begun to secure replacement supplies elsewhere, such as Egypt and India. By late 1864, Captain McKay had been reassigned to a combat role, leading infantry against Union armies. The Confederacy's employment of a skilled sea captain to lead ground assaults was surely a misuse of McKay's talents, but the penultimate year of the American Civil War there were far more extreme measures in place demonstrating the imminent collapse of the rebellion.[14]

As important as Florida was, and its Gulf Coast ports, no other Southern port could compare in size and capacity to New Orleans. With experienced harbor crews and captains, a wide variety of ships home ported there, and well-developed trade routes to Cuba, the rest of the Caribbean, other US ports, and even Europe, New Orleans was well positioned in 1861 to serve as the entryway for supplies into the Confederacy. The Union capture of New Orleans on April 24, 1862, greatly hindered Southern trade, as well as Confederate plans to expand trade through the city.[15] While many Confederate ships escaped from New Orleans to Havana and elsewhere to continue their operations in exile from their home city, the loss was still embarrassing and a great hindrance to blockade running throughout the Caribbean. By the end of 1862, Mobile also, though still in Confederate hands, was under constant and effective surveillance by the US Navy, now imposing a genuine and constricting blockade.[16]

The Confederate navy was unable to keep pace with the major naval construction efforts of the United States. Without the shipyards and capital required to construct dozens of ships of the line, the Confederacy had to rely on foreign purchases and on converting existing civilian craft to augment its naval capabilities. Established by the Confederate Congress in February 1861, the Confederate navy had impossible tasks: keep Southern ports open to foreign commerce, defeat the blockade, and carry out offensive operations against US commercial shipping, to weaken Union access to world markets, while at the same time maintaining access by the Confederacy. With forty warships at most under its flag, and frequently far fewer, the Confederate navy faced a daunting challenge. Naval spending was a low priority for Jefferson Davis, with a tiny budget and few available personnel, despite the obvious importance of overseas commerce in the Confederacy's foreign strategy, and it languished from neglect, apart from a few ships of note.[17] Despite all this, however, Confederate navy secretary Stephen Mallory's force did achieve some substantial successes, early in the war, through the use of ironclads, commerce raiders, privateers, and blockade runners. So effective was the Confederacy at sea in 1861 and early 1862, for example, that the Union dramatically increased its naval spending and directed assaults—successful in each case—against Southern bases such as New Orleans, Port Royal, Pensacola, and Fort Hatteras. The losses of these ports then greatly hindered Confederate naval campaigns.[18]

Spain's tolerance for smuggling and blockade runners was a significant aid to the South, and this also extended to its restored colony of Santo Domingo. In early 1863, the CSS *Alabama* briefly used Dominican waters and port as a refuge, sallying forth to raid US shipping then returning to this Caribbean sanctuary.[19] This collaboration was enabled by the colony's initial enthusiasm for the South, as the majority of Spanish officials and creoles supported the Confederate cause. Even after Southern fortunes declined, by late 1862, profits from tolls, port fees, tariffs, and the purchasing of supplies for the ships while docked ensured continued tolerance for Confederate vessels.[20]

Realizing the necessity of Spanish goodwill, the CSA made additional efforts in 1862 and 1863 to convince Spain to enter an alliance. Even a limited arrangement, perhaps only for cooperation in the Caribbean, would have posed a challenge for the United States. However, absent a decisive rebel victory or intervention by France or the United Kingdom on behalf of the Southern government, there was little chance of such an accord.[21] In addition to the profits earned through hosting Confederate ships, Spain also derived another important benefit: greater freedom of maneuver in the Caribbean, an area of primary interest for the Spanish government since the arrival of Christopher Columbus in the late fifteenth century.[22]

Despite some hope that Spain might provide port facilities for the construction of Confederate warships, this did not come to pass. Britain and France were more accommodating, and Spain did not have sufficient shipbuilding capabilities to be of much use. Many of the warships built entirely in Spain for the Spanish navy were obsolete sailing vessels, more appropriate for eighteenth-century than nineteenth-century warfare. For the Spanish government, however, the construction of warships from their own resources was politically important and kept such facilities as Spain did have at full employment throughout the 1860s.[23]

Spain's arguments to US emissaries also made American protests difficult. While Spain had accorded belligerent rights to the Confederacy, the United States had not. If Spanish officials in Cuba began to differentiate between US- and CSA-flagged vessels, would this not grant the very recognition to Southern ships against which the United States was arguing? To treat these two kinds of ships differently would be to grant de facto diplomatic recognition by Spain, which the United States surely did not want and the Spanish government had not authorized. Thus, American diplomats were unable to press their case too vigorously, as they hoped to avoid confrontations that might force Spain to defend its sovereignty and national honor with force, and their efforts to block Confederate shipping remained at the level of verbal protests and rapid dissemination of information on the location and conditions of these ships to the nearest US Navy captains, in hopes of interception and interdiction.[24]

At times, however, the US Navy became more involved than merely in efforts to monitor Confederate shipping. Union ships violated Spanish territorial waters dozens of times, chasing or even destroying CSA blockade runners, merchant vessels, and warships. The most famous incident involved the USS *Montgomery*, which on October 7, 1862, chased and boarded a British ship while in Cuban waters. The US Navy forced the British vessel to run aground, despite its flying the Spanish flag. The ship caught fire and suffered substantial damage. Spain demanded satisfaction, and the United States forced the ship's captain, Charles Hunter, to resign from the navy.[25]

Although Spain did not completely embrace the CSA, its tolerance for Confederate warships in Havana infuriated the United States. The US minister in Madrid, Gustavus Koerner, and Secretary of State Seward protested vigorously at the liberties allowed to the CSS *Florida* in January 1863, when similar treatment was denied to a Union ship, the USS *Massachusetts*, two days later. After sinking or capturing several US ships, the *Florida* arrived in Havana on January 21 and was allowed to make repairs and take on supplies before sailing again to wreak more havoc. General Serrano defended Spain's right to allow the *Florida* to dock, given the belligerent rights granted to the Confederacy. At the same time, Spanish authorities also reminded Minister Koerner in Madrid, who raised the issue repeatedly, that the ship had left the port of Havana within the required twenty-four hours and had not fired on US ships while within Spanish territorial waters.[26]

Koerner came away unsatisfied from his meetings with Spanish officials, as were US consular officials in Cuba who made similar protestations; this would not be the last time they protested Spain's tolerance for Confederate warships. While it was harder to hide Confederate warships, Koerner would later complain that blockade runners and other smugglers were often allowed unofficially to stay past the twenty-four-hour limit or to bend the rules by putting to sea and then returning as soon as they had left the immediate vicinity of the port. Spain's assistance in this made a substantial contribution to the South's ability to wage war against the Union in the Caribbean, and to smuggle essential supplies into the war zone and commodities out of it.

Spain was somewhat reluctant to take on new challenges in the Caribbean. Its intervention on Santo Domingo was, by 1862, going badly. Less deadly, but perhaps even more chastening, was the unilateral withdrawal of its forces from Mexico by its commander General Juan Prim. Spanish soldiers, who had arrived in late 1861 to collect debts owed by the Mexican government, had left in mid-1862, leaving behind their French allies. Prim feared being entangled in French imperial ambitions in Mexico and had signed an agreement with the Mexican government to resolve the debt issue, but the withdrawal was nonetheless very unpopular in Spain. There were so many protests in Madrid and elsewhere that General Prim delayed his trip home by visiting the United States. He traveled through New York, met with Secretary of State Seward and President Lincoln in Washington, DC, observed the Army of the Potomac, and inspected a prison in Philadelphia. He finally returned to Spain on August 5 and to Madrid on September 18, 1862. Upon his return home, he became a liberal opponent of the monarchy and worked to end the reign of Isabel II.[27] Despite Spanish efforts to shed their identification with the French campaign in Mexico, this was difficult to achieve completely. Under intense pressure from Paris, in June 1864, Spain recognized the government of Emperor Maximilian, the Austrian archduke imposed on Mexico by the French army. Faced with continual armed resistance and overthrown in April 1867, Maximilian was never secure in his rule nor internationally recognized.[28]

The American Civil War had a major disruptive influence on the Cuban economy. As tied as it was to the United States, Cuba saw its sugar exports collapse during the opening phases of the war. The naval war in the Caribbean, which saw the Union blockade and attacks on Southern ports escalate, interrupted normal commercial traffic in the Gulf of Mexico and Atlantic coastline. As a consequence, Cuba entered a major economic depression, as it attempted to find substitute markets in Europe. Additionally, US tariffs increased in order to fund the Union's war effort and reduced profits on those cargos that did make it to the United States. Sugar prices fell, even as Spain raised the tax burden in Cuba to pay for its own increasing defense expenditures on behalf of the island. Seeing the results of the war, initial creole enthusiasm for the South had diminished by 1862–1863, as Cuban financial losses continued.[29] Ironically, it was just as residents of the Spanish colony were losing interest that Confederate leaders, including Judah Benjamin, began to consider Spain a more likely candidate for an alliance than Britain and France, both of whom had frustrated the rebel government with their refusal to extend diplomatic recognition.[30]

As the Union blockade became more effective in 1863 and as Southern ports fell to occupation in 1863 and 1864, blockade running became less possible. Arms and other supplies procured in foreign ports—whether openly or under cover of ostensible sales to fictional third nations—languished without any practical means to import these desperately needed goods into the Confederacy. By late 1863, Havana was frequented far less by the few remaining Confederate ships, and Cubans had no means to increase their own carrying capacity or the numbers of merchant vessels.[31] Even more critical, many of the merchant vessels that since 1861 had enriched themselves through sales of goods to Southerners at inflated prices had been sunk or captured by the US Navy—or had calculated that the odds of this happening were so great that any potential profits could no longer entice them to violate the blockade. Even with the decline of Confederate smuggling, between the United States and Spain bad feelings remained over Confederate use of Havana—a permanent point of contention between two nations that already had a long list of mutual grievances dating back to the American Revolution.

Cooperation with the Confederacy in theory became easier with the creation in Spain of the Ministerio de Ultramar (Overseas Ministry) in

1863. The new ministry was intended to consolidate all colonial affairs in one cabinet-level office, but in a sense, it came about just as Spanish enthusiasm for an expanded empire began to wane, as the country confronted the reality of rising military expenses and the deadly occupation of Santo Domingo. Even at the height of O'Donnell's expansive vision, Spain did not dedicate sufficient interest, resources, or personnel to its empire and thus lost opportunities to gain territory or resources. Spain had exhausted itself at the very moment that much of the rest of Europe was beginning the second major phase of modern imperialism, when even small nations such as Belgium, the Netherlands, and Italy began carving up new colonies from available terrain in Africa and Asia. Apart from modest expansion of its enclaves in North Africa, especially in the early twentieth century, the era of Spanish territorial conquest was over.[32]

By the end of 1863 the Emancipation Proclamation, issued the first of that year, had changed public discourse in Europe over the American Civil War. Rather than being an issue of states' rights and sovereignty, which resonated in liberal Europe, the debate now focused more on black enslavement. Slaveholders in the Confederacy—and their European supporters—were hard-pressed to defend against the proclamation, which encouraged slave escapes throughout the South.[33] Confederate diplomats had long suffered the resistance to their cause based in European antipathy toward slavery. In Spain, especially after the proclamation became known, the war was seen less as an uprising against Yankee domination and more as a battle between those who supported free labor and those who supported slavery. In this debate, Spanish liberals came to identify increasingly with the cause of the Union. This was a difficult climate for Prime Minister O'Donnell who, as leader of the Liberal Union, was in the awkward position of arguing for closer collaboration with a state—the Confederacy—at odds with many of the fundamental beliefs of his party, and he was not the only one who felt discomfort at dealing with the American Civil War. Liberal opinion became more pro-Union, but many Spanish liberals retained personal or familial economic ties to Cuba. Conservatives were unwilling to be seen as enthusiastically pro-slavery and also wanted to avoid giving Prime Minister O'Donnell the political and military victories that might have come with a more successful foreign policy. These factors strengthened Spanish inclinations toward neutrality, a tendency reinforced by Spain's dependence on Britain and France, and its reluctance to take on more missions in the midst of the Dominican campaign.[34]

While frustrated in its efforts to gain diplomatic recognition from Spain or any other nation, the Confederacy did gain access to port facilities, in Mexico. In that nation, also in the midst of a civil war, Confederate trade flourished, facilitated especially in northern Mexico by the regional warlord Santiago Vidaurre, governor of Nuevo León and Caohuila. Vidaurre sold war materiel to the Confederates—"lead, copper, saltpeter, gunpowder, and textiles," in exchange for cotton and other considerations. Because of the unsuitability of the port, the insecurity of using it in the midst of a Mexican insurgency, its distance from most Confederate armies, and the poor infrastructure capable of managing these events, Matamoros was never able to replace New Orleans, however. Additionally, difficulties in securing arms and ammunition in Mexico meant that prices were often much higher than on the global market. Still, many essential products did come through the booming port city of Matamoros, which funneled trade from Europe and the Caribbean to the Confederacy and continued as a major loophole in the ever more effective Union blockade.[35]

So tied economically and politically was Matamoros to the Southern rebellion that, in late 1861, the Mexican governor even proposed an alliance to the Confederacy, with a new state under his personal rule to be called "The Republic of Sierra Madre." His secessionist government would then form an open alliance with the Confederate secessionists, and together they would stand against the United States and the Mexican Republic. Fearing this would alienate not only France but also Britain and Spain, Jefferson Davis declined the offer of mutual recognition. While nominally aligned with President Benito Juárez and the liberals and in opposition to Mexican conservatives and Emperor Maximilian, in practice Vidaurre was independent until mid-1864, when Juárez occupied northeast Mexico. This defeat drove the former governor into the arms of Maximilian, whom he served until the collapse of the Austrian's regime. Vidaurre, like Maximilian, was executed by the Mexican government in 1867, after its final victory over the conservative and Catholic forces that had fought tenaciously against liberalism in Mexico since at least the 1840s.[36]

The Mexican port city of Matamoros, under Governor Vidaurre, served as a conduit for Confederate trade with Spain and other European states, with its shipping often routed through Havana or other

Spanish ports in the Caribbean. It was a booming and prosperous town as a result of the opportunities available through running the blockade, and its population rose to over fifty thousand during the war from just a few thousand before the conflict. Hundreds of cargo and passenger ships passed from Matamoros to or through Havana, with a regularly scheduled packet line—small, fast steamships delivering mail, personnel, and limited cargo—traveling between the two ports. Shipping companies based in London, New York, or regionally in British Honduras (Belize), Nassau, Bermuda, or other Caribbean ports made substantial profits from the smuggling and blockade-running trade conducted in Mexican waters—sovereign territory just outside the reach of the Union navy.[37]

By 1864–1865, as the Union's victory at sea became apparent, normal trade ties between Cuba and the United States gradually resumed. Even powerful Confederate surface raiders such as the CSS *Florida* and CSS *Alabama* had seen their naval careers end in capture or destruction by late 1864.[38] Blockade running continued until the end of the war, with shipments traveling from Bermuda and other ports to Havana as late as April 8, 1865, but these were only echoes of what had been a major effort in earlier years. Cargoes that made for Havana in early 1865 were hoping to find a way to Galveston or other final Confederate redoubts, but the surrender at Appomattox ended these last efforts.[39] With the reduction of the Confederate threat to US shipping, exports of Cuban sugar and tobacco to the United States eventually returned to prewar levels. These two commodities—sales of which had fallen precipitously early in the war, with the resulting trade collapse leading to a depression in Cuba—began to find their way again into merchant fleets and overseas markets. Cuba's exports to Europe, which had temporarily replaced some of what had been sold to the United States, subsided somewhat with the restoration of normal commerce so that, for 1865, the United States was once again purchasing over 60 percent of the sugar and sugar cane grown in Cuba.[40] Notably, these crops were also returning to Southern ports, but in a dramatically changed context: New Orleans, Mobile, and other former Confederate ports were now operating on behalf of the Union and the Union armies that occupied much of the South.

Spain and the Confederacy had collaborated in every way possible in the Caribbean, consistent with Spain's declared neutrality. By granting belligerent rights to the Southern rebels, Spain enabled

Confederate ships to take advantage of Havana as a safe harbor, against the superior firepower and more numerous ships of the US Navy. While in the end it was other factors that caused a decline in CSA fortunes, principally the accelerating losses of its own terrain and cities, the Confederacy nonetheless took advantage of the friendly terrain of Cuba to maximize the damage against US commercial shipping and the US Navy. Cooperation between Spain and the Southern rebels had been in the best interests of both nations. Southern warships, cargo vessels, and blockade runners gained a safe haven within reasonable distance of Confederate shores, while Spain not only gained fees and tariffs from the ships that visited Havana and other ports but also provided material aid to the South, a rebel force causing tremendous losses to the United States, a nation that had in its turn caused grievous damage to the Spanish empire and had ongoing ambitions to do even more.

Chapter 7

Opportunism and Delay

Spain's hesitancy to join in an alliance with the Confederacy reflected not only its weak international position and subordination to France and Britain but also a feeling of deep ambivalence about the Confederacy. Spain believed that the South, if successful, would once again try to take over Cuba, but it would be "weak and easier to stop than the previous giant had been." In the decades preceding the Civil War, after all, Southern politicians had been at the forefront of the annexation of Florida, the Mexican-American War, filibustering efforts to claim Cuba, as well as attacks on Catholicism. Similarly, the Confederate government viewed Spain as a nation of "irreversible decadence" that was destined to lose its remaining colonies and influence, leaving the CSA in a position to seize Cuba, Puerto Rico, and other territories. Why enter an alliance with a weak nation that would be an easy mark after the Confederacy defeated the Union? With these contradictory agendas and the lack of mutual respect, it is no surprise the two states were never able to agree to become partners in an anti–United States coalition. Suspicion of each other's motives and long-range plans were enough to prevent this, despite many commonalities in social systems and mutual antipathy toward the United States. Nonetheless, there was a possibility that the two states could overcome their distrust and countervailing interests given the even greater fear each one had of the North. While there may have been some ambivalence between Richmond and Madrid, no such confusion permeated each one's relations with Washington, DC. The United States was the enemy of both the Confederate States of America and the Kingdom of Spain, and in this mutual condition perhaps were the makings of a coalition agreement between the two nations.[1]

The Confederacy's hesitation concerning an alliance with Spain was enhanced by the reality of Madrid's dependence on France and Britain, who together determined possibilities for substantial external support to the Confederacy. By late 1863, the Confederates had lost hope in a public show of support from Europe, whether in the form of diplomatic recognition or even open intervention. A clear display of Southern frustration came in October 1863, when the Confederate cabinet voted to expel all British diplomats from Southern territory. This was after all a logical move, given that there was no justification for Britain to maintain consuls in the territory of a state it did not recognize. Even more, the decision reflected the growing tensions between Richmond and London over Confederate conscription of British subjects. This measure came just months after the Confederacy had prohibited direct contact between foreign consuls on Confederate soil and their nation's ministers or ambassadors in Washington, DC. All communication after June 1863 had instead to go through foreign or neutral ports rather than passing through the belligerent lines of the Civil War. Diplomats accredited to the Union had no place operating through representatives resident in the Confederacy. Since most of these consuls were British (France, Spain, and other nations only having a handful of diplomats still in Southern cities by 1863), it was the British who were most unhappy at this measure. Legally, the Confederates were again correct, but they were also taking actions that countered their own interests. For a state hoping for international recognition as one route to force a negotiated settlement with the Union, this move, however psychologically satisfying, drove the British even closer to Washington's position that the Confederate states did not deserve consideration as a legitimate power.[2]

The withdrawal of Southern agent James Mason from Britain to the European continent, also to protest British policies toward the Confederacy, was another gesture that, however justified as morally necessary in the eyes of Southern leaders, also undermined their chances for even minor diplomatic victories—at a time when these were as desperately needed as battlefield triumphs by General Robert E. Lee and his fellow rebel generals. While the Southerners' frustration was understandable, their withdrawal from British politics mortally weakened the pro-Southern faction in Parliament and was seen as an unnecessary abandonment by those who had staked their reputations and political strength on demonstrating the longevity and worthiness of the Confederacy. If the rebel government in Richmond was not capable or willing to maintain a representative in the capital of the world's most powerful empire, this did not speak well to its overall persistence or long-term prospects.[3]

In his address to the Confederate Congress in December 1863, President Davis expressed his disappointment at the unwillingness of neutral European states to align with the cause of the South. Davis even denounced the shift in European attitudes in the direction of the Union, characterizing it as "positively unfriendly," specifically blaming France and Britain for prolonging the war and aiding Lincoln's government. His subsequent speech was a litany of complaints against the British, focusing on their toleration of the Union blockade of Southern ports and the unwillingness of the British to extend diplomatic recognition. Far from anticipating international intervention, by this point in the war, the Confederacy was reduced to complaining about its treatment by foreign nations. The anger of Davis toward the British did not extend in full toward the French, as his brief words on France's occupation of Mexico leave open the possibility that the French military occupation was of no concern to the South. Given the military difficulties experienced by the Southern armies, this very well could have been the case. While it would be going too far to say that Davis would have welcomed a permanent French presence in Mexico, in the context of 1863 and 1864, the French forces there were viewed with more alarm in Washington than in Richmond.[4]

By late 1863, Confederate diplomacy had come to focus almost exclusively on France and Spain, as relations with Britain had deteriorated significantly in the aftermath of the expulsion of British consuls from the South and the withdrawal of George Mason from London. Parallel to this, Confederate agents had shifted their purchases of warships and other military equipment almost exclusively to France. American legal successes in the British courts, arguing that such sales violated the United Kingdom's neutrality laws, were also a powerful incentive to relocate acquisition efforts across the channel.

During the fall of 1863, the Confederates had nine major warships being built or repaired in France, with smaller vessels and other military equipment also being produced in French ports and arsenals. These efforts soon came to disappointment, however, through the efforts of American diplomats to pressure the new pro-Unionist French foreign minister, Edouard Drouyn de Lhuys, who in turn convinced the emperor that to allow these ships to depart French waters would threaten the occupation of Mexico. The French liberal opposition also undermined the emperor's original intent, making public through their newspapers and journals the government's tolerance for Confederate shipbuilding.[5] Far from linking the fate of French control over Mexico to the survival of the Confederacy, Napoleon III had now become convinced that aligning with the South would cause his entire Mexican adventure to unravel—in the face of American hostility and British indifference. The French Marine Ministry, this time supported by the emperor, in May 1864 ordered the shipbuilding companies to find alternative buyers for the warships; the Confederate plan to rely on France thus met with disaster.[6] Napoleon III even prevailed upon Ferdinand Maximilian, the Austrian archduke who in January 1864 became Emperor Maximilian of Mexico, to reject recognition of the Confederacy, despite the absolute necessity for friendly relations on Mexico's northern border.[7]

Despite the French movement away from recognition, the United States remained concerned that Napoleon III might seek an alliance with the Confederacy in order to bolster his adventure in Mexico. Fears of this possibility led Secretary of State Seward to seek clarification from the French government, directing William Dayton, the US minister in Paris, to seek consultations with the French foreign minister at the earliest opportune time. Did the emperor have plans to make common cause with "the insurgent cabal in Richmond" against the United States? Were the rumors true that France was developing plans to seize Texas or reestablish control over the Mississippi? While asserting the dubious nature of these rumors, Seward also encouraged Dayton to remind the French of their "unfriendly attitude." The French position, adopted along with Britain and Spain in 1861, lent some credibility to fears of foreign intervention in the American Civil War. France had, by considering intervention, acted in ways considered "very injurious to the United States, by encouraging and thus prolonging the insurrection." The French occupation of Mexico and their plans to maintain a monarchy there despite the wishes of the Mexican people for a republic were also causing ongoing suspicions within the United States.[8]

Spain continued to follow French and British leadership in 1863 and remained willing to recognize the Confederacy if either of the two Great Powers did so. At the same time, Spain's diplomats began to hear rumors of another outside intervention in the American Civil War. In this case, it was not a foreign power involving itself to preserve the Confederacy. Instead, Spain suspected that Russia was considering entering the war on the side of the Union. Noting the growing ties between the Union and the Russian empire, including Russian fleets' making visits in the Atlantic and Pacific ports as well as the warm ties between the two states, Spain suspected this all might lead to an open alliance. Tsar Alexander II had made no secret of his enthusiasm for the Union and his opposition to slavery in the Confederacy, but this rumor had little substantiation. It did give Spain pause, however, at a time when its enthusiasm for the South was waning. While not decisive, fear of Russian involvement—which could have had a negative impact on Spain, especially in the Pacific—was one more negative factor weighing against recognition of the Confederacy and intervention on its behalf. Indeed, the United States and Russia did have close ties, leading Secretary of State Seward to reject an 1863 proposal from the French to join them, as well as the Austrians and British, in an intervention in support of an anti-Russian revolt in Poland.[9]

With external trade nearly nonexistent, the Confederacy nonetheless tried to keep tight control over the handful of shippers who were still willing to defy the Union blockade. In March 1864, the CSA issued a new set of regulations, intended to encourage exports, discourage imports, and gain revenue. These provisions on foreign commerce mandated that all ships engaged in trade between Confederate and foreign ports had to post bond, allow the Confederate government use of at least 50 percent of cargo space, and pay significantly higher tariffs on imported goods. These measures probably reduced even further the already minuscule numbers of blockade runners willing to risk seizure or sinking by Union warships and again demonstrate the ongoing inability of Confederate leaders to act in their own interests in relation to other states. The trade that continued after this point was probably confined even more to smugglers, violating both Confederate and Union rules with equanimity.[10]

President Davis believed, with some justification, that private blockade runners were extorting the South by purchasing cotton and tobacco for export at low prices and returning little in the way to the Treasury. Given the difficulties in navigating through the Union blockade, especially as this cordon became more real than notional after 1863, it is no surprise that smugglers expected great profits for the risks they undertook. Confederate regulations could not divert Union warships from Southern waters, discourage Union armies from seizing Southern ports, or force Britain, France, or other European states to grant favorable trade terms and renew merchant shipping to New Orleans, Mobile, and other ports.[11] The minimal levels of trade passing between the Confederacy and foreign nations was unlikely to change in any significant way so long as the dangers inherent in running past Union warships continued, whether merchant ships sailed under the stars and bars or the banners of neutral states. Despite complaints from many Confederate congressmen and senators, the regulations remained intact to the end of the war.[12]

The remainder of 1864 witnessed the continued shrinking of the Confederacy as Union armies advanced on all fronts. Even so, foreign affairs remained an issue for Jefferson Davis, as he found reason to denounce British—and to a lesser extent, French—policies toward the South. Early in his first speech to the Second Confederate Congress in May 1864, he accused the European states of "disregard of duty and treaty obligations," because of their acceptance of the Union blockade of Southern ports and their unwillingness to recognize the legitimacy of Confederate independence. His recognition that "every avenue of negotiation," whether with the United States or foreign powers, was "closed against us" was a final admission that it would be on the battlefield that the survival of the Confederacy would be decided. No help was coming from across the Atlantic, barring a dramatic reversal of Southern military fortunes.[13] This may have always been the case, but Davis's public comments put an end even to the idea that the British, French, or Spanish would rescue the South. The hopes of the Confederacy would rely on increasingly inadequate field armies and state militias, both under unrelenting pressure from the Union and yielding ever greater sections of terrain to their enemy. With the possibility of foreign intervention nearly gone in late 1864, Confederate leaders tried at least to sow doubt in the minds of Europeans about the wisdom of identifying completely with the North. Judah

Benjamin, for example, issued dire warnings in October 1864 about the financial solvency of the United States, speculating that loans issued by European banks to Washington, DC, might never be repaid. Benjamin also cautioned Britain, France, and Spain that Lincoln's government would have no limitations on it if the South were to be defeated, and Europe's remaining colonies in the Americas would again be vulnerable to revived Yankee aggression.[14]

Even as Britain, France, and Spain discarded the idea of recognition, forced mediation, and intervention, the idea remained alive because of US domestic politics. The Democratic presidential candidate in 1864 was General George B. McClellan, former commander of the Army of the Potomac and Union armies until being dismissed by Lincoln in November 1862. The platform of the Democratic Party called for a negotiated end to the Civil War, under conditions that would guarantee the survival of the Confederacy. Under this platform, it was not inconceivable that foreign states would become involved. Indeed, this was the argument successfully articulated by pro-Lincoln forces: an armistice with the Confederacy would lead to immediate foreign recognition.

> France, England, Spain, Austria, and Belgium, would acknowledge the sovereignty of the Confederacy forthwith, and make treaties with them, the commercial classes of which would hourly bribe those powers to help the Rebels while the war lasted. . . . The Rebellion, materially re-invigorated and morally braced by the recognition and promised support of the British, French, Spaniards and Austrians, would be strong enough in September '65, to stalk into the Peace Commission at Richmond in the person of Jeff. Davis, and say: "This affair must come to a conclusion. All negotiations for a peace with the Confederate States must be based upon the recognition of their independence."[15]

The fear of foreign intervention was one factor bolstering Lincoln's candidacy, but he faced long odds. Opposed in the general election not only by McClellan but initially by General John C. Frémont representing the Radical Democracy party, Lincoln was not expected to win. A fierce media campaign, victories by Union armies, and Frémont's unexpected dropping out of the race, however, gave the victory to Lincoln. His assassination followed his inauguration by only six weeks, an unexpected end to the president's second term in office.

By the end of 1864, Davis was still assigning "moral responsibility" to Britain and France for their failure to recognize the Confederacy. In a November speech to the Confederate Congress his complaints about their behavior became less immediate, however, even seeming to refer to the ongoing war in the past tense. Despite his spare comments promising future reversals, his argument shifted to declarations that the Union could not afford to endure its "exhaustive drain of blood and treasure" against Confederate armies. The mood of Southern politics had shifted dramatically—from the confidence of 1861 to grim hopes of survival in 1864, none of which were any longer placed in overseas capitals.[16] From winning an outright victory by campaigning against the North, the South was now committed to wearing down the Union army through a costly war of attrition, fought in Confederate territory. Under this scenario, European states were most likely to observe the war from as much distance as possible, so long as the soldiers of the Union army continued their inexorable advances into Southern territory. The end of the war now seemed in sight in mid-1864:

> Sherman was on the outskirts of Atlanta and Grant was pushing Lee to the outer defenses of Richmond. The Confederacy was cut by Union control of the Mississippi, and Sherman was preparing to further separate the struggling nation. The military situation was hopeless, but the bloodletting continued as a proud people continued the fight. The only hope to salvage the Southern nation in any recognizable form was through a negotiated settlement.[17]

Unfortunately for the South, the chances of negotiations were as diminishing as those of international recognition or mediation. A final bout of flailing initiatives in late 1864 and early 1865, including proposals to emancipate Southern slaves in exchange for recognition, did little to change the dynamics of the international context. Whatever their initial sympathies for the South or preference for a divided United States, the European powers had accepted that a Union victory was all but certain.[18]

Spain's interest in the American Civil War declined precipitously in 1864. Hoping to extricate itself from Santo Domingo, at the same time it found itself in another conflict in the Americas—in this case against Peru and Chile, and later Ecuador and Bolivia, in what became known as the Chincha Islands War (1864–1866). Spain's initial involvement emerged from a set of misunderstandings and personal affronts, which transformed what was supposed to be a goodwill mission by the most impressive warships in the Spanish navy into a series of naval battles and other skirmishes over public honor, claims by Spanish citizens, and even control over Peruvian guano. In this context (an actual shooting war against another nation), the seemingly lost cause of the Confederacy elicited even less enthusiasm and interest in Spain. Sherman's march on Atlanta, for example, did receive a brief mention, but these accounts remained shorter and less prominent than even minor events occurring much closer in Europe. For Europeans in late 1864, the American Civil War was effectively over, with the obvious collapse of Confederate armies reported in dispatches from the United States.[19] A comprehensive view of the war, reported as part of the *Almanaque de Mundo Militar* (Almanac of the military world), described 1864 as a year in which the war "between the States that had been once United" continued "with the same fury" and, with the reelection of Lincoln, would continue to be bloody.[20]

With the prospects for Union victory becoming more certain every day, by the end of 1864 Lincoln was taking a tougher line against the European powers. While the first three years of the war had been tremendously difficult and at several points seemed poised to become disastrous for the Union, those days were long past when the president gave his State of the Union message to the Congress on December 5, 1864. He had therefore the luxury of expressing himself more freely in regards to Spain. While not explicitly threatening toward Spain, Lincoln's address mentioned the war in Santo Domingo, referring to it as a "civil war . . . apparently without prospect of an early close," and discussed US efforts against the slave trade.[21]

Although international law allowed Spain to let ships of either side use its ports to take on provisions and make brief repairs (policies adopted also by France and Britain), in practice these rules favored the Confederate navy. Union ships controlled the seas and could use US Navy bases and civilian harbors without fear of attack, but the CSA fleet of blockade runners and raiding vessels was on the run. As the Union blockade became more effective and Southern ports fell to bombardment and ground assault, neutral Spanish and British harbors became increasingly attractive. While Confederate ships used Cuban harbors most frequently, on several occasions they also made extended use of ports in Spain itself, primarily to make repairs and seek temporary protection from Union warships but also to take on supplies, offload prisoners, sell prizes, and recruit for their crews.

The most controversial incident involved a Confederate warship, the CSS *Stonewall*, that arrived at the northern Spanish port of El Ferrol on February 3, 1865. The vessel was an ironclad purchased illegally through French and Danish intermediaries, and it arrived to make necessary repairs after enduring a winter storm and damage caused by unexpectedly heavy seas. Its captain, Thomas Jefferson Page, had orders to proceed to the Azores, and then to the Atlantic Ocean to attack Union warships and shipping. Even though the *Stonewall* should have left the Spanish harbor within twenty-four hours, it remained until March 24—well over six weeks. While the metal-encased hulk was intended as a naval superweapon, which might single-handedly change the course of the war at sea, it was notoriously unsuitable for combat on anything but "the smoothest of seas." Its armor was nearly invulnerable to Union cannon, but its main gun was hard to maneuver, and its coal capacity limited it to cruises of five days or less.[22]

Stalked by two Union warships (both hopelessly outmatched by the ironclad in armor and armaments and unwilling to test themselves against the behemoth), the *Stonewall* made its way safely to Havana, having stopped in Lisbon to take on supplies before crossing the Atlantic. On May 19, Captain Page sold the ship for $16,000 to Spanish colonial authorities, who then, in July, turned it over to US authorities for the same amount. For weeks, the struggle over the disposition of the CSS *Stonewall* had constituted a major diplomatic fight between Spain and the United States, and its resolution, which it took the defeat of the Confederacy to resolve, remained unsatisfactory to the Americans.[23] Even in the final resolution of the matter, the Spanish government reserved admitting judgment on whether the United States was within its rights under international law in receiving the warship—but the Spanish voluntarily put aside the issue in the interests of repairing strained relations. Even so, the crisis and its slow resolution were reflective of the antipathy between Spain and the United States.[24]

On April 9, 1865, General Lee surrendered Confederate forces at the courthouse in Appomattox, Virginia, thus ending the Civil War. The war, which had never received a great deal of attention in Spain, did earn a dramatic note in one newspaper: "Richmond has been taken. The Army of Lee has been annihilated. The victory has been complete. The war can be considered ended. God be praised, that He has granted the greatly desired peace to the United States." While not all newspapers were so colorful in their language, the final end of the war was welcomed in Europe as much for the clarity of the victory and the expected return of normal commerce as for any particular partisanship remaining for either camp, Confederacy or Union.[25]

While it would be easy to say that relations between Spain and the United States had deteriorated during the conflict, in fact they had never been particularly good. The Confederate temptation, although ultimately rejected by Madrid, had been seen by Washington as a real possibility, but ties between Spain and the United States had been poor for decades preceding these discussions. The perception in the United States that Spain with France had been open to an alliance with the now defeated Confederacy revived the anti-Catholic and anti-Spanish sentiments in public opinion. The Ten Years' War, an insurrection in Cuba that began in 1868, once again revived US interest in the potential for annexing Cuba, an interest that remained active until the Spanish-American War of 1898. In the aftermath of that conflict, the United States ultimately decided not to annex Cuba, despite having the means to do so. The dream of the filibusters, Southern politicians, and believers in Manifest Destiny was in the end not achieved—as a result of the objections of then president William McKinley and others against the creation of an American overseas empire. Cuba did become an effective colony of the United States, however, with its economy and political system dictated.[26]

In a sense, while Spain's potential involvement in the American Civil War could have transformed the conflict, its dalliance with the possibility merely confirmed the antipathy felt by many Americans for Spain. Although there had been clear tensions and conflicts before 1861, these disputes ensured that after the war Spain would be considered even more as a weak, corrupt, and incompetent power. As such, in American opinion, Spain would continue to be regarded as clearly undeserving of its prize possession, the most important territory in its empire, Cuba, the Pearl of the Antilles. The final result of these feelings toward Spain, as well as the ongoing perception that Cuba was within the natural sphere of American influence, was of course the Spanish-American War of 1898, which ended as badly for Spain as it possibly could have, with the loss of the rest of its empire.

Spain's revived imperial ambitions were checked significantly during the period of the American Civil War. Although an alliance between Spain and the Confederacy never came to fruition, there was a convergence of interests in the Caribbean and in the two states' shared objective of weakening the United States. In the end, both were disappointed. Of course, the collapse and ultimate surrender of the Southern rebels ended the cause of the Confederacy in absolute terms, but Spain also suffered reverses. Most notably, its humiliating defeat in Santo Domingo, where indigenous rebels drove out the modern Spanish army, destroyed any hopes for a major imperial revival in the Americas. Also contributing to the diminution of Spain's grandiose vision was its pyrrhic victory in the Chincha Islands War, a naval conflict between Spain and its former colonies of Peru and Chile. In this conflict, Spain consistently emerged as the tactical victor, seizing islands and sinking Latin American fleets. In the end, however, Spain accepted a strategic defeat as it was unable and unwilling to follow through on its absolute mastery of the sea with a costly land invasion. The final armistice was not signed until 1871, with peace treaties following years later, but the major fighting had ended by 1866. The lessons of Santo Domingo—avoid ground operations in hostile terrain—had already been incorporated into Spanish strategic thinking. Spain emerged from this conflict with a stronger reputation for the navy than the army had accumulated from Santo Domingo, but it was nonetheless a blow to national pride to have to withdraw without a final victory, a territorial or financial gain, or even a gesture of subordination by the Latin American republics it had faced in the Pacific and along the shoreline. While the Spanish fleet had fought more expertly than those of the Allies—principally Peru and Chile—and had endured fewer losses of men and ships, Spain was fighting in hostile waters, away from supply and friendly bases, against two nations that considered themselves to be in a war of self-defense. Absent a major ground assault on Lima and Santiago, it was difficult to see how else to conclude this war, other than in the diplomatic compromise effected at the end between Spain, Chile, Peru, Ecuador, and Bolivia.[27]

Spain did not, however, return to its abject international weakness of the 1820s and 1830s. The Spanish navy continued to procure new warships throughout the late nineteenth century, and the army did its best, given the ongoing political uncertainty, to improve training, personnel, and equipment. Still, Spain proved unable to maintain control of the last remaining territories in its American empire when the United States declared war in 1898. The Spanish-American War was not as absolute or as easy a victory as some US leaders had predicted, but in the end Spain did lose Cuba, Puerto Rico, Guam, and the Philippines to the United States. Spain continued to control small enclaves in North Africa, but the Spanish empire effectively ended with the close of this war. The disastrous catastrophe of 1898 capped a century of tumult and mercurial moments and finally brought to a close five hundred years of a Spanish imperial presence in the Americas. The American Civil War would be the last major war in which Spain could have played a strategically significant international role. Even at that point, its ability to do so rested at least as much on the sufferance of Britain and France as on its own military strength and geographic imperatives. For all the dreams of Spanish leaders during the nineteenth century, it had been many years since Spain had been truly autonomous and powerful. Its remaining on the sidelines in the American Civil War, while yet engaging in minor expeditionary efforts, reflected a realistic result for what was after all, despite its regional significance in the Caribbean and its ambitions in the Americas, a minor global power.[28]

Conclusion

The American Civil War officially ended for Spain even later than it did for the Confederacy, when, on June 5, 1865, Spain withdrew its recognition of Confederate belligerent rights. Even though this gesture was a formality, coming almost two months after General Robert E. Lee's surrender of April 9, still in this action Spain showed its sympathy toward the defunct Confederate States of America, by being the last European state to do so. Britain had withdrawn belligerent rights on June 3 and France on May 30.[1] It is possible to assign too much significance to this delay, but it was in keeping with the poor relations between Spain and the United States that both preceded and followed the American Civil War. Spain also allowed a handful of Confederate leaders, including General John C. Breckinridge, to escape to Cuba with a few dozen supporters and family members in advance of the Union armies and their probable capture. Breckinridge, a former vice president of the United States, had served as the last secretary of war in the Confederate government. Despite US diplomatic protests, Spain later allowed Breckinridge to leave for refuge in Great Britain, where he remained until a federal amnesty allowed him to return safely to reside in the United States in 1869.[2]

The delays by Spain, France, and Britain in complying with US demands after the end of the American Civil War would not have been a surprise to Secretary Seward had he noted the development of relations between the Confederacy and these three European powers. At every critical juncture, these three countries responded, not to the needs of the Confederacy or even to their own stated moral imperatives, but to their own national interests. While the European states looked upon the American Civil War with great concern and preferred to see two American nations emerge in place of one larger one, their greater fear was to become engaged in another distant conflict. The dread of another war on the scale of the Napoleonic struggles haunted the courts and parliaments of Europe. While Spain's occupation of Santo Domingo and France's occupation of Mexico brought major formations of European combat troops into the Western Hemisphere, these military operations also limited the power of both nations to contemplate additional expeditions. Similarly, British fears of a conflict on the European continent—over Poland, Italy, or some other dispute or entanglement—caused hesitation even among the most strident British advocates for the Southern cause to encourage direct involvement in the American Civil War.

Ironically, the conviction in the royal courts of Europe that the Union could not defeat the South—a message reinforced by Confederate propagandists and agents—accrued against the cause of the CSA. Convinced that the Union could not achieve a total military victory over the armies of the Confederacy, there seemed less urgency to involve the European states in forcing the inevitable negotiated settlement. France, Britain, and Spain, it seemed, could reap the benefits of a divided North America without alienating either of the two republics, both of them expected to survive, providing markets and other forms of engagement. In truth, the interests of all three nations, especially Spain, were best served by a war between the Confederacy and the Union that did not end but instead continued to divert the strength of the United States away from Latin America, from economic prosperity, and from interest in the affairs of other nations. Even a negotiated settlement between Confederate and Yankee governments would presumably have given both a free hand in the Americas: potentially two governments—the CSA and USA—would be then vying for control over Cuba.[3]

Spain's chief diplomat to the United States, Gabriel García Tassara, could view with some personal relief that the American Civil War had ended without Spain's entrance into the conflict. Unlike other Spanish politicians, Tassara had always been wary of entanglement with the Confederacy, recognizing the superior economic and military strength of the United States. His health always precarious, Tassara had rarely intervened in a significant way to achieve this or other goals of Spain, but he could nonetheless also be pleased that Cuba remained a Spanish colony. With his medical condition deteriorating and major changes in Spanish domestic politics, Tassara was recalled from his posting at the end of 1866. The stress of the diplomat's ten years in the United States might have been a contributing factor to his death in Madrid in 1875, at the age of fifty-seven.[4]

The Spanish army remained formidable, on paper, with just over 200,000 on its rolls at the end of 1865. Of these, however, almost 70,000 were reservists, with little in the way of equipment or training upon the conclusion of their active service, and an additional 12,000 were Guardia Civil, the national paramilitary rural police. Of the regular army forces there were 50,000 infantry, 17,000 mountain troops, 12,000 riflemen, 10,000 cavalry, 10,000 artillerymen, and just under 4,000 engineers. After a decade of deployments and the debilitating occupation of Santo Domingo, the strength and reputation of the Spanish army would take some time to recover to its pre-1861 position.[5] In its colonies, Spain had an additional 45,000 soldiers in Cuba (one-third of these were reservists), plus 11,000 in Puerto Rico (60 percent reservists), 11,500 in the Philippines, and 200 in Spanish Guinea, with the latter two colonial forces comprised entirely of active duty personnel.[6] Still, all of Spain's overseas efforts in the 1860s—Mexico, Indochina, Santo Domingo, the War in the Pacific—ended in retreats or withdrawals and had been begun only with the tolerance, indifference, or support of France and Britain. By 1866, Spain's brief period of overseas activity ended, and the country remained isolated and inactive internationally until the Spanish-American War, other than fighting internal wars in the peninsula and in the colonies.[7] On the positive side, it could be argued that Spain won out by not losing. Its empire in 1868—at the time of Isabel II's fall from power—was, with the modest Moroccan acquisitions, slightly larger than when the queen first ascended the throne in 1833. Given the perception of Spain as a power in decline this was, in contrast, an achievement. Despite its defeats, or perhaps because of them, the country's overall international profile was also higher.[8]

The negative feelings engendered between Spain and the United States during the American Civil War—over the occupation of Santo Domingo, support to Confederate blockade runners from Havana, the persistence of slavery in Cuba, and the accurate perception that Spain was intrigued by the possibility of a CSA victory—persisted well after 1865. During the Ten Years' War (an insurgency for Cuban independence in 1868–1878), American politicians and newspapers made no secret of their hopes for Spanish defeat. By the 1880s, American commercial interests, along with an increasing number of Americans who advocated for a larger US role in the Caribbean and the world, revived the antebellum Cuban annexationist dream. The Spanish-American War of 1898 and its ultimate result were not unexpected. Advocates for an American empire had been hoping to gain control of the island throughout the nineteenth century. Spanish insistence that the United States should not support Cuban rebels in the 1890s, highlighting the neutrality of Spain during the American Civil War as model behavior, remained unconvincing to many Americans. Spain had, after all, considered an alliance with the Confederacy, collaborated openly with it in the Caribbean, and supported French and British proposals for outside arbitration. None of these measures characterized a completely neutral nation, which is what Spain demanded of the United States in the 1890s. In 1898, of course, the United States went far beyond what Spain had done during the 1860s, so perhaps serving as a model would have been a better outcome.[9]

While enmity between Spain and the United States persisted, even increased, in the aftermath of the American Civil War, the same was not true of relations between the US and Great Britain—the world's true superpower of the 19th century. The American Civil War did not see any significant foreign intervention, but in its aftermath, the United States took measure of what had occurred in relation to overseas powers. Realizing the importance of ties to Britain, which throughout the Civil War had been the key nation in determining the actions of France and Spain, American diplomats focused on settling the economic and political disputes that had emerged between Washington and London.

Consul Dudley in Liverpool, in particular, fought successfully to gain financial compensation from the British government for its tolerance of Confederate shipbuilding and outfitting. After a number of cases worked their way through British courts, in 1872 an international tribunal awarded the United States $15 million for damages caused by Confederate warships built in the United Kingdom. Although this fell short of the initial $2 billion demanded by the United States, it was a significant amount, given that the British government expected no financial penalty for its actions. Within a few years, these payments allowed the United States and the United Kingdom to move beyond the aftermath of the American Civil War and to improve ties dramatically. The two nations had such a convergence of commercial, political, and military interests that the late nineteenth and early twentieth centuries saw movement toward genuine cooperation and eventual alliance. Relations between Great Britain and the United States improved dramatically after the War of 1812, which had seen the United States as a de facto ally of Napoleon Bonaparte against England and its allies. During the 1820s and 1830s, the two primary English-speaking states developed a practical coalition, with both nations agreeing to limit European imperialism in the Americas, in favor of open commercial relations. These ties in the early nineteenth century, based on common culture and political heritage, became a wartime alliance during the two world wars and the global Cold War that followed in the twentieth century.[10]

France under Emperor Napoleon III had been the most sympathetic to the Confederacy of the major powers, even if mostly only behind closed doors. In the aftermath of the American Civil War, France became less significant to the United States, however. French intervention in Mexico, in the attempt from 1861 to impose the rule of Austrian Archduke Maximilian, by 1867 had failed, resulting in the withdrawal of French forces and the execution of Maximilian. Emperor Napoleon III himself fell from power in 1870, when in a major humiliation he was captured by the German army during the Franco-Prussian War. The leaders of the French Third Republic after 1871 were far less interested in the Western Hemisphere and focused instead on North Africa and Southeast Asia as venues for imperial conquest. Even more important, the French realized that their political and military resources needed to be directed toward the East, where the newly created German empire was now the greatest continental power. The failed attempt to maintain Austrian Archduke Maximilian as emperor of Mexico was the last major intervention in the Americas by France, a dramatic reversal for a nation that had contended for dominance in North America since the sixteenth century. After belatedly recognizing Maximilian's Mexican regime in mid-1864, Spain withdrew this diplomatic concession in late April 1867, less than three months before Benito Juárez entered Mexico City and executed the Austrian monarch.[11]

The costs of Spain's increased overseas military deployments in the 1850s and 1860s had been dramatic. The burden on the national Treasury for the additional operations (including in Mexico, Morocco, Santo Domingo, and other minor operations), including all extraordinary expenditures beyond programmed salaries, was two million reales expended—five times all expenses for the occupation of Santo Domingo, 1861–1865. The human costs including deaths, disease, and injuries, had also been high: ten thousand casualties in Morocco, thirty thousand in Santo Domingo, four thousand in Indochina, and hundreds more in Mexico and other operations. Spain's total losses in these two decades were forty-five thousand, including over ten thousand deaths to battles and disease.[12] This was a high price to pay for gains which were, in most cases, ephemeral. Spanish glory faded quickly, left behind by the expeditionary units that had arrived with such great ambitions in Mexico, Santo Domingo, and other theaters of operations on three continents.

Both the Kingdom of Spain and the Confederate States of America believed that they were natural allies and could arrive at recognition and even perhaps an alliance to confront the United States. Despite these sentiments, expressed privately and publicly by key leaders in both governments, the two states were too encumbered by other challenges to pursue this option. Even enabled by the sporadic efforts by other nations, especially the French, to force an armistice or mediated settlement on the belligerents, Union strength on the battlefield was never so weak as to allow for a Southern diplomatic victory. Similarly, the weakness of Spain in the international system and its ongoing catastrophe in Santo Domingo prevented it from pursuing a defensive alliance with the Confederates. In the event, such an agreement—absent direct support from France and Britain—would have mattered little and been hard to implement in the face of resistance by the United States. While there was some value in the threat of foreign intervention, its actual success against a mobilized and industrialized United States would have been problematic.[13]

The irony is that, if battlefield victories by the CSA had made possible an agreement with Britain, France, and Spain, Madrid would have been of minimal aid to the South. The Confederates, consumed with the struggle with the Union, would similarly have been of little help as a Spanish ally. When Spain would have been of the most help to the South, it was also least likely and able to provide it. "Natural allies," perhaps, but Spain and the Confederate States of America—even had they concluded a treaty or other formal arrangement—would have been distant friends, of modest aid on critical matters: more or less the actual experience that existed between them during the American Civil War.

Notes

Introduction

1. Robert May, *The Union, the Confederacy, and the Atlantic Rim* (West Lafayette, IN: Purdue University Press, 1995), 1–2.

2. James Morton Callahan, *Diplomatic History of the Southern Confederacy* (1901; reprint, New York: Frederick Ungar, 1964), n129.

3. Edwin Pratt, "Spanish Opinion of the North American Civil War," *Hispanic American Historical Review* 10.1 (February 1930): 14–25.

4. Murillo cited from Juan Batista Vilar, "Las relaciones internacionales de España, 1840–1874," in *España siglo XIX*, ed. Javier Paredes Alonso (Madrid: Editorial Actas, 1991), 235. Unless otherwise indicated, all translations are my own.

5. James W. Cortada, *Spain and the American Civil War: Relations at Mid-century, 1855–1868* (Philadelphia: American Philosophical Society, 1980), 103.

6. Charles M. Hubbard, *The Burden of Confederate Diplomacy* (Knoxville: University of Tennessee Press, 1998), xv–xvi, 3, 7, 18–19, 21, 23–25, 122–24, 153–56.

7. Lynn Case and Warren Spencer, *The United States and France: Civil War Diplomacy* (Philadelphia: University of Pennsylvania Press, 1970), 1.

8. Antonia Pi-Suñer Llorens and Agustín Sánchez Andrés, *Una historia de encuentros y desencuentros* (Mexico, D.F.: Secretaría de Relaciones Exteriores, 2001), 164–65.

9. Callahan, *Diplomatic History*, 66.

10. Philip Van Doren Stern, *When the Guns Roared: World Aspects of the American Civil War* (New York: Doubleday, 1965), 59, 117–18.

Chapter 1

1. Manuel Allendesalazar, *Apuntes sobre la relación diplomática Hispano-Norteamericana, 1763–1895* (Madrid: Ministerio de Asuntos Exteriores, 1996), 201.

2. Perry McCandless, *A History of Missouri* (Columbia: University of Missouri Press, 2000), 266; C. Stanley Urban, "The Africanization of Cuba Scare, 1853–1855," *Hispanic American Historical Review* 37.1 (February 1957): 29–45.

3. Cortada, *Spain and the American Civil War*, 5.

4. Daniel Carroll, *Henri Mercier and the American Civil War* (Princeton, NJ: Princeton University Press, 1971), 3–4.

5. Case and Spencer, *United States and France*, 16–17.

6. Thomas E. Chávez, *Spain and the Independence of the United States: An Intrinsic Gift* (Albuquerque: University of New Mexico Press, 2002).

7. Rodrigo Botero, *Ambivalent Embrace: America's Troubled Relations with Spain from the Revolutionary War to the Cold War* (Westport, CT: Greenwood Press, 2001), ix.

8. Cortada, *Spain and the American Civil War*, 6–7, 231.

9. Humphrey Desmond, *The Know-Nothing Party: A Sketch* (Washington, DC: New Century, 1901), 11.

10. Carroll, *Henri Mercier*, 55; Harral Landry, "Slavery and the Slave Trade in Atlantic Diplomacy, 1850–1861," *Journal of Southern History* 27.2 (May 1961): 184–207.

11. James W. Cortada, *Two Nations over Time: Spain and the United States, 1776–1977* (Westport, CT: Greenwood Press, 1978), 62–63.

12. Raúl Figueroa Esquer, *Entre la intervención oculta y la neutralidad estricta: España ante la Guerra entre México y Estados Unidos, 1845–1848* (Mexico City: Secretaría de Relaciones Exteriores, 1999), 17, 193, 247–50, 287–91, 321, 327–29.

13. Matthew Karp, "A Hemispheric Defense of Slavery: The South and American Foreign Policy, 1840–1845" (paper presented to the Southern Historical Association, Louisville, November 7, 2009).

14. Robert May, *The Southern Dream of a Caribbean Empire, 1854–1861* (Baton Rouge: Louisiana State University Press, 1973), 7.

15. Cortada, *Spain and the American Civil War*, 14.

16. Karp, "Defense of Slavery"; Michael Schoeppner, "Quarantining an Epidemic: British Emancipation, Northern Abolitionism, and the Negro Seamen Acts" (paper presented to the Southern Historical Association, Louisville, November 7, 2009).

17. Luis Martínez-Fernández, *Torn between Empires: Economy, Society, and Patterns of Social Thought in the Hispanic Caribbean, 1840–1878* (Athens: University of Georgia Press, 1994), 12–14.

18. Batista Vilar, "Las relaciones internacionales de España," 233.

19. Tom Chaffin, *Fatal Glory: Narciso López and the First Clandestine War against Cuba* (Charlottesville: University Press of Virginia, 1996), 9–10, 20–21, 200; Cortada, *Two Nations over Time*, 71–73; Antonio Rafael de la Cova, *Cuban Confederate Colonel: The Life of Ambrosio José Gonzáles* (Columbia: University of South Carolina Press, 2003).

20. Michael Stevens, "Two Flags, One Cause—A Cuban Patriot in Gray: Ambrosio José Gonzáles," in *Cubans in the Confederacy*, ed. Phillip Tucker

(Jefferson, NC: McFarland, 2002), 176–80, 183–85, 189–91, 201–2.

21. De la Cova, *Cuban Confederate Colonel*, xxi–xxiii, 3.

22. Martínez-Fernández, *Torn between Empires*, 21–23, 38; Cortada, *Two Nations over Time*, 71–73; Cortada, *Spain and the American Civil War*, 12.

23. May, *Southern Dream*, 8–11.

24. Joseph Durkin, *Confederate Navy Chief: Stephen R. Mallory* (Tuscaloosa: University of Alabama Press, 1954), 108.

25. May, *Southern Dream*, 11–19.

26. Ibid., 24.

27. Louis A. Pérez, *Cuba: Between Reform and Revolution*, 2nd ed. (Oxford: Oxford University Press, 1995), 110, 111, 113; Cortada, *Spain and the American Civil War*, 14.

28. De la Cova, *Cuban Confederate Colonel*, 29.

29. Ibid., 35–37, 71, 76–82.

30. Ibid., 42, 49–65.

31. Ibid., 95–100.

32. James Johnston Pettigrew, *Notes on Spain and the Spaniards, in the Summer of 1859, with a Glance at Sardinia* (1871; reprint, Columbia: University of South Carolina Press, 2010), 422.

33. Urban, "Cuba Scare, 1853–1855."

34. De la Cova, *Cuban Confederate Colonel*, 47–48.

35. Cortada, *Spain and the American Civil War*, 8–9, 11–13.

36. US Department of State, *Case of the Black Warrior, and other violations of the rights of American citizens by Spanish authorities* (Washington, DC: Beverely Tucker, Senate printer, 1854), in University of Nebraska Special Collections; Cortada, *Spain and the American Civil War*, 8–9, 11–13.

37. Cortada, *Spain and the American Civil War*, 11, 13.

38. May, *Southern Dream*, 35–41.

39. Cortada, *Spain and the American Civil War*, 24–25.

40. Cortada, *Two Nations over Time*, 76.

41. Ibid., 68.

42. May, *Southern Dream*, 61–67.

43. Martínez-Fernández, *Torn between Empires*, 55, 62–63, 97; Cortada, *Spain and the American Civil War*, 22.

44. James Buchanan, 1860 State of the Union Address, December 3, 1860, in *Messages and Papers of the Presidents*, ed. James D. Richardson (Washington, DC, 1897–1917), 5:656 ff., at http://teachingamericanhistory.org/library/index.asp?document=946.

45. Cortada, *Spain and the American Civil War*, 20–21.

46. Democratic Party Platform of 1860, 18 June 1860 (Douglas Faction), Baltimore, Maryland, at http://teachingamericanhistory.org/library/index.asp?document=79.

47. Democratic Party Platform of 1860, June 1860 (Breckinridge Faction), Richmond, Virginia, at http://teachingamericanhistory.org/library/index.asp?documentprint=958.

48. Mario Mendez Bejerano, *Tassara: nueva biografía crítica* (Madrid: J. Pérez, 1928), 7, 17–18, 87–88, 101–2.

49. Cortada, *Spain and the American Civil War*, 104.

50. May, *Southern Dream*, 172–84; Cortada, *Spain and the American Civil War*, 27.

51. Cortada, *Spain and the American Civil War*, 26, 29.

52. Case and Spencer, *United States and France*, 21, 24.

53. Carroll, *Henri Mercier*, 57.

54. Case and Spencer, *United States and France*, 32–34.

55. Cortada, *Spain and the American Civil War*, 57.

56. Ibid., 82.

Chapter 2

1. Eduardo González Calleja and Antonio Fontecha Pedraza, eds., *Una cuestión de honor: la polémica sobre la anexión de Santo Domigo vista desde España, 1861–1865* (Santo Domingo: Fundación García Arévalo, 2005), 18–19; Cortada, *Spain and the American Civil War*, 3, 8.

2. Germán Rueda Hernanz, *Isabel II* (Madrid: Arlanza, 2001), 213–14.

3. Batista Vilar, "Las relaciones internacionales de España," 220–23.

4. Carlos Navarro y Rodrigo, *O'Donnell y su tiempo* (Madrid: Biblioteca Universal Económica, 1869), 176–77, 194–95.

5. Pettigrew, *Notes on Spain and the Spaniards*, 423–25.

6. Cortada, *Spain and the American Civil War*, 3–8; José Luis Herrero, *El ejército español en el siglo XIX* (Madrid: Cuadernos para el Diálogo, 1975), 25; Rueda Hernanz, *Isabel II*, 213–14, 232; Daniel Headrick, *Ejército y política en España, 1866–1898* (Madrid: Editorial Tecnos, 1981), 34–35, 46–47, 49, 270–71, 273.

7. Batista Vilar, "Las relaciones internacionales de España," 220–21, 230–31, 235, 247.

8. Fernando Fernández Bastarreche, *El ejército español en el siglo XIX* (Madrid: Siglo XXI, 1978), 42.

9. Headrick, *Ejército y política en España*, 52–53.

10. Fernando Fernández Bastarreche, "La organización del Ejercito y de la Armada en España, 1750–1870," in *Los ejércitos y las armadas de España y Suecia en una época de cambios, 1750–1870*, ed. Enrique Martínez Ruiz, Magdalena de Pazzis Pi Corrales, Juan Torrejón Chaves (Cádiz: Universidad de Cádiz, 2000), 57, 129, 130, 132; Headrick, *Ejército y política en España*, 73.

11. Pettigrew, *Notes on Spain and the Spaniards*, 408.

12. Enrique Martínez Ruiz, "Condiciones básicas del reclutamiento militar en España, 1768–1885," in Martínez Ruiz, de Pazzis Pi Corrales, Torrejón Chaves, *Los ejércitos y las armadas de España*, 176.

13. Headrick, *Ejército y política en España*, 101–2.

14. Stanley Payne, *Politics and the Military in Modern Spain* (Stanford: Stan-

ford University Press, 1967), 470; Headrick, *Ejército y política en España*, 100.

15. Headrick, *Ejército y política en España*, 46, 267, 270–71.

16. Albino Feijóo Gómez, *Quintas y protestas social en el S. XIX* (Madrid: Ministerio de Defensa, 1996), 42, 48, 52, 287, 355, 478.

17. Pettigrew, *Notes on Spain and the Spaniards*, 405–6.

18. Headrick, *Ejército y política en España*, 143.

19. Ibid., 49.

20. F. de Bordejé y Morencos, *Crónica de la marina española en el siglo XIX (1800–1868)*, vol. 1 (Madrid: Ministerio de Defensa, 1999), 270–71.

21. Agustín R. Rodríguez González, *La Armada Española, la campaña del Pácifico, 1862–1871* (Madrid: Agualarga, 1999), 7–8.

22. Ibid., 22–23.

23. Stanley Payne, *El Ejército y sociedad en la España liberal, 1808–1936* (Madrid: Akal, 1977), 36; Sumner Welles, *Naboth's Vineyard: The Dominican Republic, 1844–1924*, vol. 1 (1926; reprint, New York: Paul Appel, 1966), 220–21.

24. Bordejé y Morencos, *Crónica de la marina española*, 1:259.

25. Headrick, *Ejército y política en España*, 38.

26. Fernando Puell de la Villa, *Historia del ejército en España* (Madrid: Alianza Editorial, 2000), 63, 74, 274, 280.

27. Headrick, *Ejército y política en España*, 273.

28. David Ringrose, *Spain, Europe and the "Spanish Miracle," 1700–1900* (Cambridge: Cambridge University Press, 1996), 64–69, 74–75.

29. Joseph Harrison, *An Economic History of Modern Spain* (New York: Holmes and Meier, 1978), 31, 33.

30. Herrero, *El ejército español*, 25.

31. Ringrose, *Spain, Europe and the "Spanish Miracle,"* 21.

32. Ibid., 240–44.

33. Pettigrew, *Notes on Spain and the Spaniards*, 391.

34. J. Sarda, "Spanish Prices in the Nineteenth Century," *Quarterly Journal of Economics* 62.1 (November 1947): 143–59.

35. Harrison, *Economic History*, 48–52; *Almanaque de Mundo Militar: Panorama Universal* (Madrid, 1865).

36. Pettigrew, *Notes on Spain and the Spaniards*, 410–11.

37. Botero, *Ambivalent Embrace*, 54–55.

38. Ringrose, *Spain, Europe and the "Spanish Miracle,"* 252–53.

39. Jaime Vicens Vives, *An Economic History of Spain* (Princeton, NJ: Princeton University Press, 1969), 617.

40. Pettigrew, *Notes on Spain and the Spaniards*, 377–78.

41. Harrison, *Economic History*, 21, 23.

42. Vicens Vives, *Economic History of Spain*, 614.

43. José Ramón Alonso, *Historia política del ejército español* (Madrid: Editora Nacional, 1974), 333–34; Rueda Hernanz, *Isabel II*, 211.

44. *El Contemporáneo* (Madrid), 4 June 1861.

45. Cortada, *Two Nations over Time*, 76.

46. Allendesalazar, *Apuntes*, 150.
47. Bordejé y Morencos, *Crónica de la marina española*, 1:257.
48. González Calleja and Fontecha Pedraza, *Una cuestión de honor*, 23–24.
49. Archivo de Ministerio de Asuntos Exteriores (AMAE), Política Exterior, EEUU, 1864–1865 LegH2407: note, 15 October 63, political director to MAE (the Ministerio de Asuntos Exteriores was the Foreign Ministry).
50. Pettigrew, *Notes on Spain and the Spaniards*, 55–56, 70.
51. Ibid., 82, 376.
52. González Calleja and Fontecha Pedraza, *Una cuestión de honor*, 39–40.
53. Pettigrew, *Notes on Spain and the Spaniards*, 408.
54. Dean Mahin, *One War at a Time: The International Dimensions of the American Civil War* (Dulles, VA: Brassey's, 2000), 198–99.
55. Case and Spencer, *United States and France*, 77–78, 108–9.
56. Emilio de Diego García, "El Ejército español a mediados del siglo XIX: posibilidades y limitaciones," in Martínez Ruiz, de Pazzis Pi Corrales, Torrejón Chaves, *Los ejércitos y las armadas de España*, 65–66.
57. Bordejé y Morencos, *Crónica de la marina española*, 1:279, 283–84.
58. *La Época*, 14 June 1861; Rodríguez González, *La Armada Española*, 24–26.
59. Batista Vilar, "Las relaciones internacionales de España," 228–29.
60. Diego García, "El Ejército español," 123.
61. Juan Prim, *Memoria sobre el viaje militar á Oriente* (Madrid: Imprenta de Tejado, 1855), 167–69, 285; Navarro y Rodrigo, *O'Donnell y su tiempo*, 55.
62. Ministerio de Defensa, *Historia de la Infanteria Española: la época de los ejércitos nacionales* (Madrid: Ministerio de Defensa, 1998), 155–59, 162, 169; Bordejé y Morencos, *Crónica de la marina española*, 1:291–92; Batista Vilar, "Las relaciones internacionales de España," 236–37.
63. Bordejé y Morencos, *Crónica de la marina española*, 1:295; Rueda Hernanz, *Isabel II*, 225.
64. Alonso, *Historia política del ejército español*, 333–34.
65. Bordejé y Morencos, *Crónica de la marina española*, 1:293–95; Rodríguez González, *La Armada Española*, 26–27.
66. Alonso, *Historia política del ejército español*, 333–34.
67. Ministerio de Defensa, *Historia de la Infanteria Española*, 579.
68. *La Época*, 1 January 1861.
69. Ibid., 19 February 1861.
70. Navarro y Rodrigo, *O'Donnell y su tiempo*, 197; Clara Lida, ed., *España y el imperio de Maximiliano* (Mexico, D.F.: El Colegio de México, 1999), 48–51, 57; Pi-Suñer Llorens and Sánchez Andrés, *Encuentros y desencuentros*, 133, 145.
71. Pi-Suñer Llorens and Sánchez Andrés, *Encuentros y desencuentros*, 148–51, 158–59, 164–65, 167–68.
72. Alonso, *Historia política del ejército español*, 338–39.
73. Payne, *Politics and the Military*, 28–29.
74. Rodríguez González, *La Armada Española*, 26–28.
75. *La Época*, 24 June 1861; Rodríguez González, *La Armada Española*, 26–29.

Chapter 3

1. Frank Lawrence Owsley, *King Cotton Diplomacy* (Chicago: University of Chicago Press, 1959), 23.

2. Jasper Ridley, *Maximilian and Juárez* (New York: Ticknor and Fields, 1992), 114.

3. *El Contemporáneo* (Madrid), 11 April, 2 and 19 May 1861.

4. Ibid., 20 April 1861.

5. Edwin DeLeon, *Secret History of Confederate Diplomacy Abroad*, ed. William C. Davis (Lawrence: University Press of Kansas, 2005), 44–45.

6. Hubbard, *Confederate Diplomacy*, 21.

7. Norman Ferris, *Desperate Diplomacy: William H. Seward's Foreign Policy, 1861* (Knoxville: University of Tennessee Press, 1976), 4–7, 30–32.

8. *La España*, 7 January 1862.

9. Cortada, *Spain and the American Civil War*, 82.

10. "Constitution for the Provisional Government," Article 2, 8 February 1861, and "Constitution of the Confederate States," Article 2, 11 March 1861, in *Messages and Papers of the Confederacy, 1861–1865*, vol. 1, ed. James D. Richardson (Nashville: US Publishing, 1905), 8–10, 46–49.

11. Jefferson Davis, "Inaugural Address," 1 February 1861, in ibid., 34.

12. Executive note, Jefferson Davis to Howell Cobb, Confederate Congress, 26 February 1861, in ibid., 57.

13. Hubbard, *Confederate Diplomacy*, 66.

14. DeLeon, *Secret History*, xiii.

15. May, *The Union, the Confederacy*, 6.

16. Ferris, *Desperate Diplomacy*, 33–34.

17. Donaldson Jordan and Edwin Pratt, *Europe and the American Civil War* (Boston: Houghton Mifflin, 1931), 193–200; Callahan, *Diplomatic History*, 200; C. Douglas Kroll, *Friends in Peace and War: The Russian Navy's Landmark Visit to Civil War San Francisco* (Dulles, VA: Potomac Books, 2007), 77.

18. Jordan and Pratt, *Europe and the American Civil War*, 248–49; Martínez-Fernández, *Torn between Empires*, 187–89; Cortada, *Spain and the American Civil War*, 59; Callahan, *Diplomatic History*, 128.

19. Cortada, *Spain and the American Civil War*, 58.

20. AMAE, Correspondencia, Embajadas y Legaciones, EEUU, 1859–1861, LegH1470: letter, 29 March 1861, Tassara to MAE, announcing appointment of Schurz; letter, 29 April 1861, from MAE to Tassara, directing him to lodge a formal protest over Schurz's appointment; letter, 18 March 1861, Tassara to MAE, announcing appointment of Clay; see also Mahin, *One War at a Time*, 203; Cortada, *Spain and the American Civil War*, 53–54.

21. Cortada, *Spain and the American Civil War*, 108–9.

22. AMAE, Política Exterior, EEUU, 1861–1862, LegH2405: letters, 11 February, 13 March 1862, Tassara to MAE; Ferris, *Desperate Diplomacy*, 143; Cortada, *Spain and the American Civil War*, 57.

23. AMAE, Correspondencia, Embajadas y Legaciones, EEUU, 1859–1861, LegH1470: letter, 29 June 1861, from Tassara to MAE.

24. Ibid., LegH1471: letter, 13 March 1861, from Tassara to MAE; letter, 11 April 1862, Horatio Perry to MAE; letter, 21 May 1862, MAE to Perry, authorizing coaling station in Cadiz.

25. AMAE, Correspondencia, Embajadas y Legaciones, EEUU, Notas, 1843–1901, LegH1490: letter, 22 April 1862, Seward to Tassara.

26. Ibid., 1859–1861, LegH1470: *Baltimore Sun*, 6 December 1861.

27. Ibid.: letter, 21 November 1861, from Prime Minister O'Donnell to Horatio Perry, chargé, US legation in Madrid; letter, 21 December 1861, from Perry to O'Donnell.

28. Ibid., *New York Daily Tribune*, 29 August, 4 December 1861; letters, 5 August, 19 September 1861, Tassara to MAE.

29. Cortada, *Spain and the American Civil War*, 46–47.

30. Pere Anguera, *El general Prim: biografía de un conspirador* (Barcelona: Edhasa, 2003), 354–56.

31. Ferris, *Desperate Diplomacy*, 168–70; Anguera, *El general Prim*, 357–59.

32. Thomas Schoonever, "Napoleon Is Coming! Maximilian Is Coming? The International History of the Civil War in the Caribbean Basin," in May, *The Union, the Confederacy*, 118; Alfred Hanna and Kathryn Hanna, *Napoleon III and Mexico: American Triumph over Monarchy* (Chapel Hill: University of North Carolina Press, 1971), 41–43; Ridley, *Maximilian and Juárez*, 16.

33. Cortada, *Spain and the American Civil War*, 48; Anguera, *El general Prim*, 369, 376–79; Hanna and Hanna, *Napoleon III and Mexico*, 43–44.

34. Harry Thayer Mahoney, *Mexico and the Confederacy, 1860–1867* (San Francisco: Austin and Winfield, 1998), 29–36, 48–58; Callahan, *Diplomatic History*, 71–76; Hubbard, *Confederate Diplomacy*, 45–47.

35. Callahan, *Diplomatic History*, 51–53; Hubbard, *Confederate Diplomacy*, 71.

36. Hubbard, *Confederate Diplomacy*, 22–26.

37. David G. Surdam, *Northern Naval Superiority and the Economics of the American Civil War* (Columbia: University of South Carolina Press, 2001), 112–13, 117.

38. Cortada, *Spain and the American Civil War*, 56–57.

39. May, *The Union, the Confederacy*, 8–9.

40. Hubbard, *Confederate Diplomacy*, 61–63.

41. Allendesalazar, *Apuntes*, 138.

42. Hubbard, *Confederate Diplomacy*, 64, 66–67.

43. Ibid., 64–67, 68–69.

44. DeLeon, *Secret History*, 53–54, 114–19.

45. Hubbard, *Confederate Diplomacy*, 70–71.

46. DeLeon, *Secret History*, 13.

47. Ibid., 35–36.

48. Hubbard, *Confederate Diplomacy*, 78–80.

49. Ollinger Crenshaw, "The Knights of the Golden Circle: The Career of

George Bickley," *American Historical Review* 47.1 (October 1941): 23–50; Randolph B. Campbell, "Knights of the Golden Circle," *Handbook of Texas Online*, Texas State Historical Association, at http://www.tshaonline.org/handbook/online/articles/vbk01 (accessed March 29, 2011).

50. Tucker, *Cubans in the Confederacy*, 4–7.

51. James M. Callahan, *Cuba and International Relations* (Baltimore: Johns Hopkins Press, 1899), 335.

52. AMAE, Política Exterior, EEUU, 1861–1862, LegH2405: letter, 16 December 1861, from Serrano to MAE; letter, 12 December 1861, Shuffelt to Serrano; letter, 13 December 1861, Serrano to US Consul-General, Havana; other letters between Serrano, Helm, and MAE, October–December 1861. See also Martínez-Fernández, *Torn between Empires*, 158–61.

53. Callahan, *Cuba and International Relations*, 336–37; Callahan, *Diplomatic History*, 77–78; May, *Southern Dream*, 245–48.

54. Allendesalazar, *Apuntes*, 138–39.

55. May, *Southern Dream*, 235–40.

56. AMAE, Política Exterior, EEUU, 1861–1862, LegH2405: letter, 12 December 1861, US Consul-General, Havana, R. W. Shuffelt to Gen. Serrano; letter, 16 December 1861, from Serrano to MAE; letter, 13 December 1861, Serrano to US consul-general, Havana; letter, 7 January 1862, Calderón Collantes to Serrano.

57. *Richmond Dispatch*, 10 February 1862.

58. Case and Spencer, *United States and France*, 75.

59. *New York Times*, 15 September 1861.

60. AMAE, Política Exterior, EEUU, 1861–1862, LegH2405: letter, 25 February 1862, Tassara to MAE.

61. Cortada, *Spain and the American Civil War*, 54.

62. Callahan, *Diplomatic History*, 77–78, 95, 124.

63. Hubbard, *Confederate Diplomacy*, 88–90, 102–4.

64. DeLeon, *Secret History*, xvi–xx; Charles P. Cullop, *Confederate Propaganda in Europe* (Coral Gables: University of Miami Press, 1969), 14–16.

65. Jordan and Pratt, *Europe and the American Civil War*, 193–99.

66. Figueroa Esquer, *Entre la intervención oculta y la neutralidad estricta*, 325–26.

67. AMAE, Correpondencia, Embajadas y Legaciones, EEUU, 1862–1864, LegH1471: letter, 1 April 1862, Tassara to MAE.

68. Pratt, "Spanish Opinion,"14–15, 17–18.

69. AMAE, Correpondencia, Embajadas y Legaciones, EEUU, 1862–1864, LegH1471: letters, 1 August 1862, 5 February 1863, Tassara to MAE.

70. Ibid., letter, 13 June 1862, Mariano del Prado (assistant to Tassara) to MAE.

71. Ivan Musicant, *Divided Waters: The Naval History of the Civil War* (New York: HarperCollins, 1995), 330; Raimondo Luraghi, *A History of the Confederate Navy*, trans. Paolo Coletta (Annapolis, MD: Naval Institute Press, 1996), 85–87; Raphael Semmes, *The Cruise of the Alabama and the Sumter (as published*

in 1864) (Scituate, MA: Digital Scanning, 2001), 69–70.

72. AMAE, Correpondencia, Embajadas y Legaciones, EEUU, 1862–1864, LegH1471: letter, 30 June 1863, Tassara to MAE; letter, 24 June 1863, Tassara to Captain General of Cuba.

73. Ibid., *Sentinel* (Richmond), 12 June 1863.

74. James M. McPherson, *Tried by War: Abraham Lincoln as Commander in Chief* (New York: Penguin, 2009), 143–45, 176–77.

75. Ibid., 187, 202; DeLeon, *Secret History*, xx.

76. Serge Gavronsky, *The French Liberal Opposition and the American Civil War* (New York: Humanities Press, 1968), 121.

77. Jordan and Pratt, *Europe and the American Civil War*, 206–7, 210–12; Hubbard, *Confederate Diplomacy*, 85–86.

78. AMAE, Correpondencia, Embajadas y Legaciones, EEUU, 1862–1864, LegH1471: *New York Herald Tribune*, 9 June 1862, reprinting intercepted notes between Rost and Spanish foreign minister Calderón Collantes, 21 March 1862.

79. AMAE, Política Exterior, EEUU, 1861–1862, LegH2405: letter, 15 March 1862, from Pierre Rost to Saturnino Calderón Collantes, minister of foreign affairs; Jordan and Pratt, *Europe and the American Civil War*, 58.

80. AMAE, Política Exterior, EEUU, 1861–1862, LegH2405: documents, 24 August 61, from R. M. T. Hunter, CSA Department of State, accrediting W. L. Yancey, Pierre A. Rost, A. Dudley Mann as special commissioners to Spain; Martínez-Fernández, *Torn between Empires*, 159.

81. AMAE, Política Exterior, EEUU, 1861–1862, LegH2405: letters, 11 and 25 October 1861, from Tassara to MAE; Cortada, *Two Nations over Time*, 84.

82. Gerald Horne, *The Deepest South: The United States, Brazil, and the African Slave Trade* (New York: New York University Press, 2007), 169–71.

83. Callahan, *Cuba and International Relations*, 336–37; Cullop, *Confederate Propaganda*, 14–16.

84. Horne, *Deepest South*, 152, 154.

85. AMAE, Política Exterior, EEUU, 1861–1862, LegH2405: letters, March–May 1862, between US Legation, Madrid, and MAE.

86. Cortada, *Spain and the American Civil War*, 89.

87. AMAE, Política Exterior, EEUU, 1861–1862, LegH2405: letter, 31 March, Perry US chargé d'affaires, Madrid, to E. S. Eggleston, US consul, Cadiz.

88. AMAE, Correpondencia, Embajadas y Legaciones, EEUU, 1862–1864, LegH1471: letter, 1 August 1862, Tassara to MAE.

89. Gavronsky, *French Liberal Opposition*, 30–31.

90. Pratt, "Spanish Opinion," 14–15, 17–18.

91. Horne, *Deepest South*, 169.

92. Martínez-Fernández, *Torn between Empires*, 160–61; Jordan and Pratt, *Europe and the American Civil War*, 246–47.

93. Allendesalazar, *Apuntes*, 159.

Chapter 4

1. Gabriel Cardona and Juan Carlos Losada, *Weyler: nuestro hombre en la Habana* (Barcelona: Planeta, 1997), 25; Cortada, *Spain and the American Civil War*, 32–33.

2. González Calleja and Fontecha Pedraza, *Una cuestión de honor*, ix.

3. Ibid., xi–xii.

4. Ibid., 11–12.

5. Ian Bell, *The Dominican Republic* (Boulder: Westview Press, 1981), 38–39.

6. Ibid., 40–41, 42–45.

7. Ibid., 45–47.

8. González Calleja and Fontecha Pedraza, *Una cuestión de honor*, x–xi.

9. Ibid., 14–16.

10. Ibid., 28–29, 31.

11. Mariano Torrente, *Política Ultramarina que abraz* (Madrid: D. A. Avrial, 1854), 282–83.

12. Joaquín Navarro Méndez, "Anexión y abandono de Santo Domingo, 1861–1865," *Revista de Historia Militar* (Servicio Histórico Militar) 84 (1998): 172.

13. González Calleja and Fontecha Pedraza, *Una cuestión de honor*, 35.

14. Ibid., xii–xiii.

15. Ibid., 36.

16. Ibid., xiii; Bell, *Dominican Republic*, 46–49.

17. D. P. Crook, *The North, the South, and the Powers, 1861–1865* (New York: John Wiley and Sons, 1974), 54; Payne, *El Ejército y sociedad*, 53.

18. Cortada, *Spain and the American Civil War*, 32.

19. González Calleja and Fontecha Pedraza, *Una cuestión de honor*, 49–51.

20. Cortada, *Spain and the American Civil War*, 33.

21. González Calleja and Fontecha Pedraza, *Una cuestión de honor*, xiii–xiv, 58.

22. Navarro Méndez, "Anexión y abandono de Santo Domingo," 174–77; "Real Decreto de reincorporación a la Monarquía española del territorio que constituía la República de Santo Domingo, firmado en Aranjuez el 19 de Mayo de 1861," *Tratados de España. Documentos Internacionales del Reinado de Doña Isabel II desde 1842 a 1868* (Madrid: Imprenta de Miguel Ginesta, 1869), 232–34.

23. Charles Hauch, "Attitudes of Foreign Governments toward the Spanish Reoccupation of the Dominican Republic," *Hispanic American Historical Review* 27.2 (May 1947): 248, 252.

24. González Calleja and Fontecha Pedraza, *Una cuestión de honor*, xiv, 89, 96, 121–22 (121–22).

25. Rodríguez González, *La Armada Española*, 33.

26. H. Hoetnik, *The Dominican People, 1850–1900: Notes for a Historical Soci-*

ology, trans. Stephen Ault (Baltimore: Johns Hopkins University Press, 1982), 2, 19.

27. Ibid., 43.

28. Navarro Méndez, "Anexión y abandono de Santo Domingo," 179–80.

29. González Calleja and Fontecha Pedraza, *Una cuestión de honor,* xvi–xvii, 128. http://www.catholic-hierarchy.org/bishop/bmonzon.html.

30. *La Época*, 22 September 1862.

31. González Calleja and Fontecha Pedraza, *Una cuestión de honor*, xv–xvii.

32. Ibid., xv.

33. Welles, *Naboth's Vineyard*, 226, 231, 238–40, 247–49 (246).

34. Cortada, *Spain and the American Civil War*, 51.

35. Ibid., 37–38.

36. Jamie de Jesús Dominguez, *La anexión de la República Dominicana a España*, vol. 1 (Santo Domingo: Universidad Autonoma de Santo Domingo, 1979), 260, 262.

37. Crook, *The North, the South, and the Powers*, 55.

38. De Jesús Dominguez, *La anexión de la República Dominicana a España*, 141.

39. Charles Tansill, *The United States and Santo Domingo, 1798–1873* (Gloucester, MA: Peter Smith, 1967), 214–15; Crook, *The North, the South, and the Powers*, 62–63.

40. AMAE, Política Exterior, EEUU, 1861–1862, LegH2405: letter, 4 February 1862, Seward to Spanish FM Calderon Collantes; Martínez-Fernández, *Torn between Empires*, 156–57; Cortada, *Two Nations over Time*, 78–79; Callahan, *Cuba and International Relations*, 332.

41. *New York Times*, 3 June 1861.

42. Cortada, *Two Nations over Time*, 80–81; Tansill, *The United States and Santo Domingo*, 215.

43. González Calleja and Fontecha Pedraza, *Una cuestión de honor*, 62–63.

44. Archivo Histórico Nacional (AHN), Sección Ultramar, Legajo 3525, Expediente 27: 1863, VIII, 24, Santo Domingo, Parte de 10 de agosto del comandante del Cibao. Archivo Militar de Madrid—Servicio Histórico Militar (SHM), Coleccion Ultramar, Caja 5746, Legajo 11, correspondencia entre el Gobierno Superior Civil de la Isla de Cuba y el Ministerio de Ultramar: letter, "Gobierno Superior Civil de la Siempre fiel isla de Cuba, secretaria, politica," to Minister of Ultramar, 14 July 1864; report from Cap Haytien re. between two and three hundred soldiers assembled for the insurrection in Santo Domingo.

45. *Novedades*, October 1863.

46. González Calleja and Fontecha Pedraza, *Una cuestión de honor*, 42–43, 54–55.

47. AHN, Sección Ultramar, Legajo 3525, Expediente 115: letter, 1 February 1864, from Tassara to Ultramar. Ibid., Legajo 3526, Expediente 13: 1863, X, 1. *Novedades* (Madrid).

48. *Baltimore Sun*, 6 December 1861.

49. AHN, Sección Ultramar, Legajo 3525, Expediente 103: letter, 25 October 1863, from Spanish ambassador in Paris to MAE, and letter, 31 December 1863, from Tassara to MAE.

50. Tansill, *The United States and Santo Domingo*, 222–24; AHN, Sección Ultramar, Legajo 3525, Expediente 104: letter, 9 October 1863, from Tassara to MAE.

51. AMAE, Correspondencia, Embajadas y Legaciones, EEUU, 1859–1861, LegH1470: letter, 1 April 1861, Tassara to Seward; letters, 29 April, 21 May 1861, Tassara to MAE.

52. James Holly and J. Dennis Harris, *Black Separatism in the Caribbean, 1860* (Ann Arbor: University of Michigan Press, 1970), 2–3.

53. Ibid., 6–9.

54. Ibid., 105–7.

55. Ibid., 107–11; Hoetnik, *The Dominican People*, 20–21.

56. AHN, Sección Ultramar, Legajo 3531, Expediente 42: documents, March–April 1863, presented to Secretario de la Real Audiencia de Santo Domingo, don Manuel de Jesús Heredia, by William L. Cazneau and Joseph W. Favens (of the Confederacy), and by B. Cainart; ibid., Sección Ultramar, Legajo 3534, Expediente 14: letter, Tassara to MAE, on meeting with Ramón Páez, a Venezuelan in New York City, representing the "West India Company."

57. AHN, Sección Ultramar, Legajo 3525, Expediente 103–6, 109–10, 112, 115.

58. SHM, microfilm, Division E, Sección a, Subgroup II, numero 6089, from 2–1–9–1 to 2–1–9–3: Real Cuerpo de Ingenieros, Comisión en los Estados Unidos, Marina, "Sistema Ericsson", 1863; report by José de Olañeta, New York, 18 December 1863; Real Cuerpo de Ingenieros, Comisión en los Estados Unidos, Marina, 1866, "Torres jiratorias de hierro, aplicadas a las defenses de tierra." AMAE, Correpondencia, Embajadas y Legaciones, EEUU, 1862–1864, LegH1471: letter, 2 December 1862, from Tassara to MAE, drawing attention to the new armored ships of the United States ("Monitores").

59. Bordejé y Morencos, *Crónica de la marina española*, 1:259, 270–71, 279, 287, 283–84; Martínez Ruiz, de Pazzis Pi Corrales, Torrejón Chaves, *Los ejércitos y las armadas de España*; Fernández Bastarreche, "La organización del Ejercito y de la Armada," 65–66.

60. AMAE, Política Exterior, EEUU, 1861–1862, LegH2405: letter, 21 May 1862, Tassara to MAE.

61. Cardona and Losada, *Weyler*, 34–35.

62. AHN, Sección Ultramar, Legajo 3534, Expediente 9: letter, 29 January 1863, Governor Felipe Rivero to Ministro de Guerra y Ultramar.

63. Navarro Méndez, "Anexión y abandono de Santo Domingo," 163.

64. Ibid., 184.

65. Cardona and Losada, *Weyler*, 26; Bell, *Dominican Republic*, 51; González Calleja and Fontecha Pedraza, *Una cuestión de honor*, xv, 112.

66. González Calleja and Fontecha Pedraza, *Una cuestión de honor*, 113, 116–18.

67. *Almanaque de Mundo Militar* (Madrid: Atlas, 1865), 38.

68. Navarro Méndez, "Anexión y abandono de Santo Domingo," 174–75, 179–80, 184, 187–88; Cardona and Losada, *Weyler*, 25–28, 31–32; González Calleja and Fontecha Pedraza, *Una cuestión de honor*, 133.

69. Holly and Harris, *Black Separatism in the Caribbean*, 80, 86.

70. Hoetnik, *The Dominican People*, 94–95.

71. Ibid., 96, 99–100, 103, 114, 175.

72. AHN, Sección Ultramar, Legajo 3525, Expediente 32: letter, 24 September 1863, Don Carlos de Vargas y Cervento to Ministro de Ultramar; ibid., Expediente 33: posters, 23 October 1863.

73. SHM, Archivo General Militar (AGM), Caja 5774, Legajo 8: "Presupuestos Generales de ingresos y gastos de la Isla de Santo Domingo correspondientes al año económico 1863–1864 por Real Orden de 12 de octubre de 1863."

74. Ibid.; AGM, Caja 5774, Legajo 9: "Presupuesto de gastos extraordinarios del Servicio del Estado por el ramo de Guerra en la Isla de Santo Domingo, correspondiente al año económico 1864–1865."

75. Hoetnik, *The Dominican People*, 64.

76. González Calleja and Fontecha Pedraza, *Una cuestión de honor*, 159, 175.

77. Marqués de Lema, *Contra el proyecto de ley presentado por el gobierno de S.M. para el abandono de Santo Domingo, sesiones de 25 y 26 abril 1865* (Madrid: Banco Industrial y Mercantil, 1865).

78. *La Esperanza*, 22 March 1865.

79. Archivo Militar de Madrid, Colección Ultramar, Caja 5746, Legajo 11, Correspondencia entre el Gobierno Superior Civil de la Isla de Cuba y el Ministerio de Ultramar: letter, "Gobierno Superior Civil de la Siempre fiel isla de Cuba, secretaria, politica," to Minister of Overseas Affairs,14 July 1864.

80. *Almanaque de Mundo Militar* (1865): 20.

81. González Calleja and Fontecha Pedraza, *Una cuestión de honor*, xviii, 202, 226; Welles, *Naboth's Vineyard*, 294, 298.

82. *La Esperanza*, 12 April 1865.

83. Valeriano Weyler, *Memorias de un general* (Barcelona: Ediciones Destino, 2004), 37–38, 53.

84. Alonso, *Historia política del ejército español*, 342; González Calleja and Fontecha Pedraza, *Una cuestión de honor*, 226.

85. Cortada, *Spain and the American Civil War*, 40.

86. González Calleja and Fontecha Pedraza, *Una cuestión de honor*, 6.

Chapter 5

1. Hubbard, *Confederate Diplomacy*, 103–4.

2. Callahan, *Diplomatic History*, 168.

3. *La Época*, 15 August 1862.

4. Case and Spencer, *United States and France*, 403.

5. While attempts to lay a transatlantic cable predated the American Civil War, it was not until July 1866 that the British established a reliable connection between Ireland and Newfoundland—more than one year too late to have been a factor in the conflict.

6. *La Esperanza* (Madrid), 1 January 1863.

7. Hubbard, *Confederate Diplomacy*, 100–101, 103–4.

8. Ibid., 69; DeLeon, *Secret History*, 23.

9. Pi-Suñer Llorens and Sánchez Andrés, *Encuentros y desencuentros*, 148, 151–52, 158; Hubbard, *Confederate Diplomacy*, 162–64; Mahoney, *Mexico and the Confederacy*, 48–49, 51–52, 58; Cortada, *Two Nations over Time*, 82–83.

10. Hubbard, *Confederate Diplomacy*, 91–97, 107–11.

11. DeLeon, *Secret History*, xvi–xx; Cullop, *Confederate Propaganda*, 123–25.

12. Case and Spencer, *United States and France*, 179.

13. Hubbard, *Confederate Diplomacy*, 114–24.

14. DeLeon, *Secret History*, 35, 151–52, 158–59, 163–64.

15. Ibid., xvi–xx; Cullop, *Confederate Propaganda*, 154–55.

16. Eugene Berwanger, *The British Foreign Service and the American Civil War* (Lexington: University Press of Kentucky, 1994), 167–68.

17. Hubbard, *Confederate Diplomacy*, 132–36.

18. AMAE, Correpondencia, Embajadas y Legaciones, EEUU, 1862–1864, LegH1471: letter, 10 March 1863, Foreign Minister to Tassara.

19. Abraham Lincoln, Annual Message to Congress, 8 December 1863. http://teachingamericanhistory.org/library/index.asp?document=426.

20. Case and Spencer, *United States and France*, 420.

21. Callahan, *Diplomatic History*, 184, 190.

22. AMAE, Correpondencia, Embajadas y Legaciones, EEUU, 1862–1864, LegH1471: letters, 5, 13 February 1863, from Tassara to MAE; *La España*, 6 March 1863; Mahin, *One War at a Time*, 101.

23. *Treaty between United States and Great Britain for the Suppression of the Slave Trade; April 7,1862*, and *Additional Article to the Treaty for the Suppression of the African Slave Trade, between the United States of America and her Britannic Majesty, of the 7th of April, 1862; concluded February 17, 1863*, at http://avalon.law.edu/19th_century/br1863.asp. *Confederate States of America—Constitution for the Provisional Government*, 8 February 1861, at http://avalon.law.yale.edu/19th_century/csa_csapro.asp.

24. José Antonio Piqueras, "La reina, los esclavos y Cuba," in *Isabel II: los espejos de la reina*, ed. Juan Sisinio Pérez Garzón (Madrid: Marcial Pons Historia, 2004), 96–97, 108.

25. DeLeon, *Secret History*, xxii–xxv, xxxi.

26. Coy F. Cross II, *Lincoln's Man in Liverpool: Consul Dudley and the Legal Battle to Stop Confederate Warships* (DeKalb: Northern Illinois University Press, 2007), 4–5, 7, 12–14, 17, 153–54.

27. Hubbard, *Confederate Diplomacy*, 145–46.

28. Cross, *Lincoln's Man in Liverpool*, 128–34.

29. SHM, microfilm, Division E, Seccion a, Subgroup II, numero 6089, 2–1–9–1 to 2–1–9–3: "Real Cuerpo de Ingenieros, Comisión en los Estados Unidos, Marina, 1863–1866."

30. Robert MacBride, *Civil War Ironclads* (Philadelphia: Chilton, 1962), 7, 11.

31. AMAE, Correpondencia, Embajadas y Legaciones, EEUU, 1862–1864, LegH1471: letter, 2 December 1862, from Tassara to MAE, on the new Monitor warships.

32. Ibid., letters, 17 April and 8 May 1863, Seward to Tassara.

33. Ibid., report, Spanish naval delegation in the United States, 21 July 1863.

34. Cortada, *Spain and the American Civil War*, 87.

35. Callahan, *Diplomatic History*, 207.

36. Owsley, *King Cotton Diplomacy*, 1, 23, 33, 446, 464; Callahan, *Diplomatic History*, 207, 208.

37. Crook, *The North, the South, and the Powers*, 314–15; Cortada, *Spain and the American Civil War*, 38.

38. *New York Times*, 25 September 1863; *La Época*, 2 February 1864.

39. *La Época*, 8 April 1863.

40. AMAE, Correpondencia, Embajadas y Legaciones, EEUU, 1862–1864, LegH1471: letters, newspaper clippings, and memos, 1862–1864, Tassara to MAE.

41. Ibid., letters, 4 September 1863, May–June 1864, Tassara to MAE.

42. Jordan and Pratt, *Europe and the American Civil War*, 214–15.

Chapter 6

1. George E. Buker, *Blockaders, Refugees, and Contrabands: Civil War on Florida's Gulf Coast, 1861–1865* (Tuscaloosa: University of Alabama Press, 1993), 1.

2. Frank E. Vandiver, ed, *Confederate Blockade Running through Bermuda, 1861–1865* (Austin: University of Texas Press, 1947), xiii, xv.

3. Thomas Boaz, *Guns for Cotton: England Arms the Confederacy* (Shippensburg, PA: Burd Street Press, 1996), 9, 67.

4. Schoonover, "Napoleon Is Coming!" 116–17.

5. Cortada, *Two Nations over Time*, 84; Musicant, *Divided Waters*, 330, 361–63; Luraghi, *Confederate Navy*, 85–87, 344; James McPherson, "The Whole Family of Man," in May, *The Union, the Confederacy*, 153.

6. Vandiver, *Confederate Blockade*, xvii–xxxvii.

7. Boaz, *Guns for Cotton*, 11, 59.

8. Martínez-Fernández, *Torn between Empires*, 163, 171–73.

9. Cortada, *Spain and the American Civil War*, 63.

10. Vandiver, *Confederate Blockade*, xli.

11. Wise, *Lifeline of the Confederacy*, 57.

12. Stephen Wise, *Lifeline of the Confederacy: Blockade Running during the*

Civil War (Columbia: University of South Carolina Press, 1988), 75–76.

13. Vandiver, *Confederate Blockade*, xx–xxi; Hamilton Cochran, *Blockade Runners of the Confederacy* (Indianapolis and New York: Bobbs-Merrill, 1958), 221–22, 224.

14. Buker, *Blockaders, Refugees, and Contrabands*, 37, 92, 146, 149, 159.

15. Wise, *Lifeline of the Confederacy*, 57.

16. Ibid., 79–80, 83.

17. Durkin, *Stephen R. Mallory*, 131, 140, 146–47.

18. Ibid., 157–58, 164–65, 186.

19. AHN, Sección Ultramar, Legajo 3534, Expediente 9: letter, 29 January 1863, Navy commander, Spanish port of Santo Domingo, to governor of Santo Domingo; Welles, *Naboth's Vineyard*, 243.

20. Martínez-Fernández, *Torn between Empires*, 176–78, 187–89.

21. Callahan, *Diplomatic History*, 98, 128–29, 168, 207–8.

22. Lida, *España y el imperio de Maximiliano*, 110.

23. Jerónimo Becker, *De los derechos de las naciones y del principio de intervención. La neutralidad y la beligerancia. España y los Estados Unidos* (Madrid: El Nacional, 1895), 33.

24. Cortada, *Two Nations over Time*, 84.

25. Cortada, *Spain and the American Civil War*, 66–68.

26. AMAE, Política Exterior, EEUU, 1861–1862, LegH2405: letter, 10 April 1863, Gustavus Koerner, US Minister, Madrid, to MAE; letter, 23 February 1863, from Serrano to MAE; letter, 21 January 1863, from R. W. Shufeldt to captain general, Havana; letter, 30 January 1863, Seward to Koerner. See also Cochran, *Blockade Runners of the Confederacy*, 259–60.

27. Anguera, *El general Prim*, 380–83; Pi-Suñer Llorens and Sánchez Andrés, *Encuentros y desencuentros*, 55–56, 158, 167–68.

28. Pi-Suñer Llorens and Sánchez Andrés, *Encuentros y desencuentros*, 180, 197.

29. Pérez, *Cuba*, 120.

30. Callahan, *Diplomatic History*, 98.

31. Wise, *Lifeline of the Confederacy*, 167–68.

32. Rueda Hernanz, *Isabel II*, 232.

33. Wayne K. Durrill, *War of Another Kind: A Southern Community in the Great Rebellion* (New York and Oxford: Oxford University Press, 1990), 139–40, 214.

34. Pratt, "Spanish Opinion,"18; Howard Jones, "History and Mythology: The Crisis over British Intervention in the Civil War," in May, *The Union, the Confederacy*, 42–46.

35. Wise, *Lifeline of the Confederacy*, 186–87.

36. Hanna and Hanna, *Napoleon III and Mexico*, 160–63; Wise, *Lifeline of the Confederacy*, 86–89.

37. Robert W. Delaney, "Matamoros: Port for Texas during the Civil War," *Southwestern Historical Quarterly Online* 58.4 (April 1955): 473–87; Hanna and

Hanna, *Napoleon III and Mexico*, 163–66; Vandiver, *Confederate Blockade*, 130, 202, 207.

38. Durkin, *Stephen R. Mallory*, 311, 322.

39.Vandiver, *Confederate Blockade*, 148; Cochran, *Blockade Runners of the Confederacy*, 60, 98, 237.

40. Allendesalazar, *Apuntes*, 184.

Chapter 7

1. Allendesalazar, *Apuntes*, 138–39, 201.

2. Berwanger, *British Foreign Service*; *Sentinel* (Richmond), 12 June 1863.

3. Hubbard, *Confederate Diplomacy*, 148–51.

4. Jefferson Davis, report to Confederate Congress, 7 December 1863, in *Messages and Papers of the Confederacy*, 1:348–59.

5. Gavronsky, *French Liberal Opposition*, 229–30.

6. Hubbard, *Confederate Diplomacy*, 156–59.

7. Ibid., 162–63.

8. William H. Seward, secretary of state, letter to William L. Dayton, ambassador to France, 26 September 1863, no. 406, Department of State, Washington, DC, at http://teachingamericanhistory.org/library/index.asp?document=536.

9. AMAE, Correpondencia, Embajadas y Legaciones, EEUU, 1862–1864, LegH1471: letter, 22 December 1863, Tassara to MAE; letter, Seward to Dayton, 11 August 1863. "The American Doctrine of Nonintervention," at http://teachingamericanhistory.org/library/index.asp?document=645.

10. C. C. Memminger, Treasury secretary, and James Seddon, secretary of war, 5 March 1864, "Official Regulations to Carry Into Effect the Act To Impose Regulations Upon the Foreign Commerce of the Confederate States to Provide for the Public Defense," in *Messages and Papers of the Confederacy*, 1:417–20.

11. Jefferson Davis, "To The House of Representatives of the Confederate States of America," 10 June 1864, in ibid., 467–70.

12. Jefferson Davis, "To The House of Representatives of the Confederate States of America," 20 December 1864, in ibid., 505–13. A similar message went to the Confederate Senate on 17 December 1864.

13. Jefferson Davis, "To The Senate and House of Representatives of the Confederate States of America," 2 May 1864, in ibid., 444–45.

14. Callahan, *Diplomatic History*, 100.

15. *New York Tribune*, 27 September 1864, editorial, "An Armistice: How It Would Ruin Us," at http://teachingamericanhistory.org/library/index.asp?document=1478.

16. Jefferson Davis, "To The House of Representatives of the Confederate States of America," 7 November 1864, in *Messages and Papers of the Confederacy*, 1:485–87.

17. Hubbard, *Confederate Diplomacy*, 165.

18. Ibid., 169–71.

19. *La Esperanza*, 10 August and 14 October 1864.

20. *Almanaque de Mundo Militar* (1865): 17.

21. AMAE, Correpondencia, Embajadas y Legaciones, EEUU, 1865–1869, LegH1472: letter, 13 December 1864, Tassara to MAE; Abraham Lincoln, Annual Message, 6 December 1864. John T. Woolley and Gerhard Peters, *The American Presidency Project* [online] (Santa Barbara, CA) at http://www.presidency.ucsb.edu/ws/?pid=29505.

22. Case and Spencer, *United States and France*, 470–71, 478–79.

23. AMAE, Política Exterior, EEUU, 1861–1862, LegH2405: extract, *London Gazette*, 31 January 1862; ibid., 1864–1865, LegH2408: letter, 4 February 1865, from Perry to MAE; order, Earl Russell, to the Lords Commissioners of the Admiralty. Cortada, *Spain and the American Civil War*, 54, 63, 70–72; Luraghi, *Confederate Navy*, 344; Musicant, *Divided Waters*, 361–63.

24. James Bulloch, *The Secret Service of the Confederate States in Europe*, vol. 2 (New York: Thomas Yoseloff, 1959), 101–5; Cortada, *Spain and the American Civil War*, 70–72.

25. *La Esperanza*, 12 April 1865.

26. *New York Times*, 22 September 1895.

27. Rodríguez González, *La Armada Española*, 35, 37–54, 64–67, 129; Cortada, *Spain and the American Civil War*, 93–103.

28. Bordejé y Morencos, *Crónica de la marina española en el siglo XIX (1868–1898)*, vol. 2 (Madrid: Editorial Naval, 1995), 175, 421–22.

Conclusion

1. Cortada, *Spain and the American Civil War*, 62–63.

2. AMAE, Política Exterior, EEUU, 1864–1865, LegH2408: letters, 3 July, 16 August 1865, Tassara to MAE.

3. Batista Vilar, "Las relaciones internacionales de España," 233.

4. Mendez Bejerano, *Tassara*, 101–2,116–17, 197.

5. Depósito de la Guerra, *Cuadro de la composición y organizacion del Ejército Español en la peninsula e islas adyacentes* (Madrid, 1866).

6. Depósito de la Guerra, *Cuadro de la composición y organizacion del Ejército Español en las posesiones de ultramar en 1866* (Madrid, 1866).

7. Headrick, *Ejército y política en España*, 34–35.

8. Pi-Suñer Llorens and Sánchez Andrés, *Encuentros y desencuentros*, 247.

9. Becker, *De los derechos de las naciones y del principio de intervención*, 33.

10. Cross, *Lincoln's Man in Liverpool*, 147–55.

11. Lida, *España y el imperio de Maximiliano*, 166–68.

12. Batista Vilar, "Las relaciones internacionales de España," 241.

13. Cortada, *Spain and the American Civil War*, 61.

Bibliography

Unpublished Primary Sources

The American Presidency Project. At http://www.presidency.ucsb.edu
Archivo de Ministerio de Asuntos Exteriores (AMAE), Madrid
Archivo Histórico Nacional (AHN), Madrid
Archivo Militar de Madrid (SHM), Madrid
Avalon Project: Documents in Law, History and Diplomacy. At http://avalon.law.yale.edu
The Hierarchy of the Catholic Church. At http://www.catholic-hierarchy.org/bishop/bmonzon.html
Teaching American History Project. At http://www.TeachingAmerican-History.org

Published Primary Sources

Newspapers and Journals

Almanaque de Mundo Militar: Panorama Universal (Madrid) 1865
El Contemporáneo (Madrid)
La Época (Madrid)
La España (Madrid)
La Esperanza (Madrid)
New York Times
Novedades (Madrid)

Other Works

Depósito de la Guerra. *Cuadro de la composicion y organizacion del Ejército Español en la peninsula e islas adyacentes*. Madrid: 1866.

Lema, Marqués de. *Contra el proyecto de ley presentado por el gobierno de S.M. para el abandono de Santo Domingo, sesiones de 25 y 26 abril 1865*. Madrid: Banco Industrial y Mercantil, 1865.

Prim, Juan. *Memoria sobre el viaje militar á Oriente*. Madrid: Imprenta de Tejado, 1855.

Richardson, James D., ed. *Messages and Papers of the Confederacy, 1861–1865*. Vol. 1. Nashville: US Publishing, 1905.

Semmes, Raphael. *The Cruise of the Alabama and the Sumter (as published in 1864)*. Scituate, MA: Digital Scanning, 2001.

Tratados de España. Documentos Internacionales del Reinado de Doña Isabel II desde 1842 a 1868. Madrid: Imprenta de Miguel Ginesta, 1869.

US Department of State. *Case of the Black Warrior, and other violations of the rights of American citizens by Spanish authorities*. Washington, DC: Beverely Tucker, Senate printer, 1854.

Weyler, Valeriano. *Memorias de un general*. Barcelona: Ediciones Destino, 2004.

Secondary Sources

Allendesalazar, Manuel. *Apuntes sobre la relación diplomática Hispano-Norteamericana, 1763–1895*. Madrid: Ministerio de Asuntos Exteriores, 1996.

Alonso, José Ramón. *Historia política del ejército español*. Madrid: Editora Nacional, 1974.

Anguera, Pere. *El general Prim: biografía de un conspirador*. Barcelona: Edhasa, 2003.

Batista Vilar, Juan. "Las relaciones internacionales de España, 1840–1874." In *España siglo XIX*, ed. Javier Paredes Alonso, 220–47. Madrid: Editorial Actas, 1991.

Becker, Jerónimo. *De los derechos de las naciones y del principio de intervención. La neutralidad y la beligerancia. España y los Estados Unidos*. Madrid: El Nacional, 1895.

Bell, Ian. *The Dominican Republic*. Boulder: Westview Press, 1981.

Berwanger, Eugene. *The British Foreign Service and the American Civil War*. Lexington: University Press of Kentucky, 1994.

Boaz, Thomas. *Guns for Cotton: England Arms the Confederacy*. Shippensburg, PA: Burd Street Press, 1996.

Bordeje y Morencos, F. de. *Crónica de la marina española en el siglo XIX (1800–1868)*. Vol. 1. Madrid: Ministerio de Defensa, 1993.

———. *Crónica de la marina española en el siglo XIX (1868–1898)*. Vol. 2. Madrid: Editorial Naval, 1995.

Botero, Rodrigo. *Ambivalent Embrace: America's Troubled Relations with Spain from the Revolutionary War to the Cold War*. Westport, CT: Greenwood Press, 2001.

Buker, George E. *Blockaders, Refugees, and Contrabands: Civil War on Florida's Gulf Coast, 1861–1865*. Tuscaloosa: University of Alabama Press, 1993.

Bulloch, James. *The Secret Service of the Confederate States in Europe*. Vol. 2. New York: Thomas Yoseloff, 1959.

Callahan, James Morton. *Cuba and International Relations*. Baltimore: Johns Hopkins Press, 1899.

———. *Diplomatic History of the Southern Confederacy*. 1901. Reprint, New York: Frederick Ungar, 1964.

Campbell, Randolph B. "Knights of the Golden Circle." *Handbook of Texas Online*. Texas State Historical Association. http://www.tshaonline.org/handbook/online/articles/vbk01, accessed March 29, 2011.

Cardona, Gabriel, and Juan Carlos Losada. *Weyler: nuestro hombre en la Habana*. Barcelona: Planeta, 1997.

Carroll, Daniel. *Henri Mercier and the American Civil War*. Princeton, NJ: Princeton University Press, 1971.

Case, Lynn, and Warren Spencer. *The United States and France: Civil War Diplomacy*. Philadelphia: University of Pennsylvania Press, 1970.

Chaffin, Tom. *Fatal Glory: Narciso López and the First Clandestine War against Cuba*. Charlottesville: University Press of Virginia, 1996.

Chávez, Thomas E. *Spain and the Independence of the United States: An Intrinsic Gift*. Albuquerque: University of New Mexico Press, 2002.

Cochran, Hamilton. *Blockade Runners of the Confederacy*. Indianapolis and New York: Bobbs-Merrill, 1958.

Cortada, James W. *Spain and the American Civil War: Relations at Mid-Century, 1855–1868*. Philadelphia: American Philosophical Society, 1980.

———. *Two Nations over Time: Spain and the United States, 1776–1977*. Westport, CT: Greenwood Press, 1978.

Crenshaw, Ollinger, "The Knights of the Golden Circle: The Career of George Bickley." *American Historical Review* 47.1 (October 1941): 23–50.

Crook, D. P. *The North, the South, and the Powers, 1861–1865*. New York: John Wiley and Sons, 1974.

Cross, Coy F., II. *Lincoln's Man in Liverpool: Consul Dudley and the Legal Battle to Stop Confederate Warships*. DeKalb: Northern Illinois University Press, 2007.

Cullop, Charles P. *Confederate Propaganda in Europe*. Coral Gables: University of Miami Press, 1969.

De la Cova, Antonio Rafael. *Cuban Confederate Colonel: The Life of Ambrosio José Gonzáles*. Columbia: University of South Carolina Press, 2003.

Delaney, Robert W. "Matamoros: Port for Texas during the Civil War." *Southwestern Historical Quarterly Online* 58.4 (April 1955): 473–87.

DeLeon, Edwin. *Secret History of Confederate Diplomacy Abroad*. Edited by William C. Davis. Lawrence: University Press of Kansas, 2005.

Desmond, Humphrey. *The Know-Nothing Party: A Sketch*. Washington, DC: New Century, 1901.

Diego García, Emilio de. "El Ejército español a mediados del siglo XIX: posibilidades y limitaciones." In *Los ejércitos y las armadas de España y Suecia en una época de cambios, 1750–1870*, ed. Enrique Martínez Ruiz, Magdalena de Pazzis Pi Corrales, Juan Torrejón Chaves, 57–66. Cádiz: Universidad de Cádiz, 2000.

Dominguez, Jamie de Jesús. *La anexión de la República Dominicana a España*, vol. 1. Santo Domingo: Universidad Autonoma de Santo Domingo, 1979.

Durkin, Joseph. *Confederate Navy Chief: Stephen R. Mallory*. Tuscaloosa: University of Alabama Press, 1954.

Durrill, Wayne K. *War of Another Kind: A Southern Community in the Great Rebellion*. New York and Oxford: Oxford University Press, 1990.

Feijóo Gómez,Albino. *Quintas y protestas social en el S. XIX*. Madrid: Ministerio de Defensa, 1996.

Fernández Bastarreche, Fernando. *El ejército español en el siglo XIX*. Madrid: Siglo XXI, 1978.

———. "La organización del Ejercito y de la Armada en España, 1750–1870." In *Los ejércitos y las armadas de España y Suecia en una época de cambios, 1750–1870*, ed. Enrique Martínez Ruiz, Magdalena de Pazzis Pi Corrales, Juan Torrejón Chaves. Cádiz: Universidad de Cádiz, 2000.

Ferris, Norman. *Desperate Diplomacy: William H. Seward's Foreign Policy, 1861*. Knoxville: University of Tennessee Press, 1976.

Figueroa Esquer, Raúl. *Entre la intervención oculta y la neutralidad estricta: España ante la Guerra entre México y Estados Unidos, 1845–1848*. Mexico City: Secretaría de Relaciones Exteriores, 1999.

Gavronsky, Serge. *The French Liberal Opposition and the American Civil War*. New York: Humanities Press, 1968.

González Calleja, Eduardo, and Antonio Fontecha Pedraza, eds. *Una cuestión de honor: la polémica sobre la anexión de Santo Domigo vista desde España, 1861–1865*. Santo Domingo: Fundación García Arévalo, 2005.

Hanna, Alfred, and Kathryn Hanna. *Napoleon III and Mexico: American Triumph over Monarchy*. Chapel Hill: University of North Carolina Press, 1971.

Harrison, Joseph. *An Economic History of Modern Spain*. New York: Holmes and Meier, 1978.

Hauch, Charles. "Attitudes of Foreign Governments toward the Spanish Reoccupation of the Dominican Republic." *Hispanic American Historical Review* 27.2 (May 1947).

Headrick, Daniel. *Ejército y política en España, 1866–1898*. Madrid: Editorial Tecnos, 1981.

Herrero, José Luis. *El ejército español en el siglo XIX*. Madrid: Cuadernos para el Diálogo, 1975.

Hoetnik, H. *The Dominican People, 1850–1900: Notes for a Historical Sociology*. Translated by Stephen Ault. Baltimore: Johns Hopkins University Press, 1982.

Holly, James, and J. Dennis Harris. *Black Separatism in the Caribbean, 1860*. Ann Arbor: University of Michigan Press, 1970.

Horne, Gerald. *The Deepest South: The United States, Brazil, and the African Slave Trade*. New York: New York University Press, 2007.

Hubbard, Charles M. *The Burden of Confederate Diplomacy*. Knoxville: University of Tennessee Press, 1998.

Jones, Howard. "History and Mythology: The Crisis over British Intervention in the Civil War." In *The Union, the Confederacy, and the Atlantic Rim*, ed. Robert May, 29–67. West Lafayette, IN: Purdue University Press, 1995.

Jordan, Donaldson, and Edwin Pratt. *Europe and the American Civil War*. Boston: Houghton Mifflin, 1931.

Karp, Matthew. "A Hemispheric Defense of Slavery: The South and American Foreign Policy, 1840–1845." Paper presented to the Southern Historical Association, Louisville, November 7, 2009.

Kroll, C. Douglas. *Friends in Peace and War: The Russian Navy's Landmark Visit to Civil War San Francisco*. Dulles, VA: Potomac Books, 2007.

Landry, Harral. "Slavery and the Slave Trade in Atlantic Diplomacy, 1850–1861." *Journal of Southern History* 27.2 (May 1961): 184–207.

Lida, Clara, ed. *España y el imperio de Maximiliano*. Mexico, D.F.: El Colegio de México, 1999.

Luraghi, Raimondo. *A History of the Confederate Navy*. Translated by Paolo Coletta. Annapolis, MD: Naval Institute Press, 1996.

MacBride, Robert. *Civil War Ironclads*. Philadelphia: Chilton, 1962.

Mahin, Dean. *One War at a Time: The International Dimensions of the American Civil War.* Dulles, VA: Brassey's, 2000.

Mahoney, Harry Thayer. *Mexico and the Confederacy, 1860–1867*. San Francisco: Austin and Winfield, 1998.

Martínez-Fernández, Luis. *Torn between Empires: Economy, Society, and Patterns of Social Thought in the Hispanic Caribbean, 1840–1878*. Athens: University of Georgia Press, 1994.

Martínez Ruiz, Enrique. "Condiciones básicas del reclutamiento militar en España, 1768–1885." In *Los ejércitos y las armadas de España y Suecia en una época de cambios, 1750–1870*, ed. Enrique Martínez Ruiz, Magdalena de Pazzis Pi Corrales, Juan Torrejón Chaves. Cádiz: Universidad de Cádiz, 2000.

May, Robert. *The Southern Dream of a Caribbean Empire, 1854–1861*. Baton Rouge: Louisiana State University Press, 1973.

———, ed. *The Union, the Confederacy, and the Atlantic Rim*. West Lafayette, IN: Purdue University Press, 1995.

McCandless, Perry. *A History of Missouri*. Columbia: University of Missouri Press, 2000.

McPherson, James. "The Whole Family of Man." In Robert May, *The Union, the Confederacy, and the Atlantic Rim*. West Lafayette, IN: Purdue University Press, 1995.

Mendez Bejerano, Mario. *Tassara: nueva biografía crítica*. Madrid: J. Pérez, 1928.

Ministerio de Defensa. *Historia de la Infanteria Española: la época de los ejércitos nacionales*. Madrid: Ministerio de Defensa, 1998.

Musicant, Ivan. *Divided Waters: The Naval History of the Civil War*. New York: HarperCollins, 1995.

Navarro Méndez, Joaquín. "Anexión y abandono de Santo Domingo, 1861–1865." *Revista de Historia Militar* (Servicio Historico Militar) 84 (1998): 163–88.

Navarro y Rodrigo, Carlos. *O'Donnell y su tiempo*. Madrid: Biblioteca Universal Económica, 1869.

Owsley, Frank Lawrence. *King Cotton Diplomacy*. 2nd ed. Chicago: University of Chicago Press, 1959.

Payne, Stanley. *El Ejército y sociedad en la España liberal, 1808–1936*. Madrid: Akal, 1977.

———. *Politics and the Military in Modern Spain*. Stanford: Stanford University Press, 1967.

Pérez, Louis A. *Cuba: Between Reform and Revolution*. 2nd ed. Oxford: Oxford University Press, 1995.

Pettigrew, James Johnston. *Notes on Spain and the Spaniards, in the Summer of 1859, with a Glance at Sardinia*. 1861. Reprint, Columbia: University of South Carolina Press, 2010.

Piqueras, José Antonio. "La reina, los esclavos y Cuba." In *Isabel II: los espejos de la reina*, ed. Juan Sisinio Pérez Garzón. Madrid: Marcial Pons Historia, 2004.

Pi-Suñer Llorens, Antonia, and Agustín Sánchez Andrés. *Una historia de encuentros y desencuentros*. Mexico, D.F.: Secretaría de Relaciones Exteriores, 2001.

Pratt, Edwin. "Spanish Opinion of the North American Civil War." *Hispanic American Historical Review* 10.1 (February 1930): 14–25.

Puell de la Villa, Fernando. *Historia del ejército en España*. Madrid: Alianza Editorial, 2000.

Ridley, Jasper. *Maximilian and Juárez*. New York: Ticknor and Fields, 1992.

Ringrose, David. *Spain, Europe and the "Spanish Miracle," 1700–1900*. Cambridge: Cambridge University Press, 1996.

Rodríguez González, Agustín R. *La Armada Española, la campaña del Pácifico, 1862–1871*. Madrid: Agualarga, 1999.

Rueda Hernanz, Germán. *Isabel II*. Madrid: Arlanza, 2001.

Sarda, J. "Spanish Prices in the Nineteenth Century." *Quarterly Journal of Economics* 62.1 (November 1947): 143–59.

Schoeppner, Michael. "Quarantining an Epidemic: British Emancipation, Northern Abolitionism, and the Negro Seamen Acts." Paper presented to the Southern Historical Association, Louisville, November 7, 2009.

Schoonever, Thomas. "Napoleon Is Coming! Maximilian Is Coming? The International History of the Civil War in the Caribbean Basin." In Robert May, *The Union, the Confederacy, and the Atlantic Rim*. West Lafayette, IN: Purdue University Press, 1995.

Stern, Philip Van Doren. *When the Guns Roared: World Aspects of the American Civil War*. New York: Doubleday, 1965.

Stevens, Michael. "Two Flags, One Cause—A Cuban Patriot in Gray: Ambrosio José Gonzales." In *Cubans in the Confederacy*, ed. Phillip Tucker, 143–224. Jefferson, NC: McFarland, 2002.

Surdam, David G. *Northern Naval Superiority and the Economics of the American Civil War* Columbia: University of South Carolina Press, 2001.

Tansill, Charles. *The United States and Santo Domingo, 1798–1873*. Gloucester, MA: Peter Smith, 1967.

Torrente, Mariano. *Política Ultramarina que abraz*. Madrid: D. A. Avrial, 1854.

Tucker, Phillip, ed. *Cubans in the Confederacy*. Jefferson, NC: McFarland, 2002.

Urban, C. Stanley. "The Africanization of Cuba Scare, 1853–1855." *Hispanic American Historical Review* 37.1 (February 1957): 29–45.

Vandiver, Frank E. ed. *Confederate Blockade Running through Bermuda, 1861–1865*. Austin: University of Texas Press, 1947.

Vicens Vives, Jaime. *An Economic History of Spain*. Princeton, NJ: Princeton University Press, 1969.

Welles, Sumner. *Naboth's Vineyard: The Dominican Republic, 1844–1924*. Vol. 1. 1926. Reprint, New York: Paul Appel, 1966.

Wise, Stephen. *Lifeline of the Confederacy: Blockade Running during the Civil War*. Columbia: University of South Carolina Press, 1988.

Index